American Scholarship

in the twentieth century

The Library of Congress Series
in American Civilization
Edited by Ralph Henry Gabriel

American

Scholarship

in the twentieth century

Eugene

MERLE CURTI, *Editor*

With essays by Merle Curti, Louis Wirth,
W. Stull Holt, René Wellek, Walter R. Agard,
Arthur E. Murphy

Harvard University Press, Cambridge, 1953

Preface

In planning a series of books on various phases of life and culture in twentieth-century United States the Library of Congress Committee on American Civilization decided to include a study of the development of scholarship. With some misgivings I accepted the invitation to prepare such a volume. It was soon clear that it would have to be a coöperative venture, for no one, it seemed to me, could learn enough about all the fields of scholarship to deal adequately with them. Professor Ralph Henry Gabriel, general editor of the series, consented to the new plan and helped in the recruitment of contributors.

The book has, I think, many of the merits and some of the limitations of coöperative works. It has been hard to avoid repetition, for we wanted to discuss the development of the several fields of scholarship in relation to each other and in the context of the changing aspects of American life. I think, however, we have reduced repetition to the minimum. Nor has it been easy to bring as much unity into the book as might seem desirable. I wanted the contributors to feel as free as scholars should feel to present as seemed best to them the contributions of scholars in their field. There are, then, differences in the approach used, though by and large all the contributors have emphasized development in time.

It was at first planned to have a separate volume on science. We therefore defined scholarship in terms of the humanities and the social studies. In many ways, however, the scientific spirit influenced studies in the humanistic and social areas. All the essays testify to this influence. With regard to psychology, the division between the social and humanistic studies and the natural sciences is unfortunate. For psychology has come increasingly to be recognized as an autonomous natural science. Yet it continues to have philosophical and social implications, and the social aspects of psychology have become more and more recognized. Professor Louis Wirth included in his essay, therefore, some discussion of psychology in its social aspects.

The reader will not find much biographical material in the essays. Had space permitted, we should indeed have liked to picture as vividly as we could some of the great personalities in twentieth-century scholarship.

The essays have been inspired by the scholar's desire to be as objective as possible. Specialists in the several fields will no doubt take exception to one or another point in a given essay. But I believe that it will be generally recognized that the essays achieve a high degree of objectivity. Implied in all of them and explicit in some is, however, an awareness of values — and the values of the authors have of course played a part in what has been selected and presented. In a few essays there is something of the programmatic — though this is subordinated to the main story.

All the contributors to the volume have been fully aware of the interdependence of European and American scholarship. In many ways, indeed, scholarship in both Europe and America is international — for the idea of a republic of letters has much basis in fact. At the same time the conditions of American life have influenced the organization and emphases and even some of the results of scholarly investigations and publications in the United States. We have tried to indicate what these have been. It is of course dangerous to generalize about national characteristics in scholarship. The contributors to this volume have been aware of the dangers.

The record as here set forth testifies to the importance of many factors that have influenced the course of American scholarship in the last half-century: to the impact of European movements and the growing sense of the opportunities and the obligations to lend a hand to scholars and scholarship in Europe in time of distress and need; to the effects of wars, depressions, and prolonged international tensions; to the increasingly generous support of American philanthropy; to the role of government in scholarship; to the significance of the freedom of inquiry and publication that the American climate has provided and the dangers to scholarship of encroachments on

that freedom; and to the problems raised both by increasing specialization and by the growing awareness of the interdependency of all
branches of scholarly inquiry. We have indicated what American
scholars have regarded as the chief limitations of American scholarship. We think we have also made clear the notable achievements
of American scholars and the priceless contributions Americans have
made through scholarship to the national well-being and to man's
long odyssey in the larger world.

The contributors to this volume acknowledge special indebtedness
to Professor Ralph Henry Gabriel, the general editor of the series,
to the Harvard University Press, and to the Library of Congress.

MERLE CURTI

Contents

American Scholarship

in the twentieth century

I ·

The Setting and the Problems

MERLE CURTI

In the first half of the twentieth century man learned many things about himself that he had never known before. Living as he did in an era of earthshaking change, he also learned much that was new about his social environment, past and present. Americans continued to share, as they always had, the important revisions and exciting developments of knowledge regardless of their place of origin. American scholars also made contributions of weight and meaning to the world's expanding knowledge of man and his social environment. No part of the national history in the last half-century is probably so little known to the majority of fairly well informed Americans as the growth of knowledge about man and the society in which he lives. Yet this story, if less sensational and revolutionary than that of the natural sciences, is no less important in terms of today and tomorrow. For it is generally agreed that man's fate now largely rests on what he does with his knowledge of the physical universe. What he does with it is in turn closely related to the status and character of the social sciences and the humanities, broadly conceived.[1]

Properly speaking, the development of knowledge in the natural sciences, the social studies, and the humanities is of one piece, for each influenced, and in turn was affected by, the others. We are here concerned, however, with the development of scholarship in the social sciences and the humanities in America in the past fifty years. Now scholarship may be defined as high competence in a delimited field of conscious and sustained inquiry for related facts, valid generalizations, and workable truths. To have full meaning, the development of scholarship must be placed within the larger context of major tendencies in every sphere of living, both in the United States and in the rest of the world. But before considering ways in which the general milieu affected such things as the support and organization of scholarship, the changing status of the scholar, and the prolonged debate about his social responsibilities, let us see what some of the major tendencies in scholarship actually were, and how they can at least in part be explained.

I

At the opening of the twentieth century both the humanities and the social sciences rested on a tradition of western scholarship in which history, political economy, philology, archaeology, and philosophy enjoyed special prestige. The succeeding fifty years witnessed a steady development in all these fields.[2] But each did not keep the relative position it held early in the century. Philology, for example, attracted in 1950 a smaller fraction of scholars than it once had, while literary history and criticism enlisted a greater proportion. No field of inquiry could boast more thrilling developments than archaeology. Yet even so, this well-established field scarcely enjoyed the relative preëminence in the scholarly world it had fifty years earlier. Philosophical studies, despite some brilliant contributions and displays of militant vigor as the period ended, only partly succeeded in meeting the challenge offered by developments in mathematics and the natural sciences.

New fields of study, only slightly cultivated in the United States of 1900, in later decades loomed large in the literature of scholarship. These included art history and criticism, musicology, cultural history, area studies concerned with the Slavic world, Latin America, the Far East, and Africa, and the newer social sciences, especially anthropology, sociology, and social psychology. Psychology is a special case in point. At the turn of the century its foundations as a natural science were well laid in the laboratories of the Old World and the New; but it was still tied to philosophy and subordinated to it. By

1950 psychology not only enjoyed a place as a leading discipline — it overshadowed philosophy. Psychology can best be considered as a natural science; but one of its branches, social psychology, which came to enjoy growing importance after World War I, must of course figure in any account of the social disciplines.

It is not hard to find reasons for these shifts in emphasis and for these new developments. Even after giving due credit to the influence of comparable scholarly tendencies abroad, it is plain that American conditions played an important role. Interest in music, the fine arts, and literature reflected the increasing wealth, leisure, and cultural sophistication of growing cities. The rise of musicology, art history, and belletristic studies followed. So too the social sciences developed rapidly in response to the requirements of the new industrial civilization. Banking, public finance, taxation, labor relations, race relations, social legislation, public administration — all these fields of practical adjustment posed insistent questions. In an attempt to answer them statistical methods were more and more refined and put to use, and newer branches of social science appeared or expanded. To name but a few, cultural anthropology, rural and urban sociology, economic history, and industrial and social psychology received great impetus from the needs of a quickly changing society. Expanding missionary enterprises and considerations of trade, war, and America's new role as a world power, stimulated directly or indirectly studies of peoples in the Far East, Latin America, and the Slavic lands. Economic, political, and cultural, as well as geographical studies and international relations, also owed much to the growing world interests of the United States. The First and Second World Wars, important factors in the consolidation of American nationalism, encouraged historians to reëxamine the American past and to help rewrite the history of the world beyond our gates. War also provided an impulse to the study of propaganda techniques and public opinion, a field that also owed something to the necessity of rethinking the meaning of democracy in a new era. These are only a few examples of the many ways in which changing emphases in scholarly pursuits reflected changing conditions in the country and in the world.

Another outstanding development of the last fifty years has been a renewal of the broad scholarly ideals of the eighteenth and early nineteenth centuries. In the last two decades many scholars have, in thinking of knowledge as a whole, reacted against its narrow compartmentalization. Buckle's contention that the chief significance of any field of knowledge lies not at its center but at its periphery has been illustrated again and again in the accomplishments of scholars who have crossed conventional boundaries. From these crossings have issued sociological jurisprudence, agricultural economics, the sociology of knowledge, social psychology, and the history of science. In addition to these crossings of fields, the second quarter of the century witnessed the integration of related elements in many fields of knowledge. The child study movement, for example, while launched much earlier by G. Stanley Hall, expanded to comprise all knowledge about infants and children. Studies of the geographic and cultural areas of the world, of the regions in the United States, and, more recently, of American civilization itself, furnished other examples of this tendency to develop interdisciplinary syntheses.[3]

Another striking feature of American scholarship during the past half-century has been the more serious and extensive application of the methods of the natural sciences to the humanities. In fact, this became a dominant tendency in these disciplines. If such applications were carried to an excessive point, as many critics in the later decades of the period argued, none could deny that they had yielded important corrections, fresh insights, and even major discoveries.[4]

The application of certain techniques of the natural sciences to the social field likewise bore fruit. As a result the emphasis shifted from the older philosophical, *a priori*, and abstract approach to that of observation, analysis, control, and in a few cases, to actual prediction of future social behavior. Thanks to the case study, the life history, the community survey, the controlled interview, and the use of statistical techniques, scholarship in the social disciplines increasingly resulted in relatively objective studies of the behavior of institutions and social groups. The scientific approach also undermined the older assumption that man is separate from nature. That he is a part of the natural order itself came to be largely taken for granted.[5]

The assumption that man is part of nature led to the concept of culture, one of the most important and emancipating of all twentieth-century contributions to knowledge in the social field. The culture, or totality of institutions, adjustments, and values binding a distinctive social group together, was recognized as molding personality and explaining variants in social behavior in the many cultures of the world. Human nature was thus seen to develop only in relation to a particular culture, and to be susceptible to change as the culture changed. The relativistic and pragmatic aspects of the culture concept which resembled rising theories in the physical sciences, promised, if fully and widely appreciated, to emancipate man from many age-old superstitions and prejudices and to provide a realistic basis for improved social relations.

In exploiting new scientific methods and assumptions, scholars also occupied themselves with methodological problems in their specific disciplines. At the same time they came to question previous assumptions upon which their work had been based, and began to think anew on the relationship of their specific disciplines to the total framework of knowledge. In short, they became concerned with the general problems of a philosophy of knowledge.[6]

These and other advances in American scholarship owed much to Europe and European trained scholars. But the striking fact has been the gradual reversal in the traditional debtor-creditor relationship between American and European scholars. Early in the present century European commentators began, though grudgingly, to acknowledge the contributions of men like Willard Gibbs, William James, Franz Boas, J. H. Breasted. and G. L. Kittredge.[7] The devastating effects of the First World War provided American scholars a challenging opportunity for leadership in the international community of learning. Americans took the initiative in the postwar years in establishing international unions of scholars — the International Committee of Historical Sciences, the Permanent International Congress of Linguists, and the International Union of Academies, among many others. Waldo G. Leland, an academic statesman

to whose initiative and labors much of the international organization of scholarship was due, has reminded us of the role of these
bodies in helping to reconcile scholars of various nationalities, a
necessary step if intellectuals were to learn from each other and to
help build the republic of letters in a peaceful world. Such international associations, often with the help of American foundations,
initiated and carried forward scores of important scholarly undertakings. Americans also worked as experts in the intellectual enterprises of the League of Nations.[8]

The totalitarian onslaught further helped to reverse the traditional American dependence on European scholarship. Many gifted
scholars from the Old World sought a haven in the United States.
The Emergency Committee on Aid of Displaced Foreign Scholars,
organized in 1933, reported ten years later that it had helped 269
foreign scholars in finding positions.

Observers, impressed by the enriching effects of this migration on
American intellectual life, recalled the impact of the fall of Con-
stantinople and the revocation of the Edict of Nantes on the flowering of scholarship in the lands to which refugees fled in earlier
centuries.[9] With the breakdown of Europe in the midst of disloca-
tion and war, the United States in the 1940's became the chief
center of learning in the world. American universities now began
to contribute, along with the foundations, to the rehabilitation of
European centers of learning. If the United States is thought of as
essentially European in culture, the geographical shift was perhaps
of no great point. But if it is regarded as the center of a new civilization, then the widely recognized prestige of American scholarship
could rightly be considered as a major factor in modern cultural
history.

Wars, revolutions, dislocations, mass poverty, and totalitarianism
were not, of course, the sole factors in altering the traditional relationship between American and European scholarship. The advances
that were made and the current eminence of American scholarship
owed much to two things. The first was the national talent for
organization. The second was the wealth that flowed into our universities and other research centers.

II

The period from the First World War to the mid-century point saw the American scholar functioning more and more through organizations. The major national organizations of humanistic and social science scholars, all well organized before 1917, became increasingly important factors in initiating and planning research, in providing for the dissemination of findings, and in organizing scholarship generally. Specialization within the larger fields embraced by the national professional organizations resulted in the formation of regional and functional groups within the frame of the older national organizations. Scholars from the various disciplines, finding a common interest, organized the Medieval Academy, the Byzantine Academy, the Oriental Institute, each with its officers, committees, research programs, and organs of publication. Following the example of the natural scientists, who established in 1917 the National Research Council to facilitate the pooling of resources in the war effort, the American Council of Learned Societies and the Social Science Research Council emerged after the war. These Councils were federations of related national professional organizations. In large measure they confined themselves to research planning, to the improvement of research techniques, to stimulating and supporting new interdisciplinary investigations, and to obtaining funds from the foundations for the support of specific enterprises in the form of fellowships, grants-in-aid, and other subsidies.[10]

Perhaps of even greater import were the surveys undertaken by the learned councils. These were of many kinds and varieties. The role of research in educational institutions, the status of the research scholar, and the financing of research, all were surveyed and commented upon by the various associations. It is impossible to say how widely those responsible for research activities used these surveys, but they must have been of considerable value to scholarship in America.[11]

The foundations themselves, led by the various Carnegie and Rockefeller organizations, did not limit their functions to providing grants to the American Council of Learned Societies, the Social Science Research Council, the national professional organizations of social scientists and humanistic scholars, the several universities, and libraries actively engaged in research programs. The foundations in all cases did approve or disapprove proposals for grants-in-aid of specific researches. But they also initiated projects and sought for creative scholars with new ideas.[12]

The constructive contributions of the professional organizations and the foundations to scholarship in the humanities and the social sciences can hardly be overemphasized. They provided the initiative or support for such important projects as the comprehensive study of the Mayan culture area, the excavations in the Near and Middle East conducted by Breasted and his associates, the Indus River valley excavations, the *Dictionary of American English*, the *Linguistic Atlas*, and the *Dictionary of Middle English*, to name only a few. It would be hard to overestimate the indebtedness to the foundations, directly or indirectly, of American contributions to musicology, the history of ideas, art criticism, and studies of the Far East, Latin America, and the Slavic lands. In all these areas the advantages of long-range planned research, conducted coöperatively on a large scale, have been amply demonstrated. In addition, the Councils and foundations provided facilities for the publication of new findings and for the training of young research scholars. Concepts and approaches deemed both novel and significant resulted from American emphases on coöperation, cross-fertilization, and organization.

But it became increasingly clear that councils, committees, professional organizations, and planned coöperative research were not open sesames to prosperity in learning. Rich returns, as is well known, often followed from unexpected directions. Many scholars continued to work best alone, unencumbered by the imperatives of committees and formal coöperation. Thoughtful authorities came to wonder how effective research planning could ever be in areas of pure theory.[13]

The increasing influence of these professional organizations raised still other questions. A leading official of one of the great foundations confessed that these agencies had sometimes overstimulated certain fields, spoiled talented scholars, and contributed to an undue emphasis on scientific techniques in humanistic studies. Moreover, in the first decades of the century, leading liberals maintained that the foundations sometimes showed prejudice in failing to support investigations that in their opinion might result in weakening the prevailing economic order.[14] Liberals also argued that the assumption by the foundations of responsibility for and direction of research discouraged government from supporting investigation in needed fields. The growing tendency of the foundations to work through professional scholars and to develop wise procedures lessened in time the force of such criticisms. But the indictment of the foundations nevertheless left an uneasy feeling in many minds.[15]

The increasing interest of business itself in research also affected the organization and support of investigation. Beginning in the last decade of the nineteenth century, a few large corporations systematically sponsored research in theoretical as well as in *ad hoc* technical problems. Frederick Taylor and others provided leadership in enlarging technological studies to include investigations of workers' efficiency and labor-management relations. Increasingly business firms sponsored researches in industrial psychology and in the pertinent fields of economics.[16] In the second quarter of the century the movement for the study of business history was also well under way. Here again, as in the case of the foundations, such developments raised the problem of freedom of research. In part, business set the problems, determined conditions under which investigation was conducted, and controlled the use of findings.

No chapter in the history of the organization and support of research could be more important than one dealing with the role of government in the support of social science and the humanities as well as the natural sciences. In the nineteenth century the interest of state and federal governments in research was expressed in exploring expeditions within the United States itself and overseas, in the subsidies to the Smithsonian Institution, in the state and federal geological surveys, in the expanding activities of the Bureau of Standards and the Census Bureau, and in the undertakings of the Department of Agriculture, both in Washington and in the experimental stations established at the state and federal supported colleges of agriculture.[17] The state universities, led by Michigan and

Wisconsin, also proved to be increasingly important agencies for the flow of public funds into research in many fields.[18]

But the great era of government supported and directed research belongs to the twentieth century. While much of this continued to fall within the field of the natural sciences, an increasing amount involved the social sciences and even the humanities. This expansion resulted from many influences: from an increasing amount of available public funds, from the problems posed by an ever more complex industrial civilization, from the exigencies of war. It is impossible here even to suggest the range and significance of government supported research, or the many agencies and institutions concerned with it. In a sense, however, the Library of Congress symbolized the development. By 1950 it housed and serviced the greatest collection of books, microfilms, manuscripts, and documents in the world, provided scholars with all sorts of aids, and initiated and conducted far-reaching projects in many fields of knowledge.

The great depression of 1929 and subsequent years occasioned a vast program of government support for scholarly activities in the social and humanistic fields. A good proportion of the three thousand projects the WPA sponsored in 1937–38 at the cost of $124,000,-000 fell within the fields of economics, sociology, history, anthropology, folk art, music and literature, philology, and related subjects. The professional organizations of scholars, the universities, the libraries, and other research centers in sponsoring the WPA cultural projects provided standards for competent execution and insured a commendable degree of freedom from political and economic pressures in the actual conduct of work. Nevertheless critics, especially in the conservative camp, contended that many of the research projects spoke the New Deal idiom. While this was less true than many maintained, still the widespread government support and overall direction of research raised the problem of objectives on the policy-making level. What, after all, were the considerations that governed the acceptance and rejection of suggestions for research, how representative of the great body of scholars were those who made the decisions, and how were the projects themselves related to professional interest? [19]

Although both the First and the Second World Wars in many

ways interfered with scholarly progress by deflecting support and personnel to military purposes, both wars increased the role of government in the organization and support of science. Government and in some degree the public itself recognized that research was not mere abstruse busy-work conducted in ivory towers but that it was a major source of strength deserving of more generous support than it had hitherto received. Scholars in every field of the social sciences and humanities discovered in the First World War that their services were needed. This was even more true in the Second World War. Government agencies called scholars in many fields to Washington as consultants. Never before had specialized knowledge played so large a role in the making and execution of policies on almost every level. The federal capital became the intellectual center of the nation. Both wars, and especially the second, accelerated investigations in many fields, demonstrated new uses of existing knowledge, and proved that research and scholarship were as necessary to war as to peace. Military and naval history, to cite a single example, flourished as never before, thanks to vast sums spent by the government in the writing of the history of the armed forces.[20]

However important and desirable all this government support of research was, it nevertheless again raised the question of the freedom of scholars to choose the types of investigation they deemed important. He who paid the piper called the tune. Further, the problem of control became sharply focused in the discussions at the end of the Second World War regarding the nature of the proposed National Science Foundation. Proponents of the social sciences pointed out the great need for more extensive and intensive researches in their field, in the public interest. One segment of public opinion expressed fear that such support might channel investigations into controversial fields, by which these "conservatives" meant "radical" areas. Groups left of the center on the other hand feared that government support might rule out important projects unacceptable to the directors of the prevailing order.[21]

The growing role in research of the foundations, of business, and of government, raised many other issues. In competing for gifted men and women in research and scholarship, government and business posed many problems for those interested in recruiting, training, and keeping young investigators in university work and in explorations not strictly *ad hoc* in character. Important research continued, of course, to be done at the universities; but more and more it moved to other centers, to government, business, libraries, and museums. Increasingly the graduate schools prepared young men and women for the practice of the professions rather than for research careers. Many believed with Howard Mumford Jones that the graduate schools in trying to train both for research and for professional practice in law, medicine, and teaching failed to do either adequately. Too often the research training program did not rise above the level of collecting data which the investigator could not evaluate and interpret with any high degree of critical imagination. Yet equipped chiefly with such techniques the young Ph.D. embarked on college teaching, unprepared to enrich youth with treasures from the great cultural tradition or to guide it to constructive roles in society by acquainting it with the new movements of thought and the current social and economic realities.[22]

Various suggestions for the solution of this problem filled the pages of educational journals.[23] Howard Mumford Jones himself proposed to gear graduate programs to general education. Chancellor Robert Hutchins, forgetting perhaps the many significant contributions to knowledge resulting from the American conjoining of theory and practice, deplored the results of the effort to combine professional training and research. In his view these functions might best be entirely separated in different institutions. The half-century ended with the whole discussion still active.[24]

Closely associated with the national fondness for organization so well exemplified in modern American scholarship has been the extraordinary development of its tools — of bibliographies, catalogues, finding lists, dictionaries, encyclopedias, microfilm, and microprint. European scholars have both admired and criticized the development. Whatever the force of their varied reactions, it is perhaps no overstatement to say that in the social and humanistic fields the new techniques of microfilm and microprint, to name but two, may prove as significant in the ultimate effects on scholarship as did the invention of printing itself. The late Robert Binkley expressed the hope that the new methods of mass-collecting might democratize and decentralize scholarship by making possible mutually advantageous coöperation between amateurs and professionals. Another depression, if one comes, may test that assumption and hope.[25]

No discussion of the organization and support of scholarship can properly ignore the problem of dissemination and communication of the results of research. In advocating the responsibility of scholars to communicate their findings, writers ranged over the whole question of the status of the man of learning in society and his responsibilities to the public, a problem to be discussed subsequently in this essay. Here it may be said that the professional organizations, the Councils, and the university presses assumed major responsibility for the dissemination and communication of the findings of scholarship. After the First World War, the rapid development of the older adult education movement (Chautauqua, summer schools, university extension, and the semipopular lecture) posed new problems for scholars. A few, including James Breasted and Charles and Mary Beard, made the best-seller list with their well-informed and readable syntheses. Many more shared their scholarship with a limited audience of nonspecialists who read such periodicals as the *Yale Review*, the *South Atlantic Quarterly*, the *Virginia Quarterly*, the *Antioch Review*, the *Pacific Spectator*, and the *American Scholar*. The university presses increasingly encouraged scholars to present their findings in a sufficiently attractive literary and nontechnical form to enlist the favor of the generally well educated man and woman.[26] New agencies in the second quarter of the century — including the Foreign Policy Association, the Council of Foreign Relations, and summer seminars (such as the one held at Princeton in 1935 on Arabic and Islamic studies) also served an important function in publicizing the work of scholars. So did Colonial Williamsburg, which offered archaeological and historical knowledge to its millions of visitors.

The movement for more widespread and effective dissemination of knowledge involved certain assumptions: that the public really wanted to know the results of scholarly inquiry, that communication would enlighten the citizenry on the great issues before them, and that a more general appreciation of the nature of scholarship would strengthen its underpinnings.[27] No body of scholars made greater effort than the Americans to communicate to the public its specialized knowledge in forms comprehensible to the average man and woman.

James Harvey Robinson, who made his reputation in research in medieval history, seemed to some fellow scholars almost a traitor when he became a widely-read popularizer with an emphasis on man's ability and duty to continue to change his institutions and his thinking. Again, popularization at times proved disconcerting to the more traditional segment of the scholarly world. Newspapers and periodicals sometimes unduly sensationalized an item of scholarship and put pressure on scholars to give opinions about matters on which they could not speak competently. But only a minority succumbed to the temptation to pontificate. Another criticism of popularization — in part justified — was that it led to oversimplification and superficiality. Despite misgivings, an ever larger number followed James Harvey Robinson in seeking to humanize knowledge, aware, as Francis Bacon was, that scholarship is not "a couch, whereupon to rest a searching and restless spirit . . . or a tower of state, for a proud mind to raise itself upon; or a fort, for strife and contention," but rather "a rich storehouse for the glory of the Creator, and the relief of man's estate." [28]

The distinction that American scholarship came to enjoy in the first half of the twentieth century rested in part, then, on generous support from industry, government, and the foundations, on crossfertilization and formal coöperation, and on the union of theory and practice which developed under American pressures and conditions. It owed much to the prevalence of an atmosphere of freedom of investigation and communication — although the new developments raised questions regarding freedom, questions to be probed in the later part of this essay. But the achievements of American scholarship must be related to criticisms that both Europeans and Americans made of it.

III

Many at home and abroad regarded American scholarship as stronger in quantitative aspects than in qualitative. To some it seemed assimilative, rather than reflective and discriminating. Insofar as they admitted the truth of this indictment, observers laid the shortcomings at the door of graduate training, where the emphasis seemed to rest too heavily on the acquisition of techniques, on turning out researchers in mass quantities, and on discouraging if not crushing the few bold and original minds.[29] To meet these defects, universities and especially foundations provided for post-doctoral fellowships. Dean Andrew West of Princeton pioneered in developing a graduate school limited to a small fellowship of scholars, in which intellectual stimulus, general culture, and broad learning were to militate against a narrow overspecialized emphasis on technical research and mere survival as hurdle after hurdle was surmounted.[30] The Harvard Society of Fellows was another experiment in this direction.

Other critics held that scholars in the humanities and social disciplines too often misapplied to their work the theories and techniques of the natural sciences. In many cases, the argument ran, these were inadequate and inappropriate. The humanities as a result were dehumanized, rendered sterile and pitifully trivial, while the social studies were bogged down with scientific methodologies which robbed them of the philosophical approach and the meaningful orientation. Such was the indictment, in the barest outline.

These convictions stimulated the appearance of a vast polemical literature which mounted in bulk during the thirties and forties. Excessive emphasis on fact-finding, on overspecialization, on trivial investigations, on antiquarianism provided the theme songs of the critics. They deplored the alleged assumption that all facts are equal, that research may be divorced from a broad cultural setting. They indicted the multitude of fact finders, with their mystical faith that if enough bricks were made, a great structure would be reared.[31] Now and again a scholar who appreciated the partial truth in the indictment struck a more balanced view. Hans Zinsser, for one, reminded the critics that a multitude must clear the underbrush if a

few, possessed of great vision, were to survey the roads to new unknown areas.[32]

Other critics of American scholarship attributed its so-called inadequate concern for synthesis and larger relationships to the multitude of pressures to which the scholar was subject. He was not left
alone to think through the meaning of his materials, to relate his
findings to the great achievements of earlier scholars in his own and
in related fields. He was bogged down with too many administrative duties, too many committees, too much teaching. All this, plus
the demands his duties as a citizen and his obligations to popularize
his learning to a larger public made on him, led, many believed, to
fragmented, unimportant publications. At the same time critics
also made their targets the inadequacies of the scholar's training, his
exclusiveness, and the resulting narrowness of his output.[33]

It became increasingly common to deplore the dullness of American scholarly publications, their lack of clarity and beauty of literary
expression. While most historians endeavored to make history conform more closely to the canons of social science some gallantly
tried to restore it as craftsmanship to the great literary tradition.
In the field of literary scholarship critics cried for grace and gaiety,
for proportion and verve. Nor was this all. Jacques Barzun argued
that scholars generally depended on out-of-date points of view and
even discredited interpretations in the peripheral fields surrounding
their own highly narrow specialties.[34] As the half-century ended
both laymen and natural scientists expressed dismay at finding that
the social sciences and humanities, after all that had been done, were
still so unsystematized, so unsure, and so indeterminate.

Yet any such verdict must be qualified. Judged even by traditional
European standards American scholarship in the first decades of
the twentieth century was substantial in quantity and competent in
quality. At its best, humanistic scholarship certainly ranked with the
most notable in contemporary Europe. In the field of the social sciences, Americans were truly creating a vigorous, original, and significant body of knowledge. But American and European scholars
alike were often misled by the tendency of American scholars to be
self-critical, to belittle the emphasis on fact-finding and the frequent
failure to relate new discoveries to traditional knowledge and to

larger perspectives. In point of fact, one of the great strengths of American scholarship was its extraordinary capacity for self-criticism, its humility, and its appreciation of the learning of other lands. In general, Europeans failed to understand this, nor was it adequately taken into account by many Americans themselves.

Moreover, it was seldom apparent to European scholars, and rarely so to Americans, that scholarship in the second quarter of the twentieth century was experiencing a redefinition and a reorientation. Profound changes in the economy and culture invited scholars to consider the relation of their work to contemporary problems and tensions, to assume a larger and more immediate responsibility to the social order of which they were a part. The responsiveness of many to this urgent call was in part explicable in terms of the value traditionally attached to humanitarianism, to the useful, to the pragmatic. At the same time this pressure on scholars to shape their work in terms of social needs enhanced the difficulty of approaching that disinterested objectivity and universality on which scholarship had properly set so high a value.

In relating the specific finding to an immediate problem or need, in crossing traditional barriers between fields of learning, in experimenting with new techniques and with coöperative approaches, American scholars were in truth pioneering. Many did not fully sense this fact, and deplored some of its implications. That it was possible for so many to move into a relatively new area of application, explains both the self-criticism here and the unfavorable view which Europeans took toward the American performance — a view which often obscured the increasingly important contributions made in the United States to knowledge in the more traditional sense.

IV

Recent decades have seen a marked weakening of the tradition of the scholar as a figure isolated from the society in which he lived. But even before the twentieth-century, scholars devoted their specialized knowledge and gifts to solving the pressing problems of society. Long before Fichte summoned German pundits to help free and strengthen the fatherland, New England Puritans, in the tradition of medieval scholars, used their knowledge in the fight against such enemies of Zion in the Wilderness as Catholics, Indians, and witches! Yet with some point Emerson in the early nineteenth century indicted American scholarship for its Alexandrian dependence on the books of other scholars, for its indifference to the living problems of nature and man. Toward the end of the century two other Harvard men spoke their minds. Wendell Phillips excoriated his alma mater for having aligned itself with the forces of privilege in ignoring the needs of the oppressed and the unfortunate. James Russell Lowell belittled the picayunish scholarship that divorced itself from the larger culture and the larger life.

At the very time that Phillips and Lowell were making their indictments of a "sterile" American scholarship, the western state universities were heroically, if often ineffectively, struggling with the problem of relating the higher learning to current human needs. With justification President Charles Kendall Adams of Wisconsin declared in 1897 that the indictment of the Harvard scholars could not have been fairly leveled at the state universities.[35]

The call for scholars to concern themselves with living public issues did not leave the private institutions untouched. Woodrow Wilson, David Starr Jordan, William Rainey Harper, Nicholas Murray Butler, and Charles W. Eliot all sounded the same trumpet call.[36] A growing number of scholars lent their talents to the solution of public questions; the Wisconsin Idea in the first decade of the present century was only the most striking example of the scholarly concern with current issues. In the state and federal agencies a growing number of university scientists and social scientists found opportunities to put their knowledge to work in the solution of problems associated with the new industrial economy.

In the First World War scholars in the humanities as well as in sister disciplines were called on for help. They did help, and with a new sense of exhilaration and satisfaction that was no doubt in part compensatory for the passivity and remoteness from actualities that many scholars had felt.[37] The depression also saw a national mobilization of the scholar as a vital part of society. Scholars shouldered new responsibilities in the public interest. In those years a growing number battled in public office for the country. Charles E.

Merriam, William E. Dodd, Wilbur Cross, T. V. Smith, Rexford Tugwell, Robert Morss Lovett, Edwin Witte, and Paul H. Douglas are only a few examples. And throughout the land scholars who stayed at their desks talked, wrote, and lectured differently because of a new concern for the forgotten man and for neglected areas of work that might help solve his problems.[38] The Second World War, of course, carried the tendency further.

Thus the secularization of scholarship moved rapidly ahead. The old-time scholar, dressing and behaving differently from most folk, whom more worldly friends regarded with the same pity and admiration that medieval knights and merchants must have shown the monks, gave way to a new type who dressed, talked, and acted very much as a man of the world. Like other men of affairs, he struggled for prestige and success in a highly competitive profession, fought for a greater measure of economic security, and increasingly immersed himself in the main stream of events.[39]

Yet far too often this struggle for status immeasurably hindered the fulfillment of his true function as a scholar. In addition, far too often his efforts at relative economic security were doomed to failure. Being a member of a profession which, theoretically at least, did not and could not measure its results in pecuniary gain, the scholar often found himself in a state of financial embarrassment. Like other members of the white collar classes in America he found that security in an economic sense became even more distant during depression periods.[40] While the scholar was usually a member of some sort of organization he found it difficult to use that organization as an economic bargaining weapon. In some educational institutions, it is true, some faculty members joined a teachers' union which was dedicated to making the economic status of the profession more attractive. But these efforts generally were not effective at the college and university level.

Despite the recognition by the lay public that scholarship was a national resource, Americans did not give the scholar the place which classical Athens and prerevolutionary China or even contemporary Europe and England awarded him. Indeed, many looked on the scholar, especially the social scientist, as a crackpot theorist if not a downright menace. Thus, for example, Frederick Prince

spoke for many fellow businessmen in declaring that "professors are
one of the chief curses of the country. . . . They talk too much.
Most professors are a bunch of cowards and meddlers. . . . You
have only to think back over the last ten years to realize the difficulties we have been drawn into through professors. The sooner
we get away from their influence, the better." [41]

V

Although at no time in any culture has the scholar's freedom
been divorced from the broader aspects of freedom or the lack of
it in the society as a whole, the issue has become more sharply
focused in twentieth-century America than ever before. The reasons are obvious. The more general participation of the scholar in
public life made him even more obviously dependent on public
support and approval than he had seemed when he kept largely
aloof in his ivory tower. That participation also made the public
more sensitive to what the scholar said and did, especially in matters
explicitly affecting the general interest. New forces and pressures
sharpened the confines of the area of free discussion and action in
general and academic freedom as part of this. As the old question
of orthodox theology versus modern science retreated or disappeared, mounting tensions in the relations between business, labor,
and agriculture set in. Associated with these were conflicts arising
over the new world role America was playing, accentuated by participation in two world wars and by a grave struggle with Soviet
Russia.

The 1890's had witnessed several threats to the freedom of academic scholars who questioned the economic *status quo*. Events in
the first decade and a half of the twentieth century suggested that
it was no less dangerous then for a university professor to speak and
write in favor of measures deemed "socialistic" or "radical." The
danger was brought home in 1914 when the University of Pennsylvania dismissed Scott Nearing, a popular professor of economics, for
socialist writings and activities. When America plunged into the
First World War, the dismissal of faculty members who opposed
that action and their persecution at the hands of an hysterical public,

emphasized anew the importance of the whole issue of academic freedom within the larger confines of the question of the civil liberties in the society as a whole.[42] The rise of Communist Russia and the fears it aroused in conservative circles in the 1920's created a sensitive area for academicians left of center. Depression augmented the potential threat to academic freedom not only in reducing the economic security of scholars along with millions of other Americans, but in focusing attention on those who lent their talents to the attempted solution of the nation's problems. As economic distress deepened, the writings and actions of the scholar took on an added significance and became more closely scrutinized. Sometimes such scrutiny resulted in loyalty oaths and in crusades for the censorship of textbooks.[43]

Finally, the advance of totalitarianism abroad, America's entrance into World War II, and the ensuing cold war with Russia, sharpened the issue of academic freedom. It became increasingly clear that if a free society was to exist in a period of reliance on military power, then the freedom of the scholar must be maintained. At least a segment of American scholars felt a deep responsibility for preserving freedom in America.

Early in 1913 a small group of scholars representing some eight major universities responded to the call of Lovejoy, Dewey, and others to meet in Baltimore to discuss the advisability of organizing an association of university professors dedicated to the exploration in a democratic fashion of the common problems of the universities, as a means of realizing more effectively, in conjunction with officials and the public, the aims of higher education. Thus was launched the American Association of University Professors. From the start the issue of academic freedom loomed large in the discussions and activities of the new organization, although it also gave much attention to the related problem of tenure and security, to professional ethics, and to the maintainance of the highest possible standards in research, instruction, and public service.[44]

The report prepared early in the history of the AAUP by the Committee on Academic Freedom and Tenure (Committee A) reflected the basic position of the Association on academic freedom and continued to guide it in this sphere. The Committee assumed that progress toward a higher civilization would follow from the continued advancement of human knowledge, from its dissemination, and from its use by experts in the service of the public. Its position on academic freedom rested on these general assumptions. The Committee maintained that the scholar could effectively function only in an atmosphere of freedom, whether in inquiry and research, in teaching, or in extramural utterance and action. Feeling that the first phase was everywhere in a sound condition, the Committee devoted itself to the latter two aspects of academic freedom. It distinguished between private colleges created for specific purposes and those institutions which were public in nature. The latter comprised not only the state universities but all those that appealed to the public for support.

The Committee maintained that if education was the cornerstone of progress, then the scholar's peculiar social function required him to reveal the results of research to fellow specialists, to students, and to the general public "without fear or favor." If the scholar was to be useful to society, society must have confidence in his disinterestedness. Hence the scholar was in no sense comparable to an employee in a business firm. The academic family must police its own ranks, lest this be done by less competent bodies. Such policing implied a sense of responsibility on the part of the scholar to his institution and to society as well as to the truth. He must in taking account of the immaturity of his students not try to indoctrinate them; he must rather stimulate them to think. In facing the public, the scholar should try to avoid hasty, intemperate statements; but it was neither possible nor desirable "to deprive a college professor of the political rights vouchsafed to every citizen." Thus it was not proper to prohibit scholars from speaking on controversial questions outside the university even when these questions fell outside their specialties. Nor was it proper to condemn academicians for lending active support to organized movements which they believed to be in the public interest.[45]

In later years succeeding presidents of the Association and succeeding reports of Committee A restated and amplified the original report. But the Association did not content itself with mere words. It defined over the years the conditions of good tenure and of proper relations between professors, administrators, governing bodies, and interest groups beyond university campuses. It is impossible to outline or even to mention the host of investigations which Committee A conducted at various institutions where charges of violation of academic freedom were made. These have been many. Yet it should be noted that most of the violations of academic freedom and tenure concerned the teaching of undergraduates or the extramural activities of the professor.

After careful investigation the Committee recommended the censuring of administrations in which the governing body failed to respect the AAUP code of academic freedom and tenure. Whether such action really achieved the desired result has been a matter of controversy. This much can be said in regard to these investigations. Usually the violation of academic freedom was attended with publicity in which the administration side of the picture dominated, if it did not monopolize, newspaper accounts. By the time Committee A had made its investigation, written its report, and tried to disseminate its findings, the harm had been done. The sober careful analysis of the reports failed to make good headlines and were all too often ignored by the newspapers; and the public, unaware of the findings, continued to entertain the original impression created by the first headlines emanating from administration sources. Thus in actuality many censured administrations went their way largely unaffected by adverse AAUP reports.

Perhaps at no time is the difficulty in maintaining academic freedom greater than in war, for patriotism and scholarship have found themselves at opposite poles as well as close supplements. In 1916 Committee A elaborated its position regarding the problem of the professor who did not accept the war as wise and desirable and necessary. That position hardly conformed with the strong stand taken in 1915 in behalf of academic freedom.[47]

With the war clouds gathering in Europe in 1939, the Association, taking note of the abridgments to intellectual freedom in 1917 and 1918, adopted resolutions calling for a sustained effort to preserve our liberties. After the country entered the war, Committee A again called upon members of the Association not to forget their role as scholars while fulfilling patriotic duties. Only if scholars continued to maintain the critical attitude, to ask basic questions, to resist drifting with the tide, could America win the only war worth winning — the war to make peace and freedom possible in the world. "If the freedom we cherish is indeed basic to our scholarship, is it too much to ask that it inspire us to act justly in a perilous time?" [48]

As late as 1944 the Committee, seeing no reason to modify its stand, maintained that events had proved its wisdom. Linking academic freedom with freedom of thought for which the war was being waged, the Committee stated that "it would be folly to draw a boundary line across the area of freedom." [49] Never before had there been greater necessity for unbiased information than there now was to meet the great problems of the postwar world. Committee A and the Association could look with a certain pride on the record during the second world conflict.

While the need in the postwar years for accurate information remained greater than ever, the pressures against such inquiry and dissemination exceeded anything that was felt during the war itself. The cold war with Soviet Russia resulted not only in purges of Communists and Communist sympathizers from faculties, but also in clamor for restrictions on academic freedom and in new loyalty oaths. The University of Washington attracted nation-wide publicity when three faculty members were discharged largely on the ground of political affiliations. The report of Committee A had not appeared by the last day of 1952; but many believed that in the report of this case would be found a key to future policies in the face of new pressures threatening to undermine academic freedom in America.

But there were other forces seeking to hamper the pursuit of freedom by American scholars. In the 1920's fundamentalists sought to restrict the teaching of theories of evolution. A special committee set up by AAUP on Freedom of Teaching in Science took strong ground. "We are never absolutely certain as to what constitutes truth, but if there is any method of insuring that what is taught is true better than that of giving investigators and teachers utmost freedom to discover and proclaim the truth as they see it, that method has never been discovered. If those who know most about a subject sometimes decide wrongly, matters are not likely to be

.mended by putting the decision into the hands of those who know less." [50] In another report two years later, the Association backed up its committee which maintained that the real issue in this question was "whether or not we wish to make an intellectual slave of every teacher in a state-supported institution and to force him to square his teaching with the dogmas of any group which succeeds in getting legislative protection for its doctrines." [51]

There were other notable stands for academic freedom. In 1928 the Federal Trade Commission revealed that numerous scholars and academicians had accepted emoluments from the large private utilities for their services in writing and teaching on the subject of power. In 1931, after long consideration, the Association went on record with a statement of principle to the effect that "no university professor who receives a fee or other compensation from any person or association interested in public discussion or testimony respecting a particular question of public importance should take part in such testimony, without making public the fact that he receives a compensation therefor, and the name of the person or association paying him said compensation." [52] The Association also viewed with disapproval the campaign of the National Association of Manufacturers in 1939 to censor school textbooks on the ground that the extracting of certain "objectionable" passages from textbooks, constituted a dangerous precedent in giving false impressions to laymen of the contents of the books.[53]

The AAUP also sharply criticized the enactment by twenty-two states of legislation requiring teachers to take oaths of loyalty. In 1936 Committee A pointedly asked: "Are teachers alone to be singled out for such treatment? . . . Loyalty is something one lives, and not something one professes, in spite of views to the contrary held by misguided patriots and owners of low-class newspapers who have no conception of what the founding fathers really meant. Laws should deal with overt acts, not with a state of mind. Intellectual honesty can only be dangerous to demagogues." [54] The Committee then restated its stand on academic freedom, pointing out that "whether we like it or not, real freedom of speech means freedom for the ideas we loathe, as well as for those we approve. The whole question of academic freedom is merely a part of the larger concept of freedom of speech in America." [55] Nor did the Association confine its interest to America alone, for it protested vigorously against the persecution of colleagues in foreign lands and coöperated with agencies designed to provide relief for persecuted scholars.[56]

But the American Association of University Professors represented only part of the academic world. An unknown number of scholars shared the position of Nicholas Murray Butler, president of Columbia, who urged that academic freedom implied the limitations imposed by a common morality, common sense, common loyalty, and decent respect for the opinions of mankind.[57] Such limitations might make a mockery of the academic freedom for which the AAUP stood, especially in times of crisis, as President Butler's position in 1917 and 1939 revealed. Others felt that the scholar should publicly express himself only in those matters on which he was qualified as a specialist to speak. But this meant the forfeiture of basic constitutional rights.

Others, for religious, racial, or political reasons, refused to subscribe to what seemed to them unlicensed academic freedom: this meant that which criticized their own position or doctrine. Roman Catholics, for example, while professing to hold views on academic freedom entirely in tune with those of the AAUP, actually came far from doing so, if official statements are evidence. The Catholic position denied the right of any scholar to "impose on the immature, the uncritical, the unwary, his own untested intellectual idiosyncrasies." This meant, in other words: "Academic freedom is freedom to teach what is true and to receive instruction in what is true. When it comes to defining what is true, Catholic education seeks the guidance not only of the natural law, but of Christ, our Lord, which is interpreted for us by the Church." Thus the scholar was in effect free to teach only that which corresponded to Catholic doctrine as determined by the Church itself.[58] In the graduate field the Catholic universities favored "the winds of competent criticism which will blow away the smoke screens of prejudice and especially of the modern agnostic and atheistic theophobia. It will be to keep the air clear so as to permit a full view of truth in its correct perspective." [59] By inference, academic freedom did not include anything that might possibly blow away the revealed truths of the Church. Whether this position was followed by all Catholic scholars cannot easily be determined.

Thus it is apparent that there was no general agreement on the meaning of academic freedom. Its variant principles rested rather on the several competing assumptions of the purpose and meaning of education. Where these assumptions differed, the understanding of academic freedom differed. It was certain that the world of higher education did not in anything like its entirety subscribe to the instrumentalist position, largely exemplified in the principles and practices of the AAUP. This position meant that academic freedom can never be single and general, but that it must be specific and plural, that it represents the optimum opportunity for hearing all sides and for making a choice of all possible avenues. It meant respect for, and protection of, the right of expression of opinions, hypotheses, and theories one might abhor, on the assumption that the greater the diversity of views, the better the chance for approximate truth.

It seemed, at the mid-century point, that this view was in the process of modification, that a more restricted view leaning toward some sort of absolutism was gaining ground. But it was impossible to weigh the relative strength of the contending views of academic freedom in the larger context of conflicting educational philosophies. In other words, the nature and degree of academic freedom that was to prevail rested on the acceptance of one or another of the differing conceptions of the place of the scholar and scholarship in society. The problem was one of defining the social responsibility of the scholar and scholarship.

VI

This problem, as we have already seen, has always been present in western civilization, and came to be ever more acute with the consolidation of industrial America and with her increasingly important position on the world stage. Despite the fact that innumerable scholars had lent a hand, as we have seen, to the winning of the two world wars and in the fight against the depression, and had further spoken out against the Nazi violation of human rights and scholarly values, some felt that American academicians were still too largely neutral in the face of momentous public questions. American scholars, Archibald MacLeish eloquently proclaimed in *The Irresponsibles*, had been woefully indifferent to the ordeal European scholarship and letters had been passing through, callously unwilling to defend the great western tradition that had nurtured them no less than their Old World colleagues, and tragically blinded by a false conception of learning as a useless personal ornament.[60] On a different but related level Robert K. Lynd indicted the social scientists. In his view scholars had, in assuming impartiality and in refusing to take a stand in current controversies, actually capitulated to dominant interests and then rationalized that capitulation as an objectivity which in fact was only a mirage.[61]

Drawing in part on earlier contentions of Paul Elmer More and Irving Babbitt, critics of the MacLeish-Lynd positions insisted that the essence of scholarship is the cultivation of the long view, the sustained courageous search for truth, irrespective of immediate pressures and dictates. One rejoinder declared that MacLeish had made the fatal blunder of asking scholars to pervert the intellect in order to defend it, that he had mistakenly defined the activities of scholarship in terms of certain other activities that are not essentially related to scholarship at all.[62]

For the most extreme advocates of each of these positions there was little or no conflict: the path of duty was clear. For the unknown but large number of scholars who have shared both objectives there was a genuine dilemma. Only a few of these succeeded, perhaps, as John Dewey so notably did, in integrating the two functions and in making significant contributions to both. For Dewey has both advanced knowledge in psychology, education, and philosophy, and fought gallantly in the forum of public opinion for the democratic values he cherished.

The implicit assumption that the man of learning is a custodian of the social conscience, of cultural and human values, has further complicated the problem of his obligations to society. This assumption was often shared both by those who advocated the application of specialized knowledge to immediate social issues and by those who emphasized the long-run search for disinterested truth. Many scholars, of course, took a much more humble and limited view of the role of the man of learning in society. But those with the ideal of custodianship failed to take into account the fact that there were other groups, vested with greater power, that similarly regarded themselves as guardians of social values: for instance, columnists, the business community, the government bureaucracy, and the church. The assumption that the scholar is in a special sense the custodian of social values further overlooked the fact that large sections of the public regarded the intellectual as peculiarly inept in decision and policy making. It is only necessary to recall the prejudice against the New Deal scholars, prejudice only partly offset by the more generally appreciated services of experts in the Second World War.[63] The problem of the scholar was thus not a conflict merely between those who felt that their chief function was to interpret, defend, and extend the cultural heritage and those who felt called on to use specialized knowledge in immediate tensions and problems. It was also a conflict between what scholars wanted to do and their ability and power to do it in view of the influence of social groups outside the realm of scholarship.

An increasingly large number came to accept a different view. They accepted the thesis that it was impossible for scholars actually to divorce themselves altogether from immediate pressures in the pursuit of learning. In their minds the scholar who believed he was entirely objective in standing apart from current controversies, only deceived himself. He was indeed in one sense taking sides, however unaware of this he might be: for in failing to take a stand, he was supporting the dominant position.

There was also a growing recognition that decision making, whether by scholars or by nonscholars, results from a kind of intuitive judgment closely related to the temperament and the values of the thinker and to fluctuations in public opinion and the pressures of effectively organized groups and interests. When scholars become practitioners, they probably rely more on such intuitive judgments than on the disinterested analysis associated with scholarship.[64] Neither the scholar who in theory divorces himself from immediate issues nor the one concerned with immediate problems has any monopoly on objectivity.

That there are differences in the degree of subjectivity is, of course, true. And none denied the supreme importance of the sustained effort to be as objective as human frailties and present techniques in knowledge-finding permit. Indeed, Charles A. Beard and Carl Becker asked whether it was not true that the scholar who faced his bias and his limitations squarely was not able to be more objective than the one who claimed for himself an unattainable disinterestedness. They urged the importance of exploring more deeply the means by which the perception of relativism might be kept from becoming mere cynicism and opportunism, and by which the intuition of values and faith might be kept from becoming a rationalized camouflage of private and group interests.[65]

A third assumption, shared alike by many scholars in both groups, was that research equals progress. In insisting on their peculiar function of guarding the great cultural heritage, the above-the-battle scholars put less emphasis than others on the idea that scholarship is the way to progress. Yet there was a widespread assumption that such was the case. On his part, the scholar concerned with service almost inevitably assumed that the application of knowledge to problems of everyday life was somehow indispensable to progress. President Van Hise of the University of Wisconsin commonly calculated the dollar and cents returns of the research the state supported at his institution and pointed to the result as progress.[66] No doubt the application of knowledge to specific life problems led to an advancing standard of living. It was also widely recognized that the solution of certain problems by the application of the results of research gave rise to new problems. To recognize this was not, however, to establish a case against science and research, as some humanistic critics believed. But it was, as such critics insisted, an argument that the results of research did not necessarily equal progress unless applications were responsibly directed toward socially desirable and ethical ends.

The humanistic rationale included — at least in certain quarters — the contention that the scholar should also stick to his last. The scholar might as an individual take part in public conflicts, but when he did so, the tools of scholarship must not be among his weapons, for these tools were sacred to the long-range search for truth. Such spokesmen as Robert Hutchins, Theodore Greene, and Henry M. Wriston insisted that scholarship already suffered too much from an oversensitivity to current issues. This, of course, was closely related to their respective positions in the educational structure, whether humanist or neo-Thomist.[67] On the other side, instrumentalists asked how, in the battles of the day, the scholar could be separated from the pursuit of truths with the instruments of scholarship.

Dissatisfied with the relativism of the second quarter of the twentieth century, many scholars reacted against it. This they did regardless of the relativistic implications of cultural anthropology, psychology, the new physics, and the philosophy of instrumentalism. They assumed that it was possible to end the world-wide moral and intellectual confusions by imposing a new unity and a new authority.[68] In the 1920's some scholars, influenced by neohumanism, found such an authority in the classical tradition. In the 1930's a few, probably a very few, scholars saw in Marxism a new coherence and authority, but after the Nazi-Russian pact there was a tendency to lose respect at least for Communist Marxism. In the 1940's some scholars found that unifying authoritative principle or synthesis in neo-Thomism, or in the great books.

But instrumentalists and relativists accepted the challenge. They replied that the great danger in an authoritarian approach was that values related to our geographic area, our institutions, our time, would be imposed as universals, as eternal truth. In failing to recognize the subjectivity of scholarship and scholars, these critics maintained, both scholars and scholarship would in effect capitulate to the dominant interests of their age. In assuming that omnipotence and universal truth were on their side, they would stifle new research and inquiry and criticism, and end by enforcing a new orthodoxy, a given absolutism.

During and after the Second World War many signs pointed to the growing vogue of what promised to become the new orthodoxy, the new absolutism. As the tension with Soviet Russia gave way to the cold war, many scholars consciously or unconsciously found an orthodoxy and a sense of security, if not an absolute, in American nationalism. They embraced more tightly the "American way of life," which scholars had long tried to define, and the more or less free enterprise system associated with political and social democracy. Both the scholars devoted to the long-range quest for truth and those committed to immediate public service saw in "Americanism" the antithesis to communism. Both assumed that the troubles with Russia resulted solely from Soviet aggressiveness, intransigence, ruthlessness, and Marxist dogmatism. They did not always ask whether the behavior they properly deplored might not be merely a symptom of a deeper, more complex situation within Russia itself and in the larger world caught in revolutionary crisis. At least some scholars in opposing communism did sound warnings against the danger of opposing communism with methods used by the Communists themselves.

The similarities of the two scholarly positions were sometimes overlooked in the heat of discussion. Both sought, in a general way, the same ends — a free society. But it was clear that means had become all important. The absolutists in adopting authority, discipline, and accepted criteria of orthodoxy seemed in some eyes to follow a path likely to make their ultimate goal impossible of achievement. But the instrumentalists in choosing the means of freedom could give no final assurance that these would lead to an assured and defined end. In the terms of the two positions, scholarship in the mid-century turmoil seemed a somewhat inadequate instrument. Yet it was by no means clear that there was any better one at hand. At the same time, the scholarly heritage of the past, and especially of the first half of the twentieth century, required a continued and sustained search for a scholarship — in conjunction with other forces — adequate to the needs of the new atomic age. The truly impressive achievements of the first half of the twentieth century gave promise that such a quest was in no sense hopeless.

II ·

The Social Sciences

LOUIS WIRTH

I

The social sciences comprise so vast a range of interests that any attempt to chart the salient direction of their development, even during so short a span of intellectual history as half a century, is bound to be presumptuous. This is especially true because what has happened to the social sciences in the last fifty years constitutes the major segment of the history of these sciences, as sciences. The scientific approach to these fields of learning has, with few exceptions, notably that of economics, been largely a product of the work of the last fifty years. The proliferation and academic specialization of these disciplines during the last half-century represents a bewildering spectacle and stands in sharp contrast to the essential unity, and to a large degree also the scientific sterility of social science scholarship in earlier periods.

The social sciences as here conceived are those studies of man which seek to discover what is true about him and his actions by virtue of the fact that everywhere and always he leads a group life. This perspective of human action furnishes the common platform for all of the social sciences and the unifying principle which makes it possible to think of them together as a single, though extensive, field of intellectual activity. What differentiates them from one another is not a difference in subject matter, for all of them are concerned with the collective life of man, but rather the characteristic questions which each social science discipline raises about this common subject matter and the characteristic concepts and method by which each seeks tenable answers to its questions.

Group life, however, exerts so pervasive an influence upon human behavior that it sometimes becomes difficult to distinguish between the studies of man that are not properly a concern of the social sciences from those that are. Thus, for instance, human geography, which is concerned with the relationship between man and his habitat, has often dealt with this nexus without due recognition of the importance of man's life in groups. This has been equally if not more true in psychology, which though obviously concerned with human behavior has often only as an afterthought taken cognizance of the group factor in this behavior. A somewhat different difficulty arises in the case of history, which is the authentic, organized record of man's experience. The exclusion of history from our account of the social sciences in the twentieth century does not imply that historical scholarship is not intimately associated with social science both as a source of indispensable data and as consumer of the findings of social science. It is also a full-fledged partner in the common quest for reliable knowledge concerning human nature and the social order. The omission of the developments in, and contributions of history from, this account is due to the circumstance that history is more fully treated in a separate chapter and rests upon the further consideration that, as a form of scholarship, it is concerned with the unique and the particular and does not seek to arrive at general propositions. The "laws" governing human conduct, which the social sciences seek to discover, can only be established by viewing historical events comparatively, by tearing them out of their particularistic contexts of time, place, and circumstance, and by translating events into things.[1]

The social sciences, with whose record of the last fifty years we shall be concerned here, comprise economics, politics, sociology, human geography, and those aspects of anthropology which have recently come to be recognized as social anthropology, as well as those aspects of psychology which are now designated as social psychology.

The failure to treat certain aspects of history, geography, anthropology, and psychology in this account of the development of the social sciences should not lead to the inference that they are irrelevant. Indeed, it is to these peripheral areas that the social scientist must turn for his postulates and for much of his data. Similarly, this account of the social sciences omits the developments in such practical fields as education, social psychiatry, social work, law, business, race relations, industrial relations, international relations, administration, and planning. While these arts, techniques, and professions are, of course, intimately related to the social sciences in that they are dependent upon them for their basic knowledge concerning man as a social being and the society in which he lives and, in turn, provide the social scientist with significant materials for study, it is manifestly impossible to include them for any detailed consideration here. It will, however, be of interest in this attempt to trace the recent developments of the social sciences to show how they have influenced such fields as history, linguistics, and psychology on the one hand, and practical social action on the other hand.

It has often been said, especially when apologizing for the scarcity of reliable social science knowledge which could furnish the foundation for scientifically guided social action, that the social sciences are, after all, very young and have had little time to develop significant bodies of reliable knowledge such as the physical and biological sciences have made available to such practical fields as medicine and engineering. This is an error which even a cursory view of the record of man's thought about himself and his world clearly reveals. Actually, interest in the understanding of human nature and the social order is amply demonstrated by some of the earliest records of history. There was a striking difference, however, between what men thought they knew about the physical world and the world of living things on one hand, and what they thought they knew about themselves and their fellows on the other. Whereas physical and biological knowledge began to be subjected to the test of experience and the scrutiny of scientific workers at a relatively early stage in its development, ideas concerning man and his relationships with his fellow men became formulated into doctrines which resisted reëxamination and modification because they became associated with the prerogatives of power holders or became encrusted with sacred and undiscussable dogmas. This is not to say that there has been unlimited freedom of inquiry in the physical and biological sciences, but rather that secularization and acceptance of the canons of scientific inquiry in these fields came earlier and proceeded at a much more rapid pace than was the case in the social sciences. In the realm of the social and the human, the quest for knowledge continued to rest on authority and speculation rather than on empirical research long after inquiry in the realm of the physical and biological had accepted systematic observation, experience, and experimentation as the tests of truth.

Another reason for the backwardness of the social sciences is the fact that, unlike the problems with which the natural sciences deal, those which furnish the subject matter of social science are also familiar to the average citizen in his daily experience and are the subject of folklore, maxims, and proverbs. Social science knowledge must break through this hard "cake of custom," as Bagehot [2] would say, and make its way in the face of this vast store of common-sense knowledge and practical wisdom which has accumulated through the ages. Hence, in the realm of the social and the human it is often difficult to distinguish between the layman and the expert. Social science expertness has difficulties in achieving the recognition which the physical and biological scientist is accorded by virtue of his demonstrable command of reliable knowledge in the form of ability to predict and control.

The relatively low prestige of social science, as contrasted with natural science, is further accentuated by the circumstance that the physical and biological sciences employ a specialized and esoteric language to which the layman can gain access only with difficulty. The social sciences, in contrast, despite the frequently heard complaint about their forbidding language, for the most part rely upon the language of everyday discourse and are, therefore, subject to the suspicion that they disguise what everybody knows in language which nobody can understand.

Finding himself supported in his own notions concerning the social issues of his world by the sacred traditions and fixed beliefs of his family, his tribe, his church, his class, his party, and his nation, the average citizen is not likely to be amenable to rational persuasion to a set of contrary ideas merely because his own ideas have been proved untenable by alleged experts. Suspecting those who disagree with him of ignorance or of bias based on self-interest, the ordinary man is not disposed to believe that the social scientist is exempt from the same sources of fallibility. The general public is skeptical of the claims of the social scientist that he has arrived at his conclusions by orderly, objective and full investigation of the facts; that he has taken all available safeguards against his own biases and errors of judgment through critical self-examination, through adopting a broad historical perspective and a comparative point of view and by strict adherence to the rule of logic and scientific proof. Whereas the correctness of the findings in physical or biological science can generally be demonstrated by experiment, by empirical proof, and by countless gadgets which have practical utility, those of social science are more likely to be accepted or rejected on the basis of scientifically irrelevant personal and social considerations. Moreover, since the problems with which the social scientist deals are characteristically controversial issues among the rival interest groups comprising society, social science runs the risk of being considered "dangerous thought," and the social scientist a "subversive" character.

In these respects social science is in a uniquely precarious position among the branches of scholarship. It enjoys neither the prestige of natural science which demonstrably has aided men in solving their practical problems, nor can it rely upon the escape clause in which the humanistic studies can take refuge, namely that they have no other purpose than to increase human understanding and elevate the human spirit. In the face of these disadvantages, it is rather remarkable that the social sciences should have achieved the wide recognition, attracted the rich material support, and infused themselves into the texture of life in America to the degree that they have succeeded in doing during the past half century.

II

From the vantage point of the present, the past half-century in the development of the social sciences in the United States may be described as a period of healthy and vigorous growth. Indeed, if the "scientific" aspect of the social studies be emphasized, it is not too much of an exaggeration to say that social science had its beginning around the turn of the century. This may be said to be true in two senses: first, that before the opening of the twentieth century the substantive knowledge concerning men in their relations with one another was vague, meager, and impressionistic; and second, that before 1900 only the first signs were visible of the pursuit of social science as an academically sanctioned professional activity.

Strict adherence to the requirements of historical accuracy (which in the field of intellectual history must be interpreted literally) calls, of course, for considerable qualification of these statements. The new century did not open on a social science wasteland. There had not only been much theorizing and a rich store of practical wisdom about man and society in earlier generations, but there was also at hand an impressive accumulation of valuable and reliable factual knowledge in many fields of social science. There was also some evidence of the intrusion and acceptance of social scientists, as such, in the expanding American institutions of higher learning.

In the eighteen-nineties and throughout the first decade of the twentieth century there was vigorous discussion among the social scientists themselves concerning their respective roles in the intellectual division of labor, the nature and scope of their subject matter, and the distinctive features of their methods. There were heated debates on whether social science was one or many; whether it was merely a "point of view" or a substantive body of specialized knowledge not already adequately treated by history, politics, and moral philosophy. Many meetings were held and learned polemics were published on whether the practitioners of the new social science could better pursue their interests if they organized themselves into distinct scientific associations. There was serious and protracted discussion about how the social sciences were to be taught, about the need for the establishment of professional journals, and about the timeliness of organizing new departments in the colleges and universities.

The social sciences in America at the opening of the twentieth century were in a mood which could be more appropriately characterized as exhuberant promotionalism than sober stock-taking. They were less concerned with systematic organization of existing knowledge and charting of the most feasible lines of scientific development than with legitimizing their existence in the academic world and counteracting the misunderstanding and lack of support of an unsympathetic public.

Although the social atmosphere of America helped to shape the nation's intellectual life in all its phases, it had more directly discernible influences upon social science than upon natural science. The rapid rate of industrial expansion of the country, the rise of the nation to the position of a world power, the growth of great industrial and business combinations and the recurrently asserted challenges of that power by organized labor and populist-agrarian movements, the disappearing frontier, the mass influx of immigrants, the plight of the Negro, the chaotic growth of cities, the everwidening slums, and the existence of widespread poverty, were part of the scene in which the nascent social sciences were seeking to make headway. As in other countries, particularly England and Germany, undergoing the travail of rapid industrialization, movements of protest and of reform were winning disciples. Literary figures were crying out against the ravages of the industrial juggernaut, against reckless individualism, against the iniquitous distribution of wealth, against wasted natural resources, and against the crippling impact of the forces released by the industrial revolution upon men and institutions.

These forces, the problems which they generated, and the social movements to which they gave momentum, had a twofold impact upon the social sciences: they furnished the social scientists with the incentives and materials for their scientific enterprises and they induced the American public, which had experienced a chastening of its faith in automatic and unlimited progress, to take the social sciences more seriously. Up to this time the greater part of the in-

tellectual leadership in the ameliorative and reform efforts had come
from the nonacademic world. The "muckrakers" were carrying
their dramatic and often shocking facts concerning the deficiencies
and abuse which they had discovered by turning their discerning
eyes to the less publicized aspects of life in America, to numerous
lecture audiences and a rapidly widening circle of readers. The settlement movement, which had taken root in the larger cities, was
furnishing new guides to philanthropic efforts and incidentally was
providing a favorable platform from which to observe the problems
and processes of social life at close range. Although trade unions in
1900 had a membership of less than a million, their spokesmen were
raising the issues of improved wages and working conditions, collective bargaining and the right to strike, the prohibition of child
labor and the control of immigration. Agrarian unrest found artic-
ulate expression in political movements emphasizing currency reform, restraint of monopolies, and regulation of railroad rates. Journalists, preachers of the social gospel, reformers, political leaders,
and popular educators were expounding their doctrines on land,
money, taxes, the tariff, the Indian, the Negro, immigration, divorce,
alcohol, religion, and empire. The unorthodox economic theories of
Marx and of Darwin found their way into the popular literature
and the mind of America. They furnished the provocation for a
reëxamination of the traditional academic thought in economics,
sociology, politics, anthropology, psychology, and law.

The character of the developing social science at the turn of the
century was significantly shaped by the dominant philosophy of the
period with its empirical and pragmatic temper, its consequent emphasis upon the actual problems of the developing American society,
its revulsion from doctrinaire metaphysics and armchair speculation, and its accent upon observation and experimentation, for
which William James and John Dewey might serve as symbolic
representatives.

Many of the most outstanding social scientists had acquired their
training in the German universities, where they had been exposed
to the new methods of history, of political science, and of psychology. Returning from their graduate studies to America, they had
brought with them the spirit of the newly established laboratories

in psychology, and of the seminars in history, political science, and economics. At Johns Hopkins University, at Columbia, and at Chicago, and in a number of other institutions of higher learning in America, these young *Doktoranden* turned the intellectual curiosity of their students to fresh inquiries into the indigenous problems of the American scene, as the crop of dissertations which was finding its way into the journals and into the newly established series of monographs convincingly demonstrated.

Though colleges had been offering courses in "social science," these courses with rare exceptions were little more than the propounding of the established orthodoxies and their defense against the heretical ideas imported from abroad or implicit in the popular reformist or revolutionary thought of dissident Americans. The new academic atmosphere of America was increasingly characterized by specialization and first-hand empirical inquiry into the realities of life. Social science came to be more and more divorced from moral philosophy and cosmic theorizing on one hand, and from impetuous reform and stubborn defense of the *status quo* on the other. This is not to say, of course, that the earlier intellectual tradition had no surviving representatives, or that these failed to resist or denounce the academic ferment that was seething; but as the years passed, the triumph of the new social science over the old social philosophy became increasingly assured. Having been, from the 1870's to about the turn of the century, dependent upon European scholarship for its ideas and methods, the American social scientists, with the beginning of the new century, gave increasing evidence of their capacity to select their own problems and to develop the methods appropriate to their scientific analysis.

Academic social science in the United States might be said to have been launched with the inauguration in 1876, at the newly established Johns Hopkins University, of critical investigations in "History and Politics." This was followed about four years later by the organization of the School of Political Science at Columbia, and shortly thereafter by the development of graduate instruction at Cornell, Harvard, Michigan, Pennsylvania, and Wisconsin, in history and related subjects. At Yale, William Graham Sumner, the chief apostle of Herbert Spencer in America, under the label of social science was expounding the classical doctrine of *laissez faire*, which he offered as the proper guide to American policy in the face of recurrent temptation and increasing pressure for state intervention. From the standpoint of the institutional acceptance of social science by the centers of higher learning in America, perhaps no event was more significant than the founding of the University of Chicago in 1892, and the incorporation into that institution, from its very beginning, of a full complement of academic departments for graduate instruction and research in all of the social science disciplines.[3]

Aside from their successful infiltration into the institutions of higher learning, the social sciences, around the turn of the century, could point to notable progress in professional organization. The American Statistical Association had been founded in 1839. The American Social Science Association, which, however, could scarcely be said to have been the ancestral body from which the present-day social science organizations directly descended, was founded in 1865. The American Historical Association was organized in 1884, to be followed a year later by the American Economic Association. The American Academy of Political and Social Science was established in 1889, the American Psychological Association in 1892, the American Political Science Association in 1903, and the American Sociological Soeiety in 1905.

As these new specialized scientific bodies arrived at professional self-consciousness, they established their own scientific organs. The American Statistical Association began to publish a Quarterly in 1888; the *American Historical Review* was initiated in 1895; the *American Journal of Sociology* was established in 1895. Similar journals in the fields of economics, political science, anthropology and psychology, both as official organs of their respective societies and privately sponsored publications of universities, came into being in rapid succession. In addition, numerous series of monographs were established to furnish outlets for the increasing volume of dissertations and other scientific writing. By the opening of the twentieth century, the social sciences could be said to have achieved academic recognition.

The first decade of the twentieth century marked a decided break with the past in the developing social sciences in the United States. American scholars who had gained their initial training and skills in Europe were now fairly firmly established in the strategic centers of higher learning. In the midst of widespread popular awareness of acute social problems and of the ferment of protest and reform they began to devote themselves increasingly to first hand observation of the social scene and a critical analysis of the varied proposals for social improvement. The echoes of Marxism, Darwinism, and Spencerian social evolution were reverberating through the academic halls, and if these new ideas did not suddenly shake the foundations of the traditional theological and metaphysical doctrines upon which the higher learning had been built, they at least generated intellectual curiosity, revitalized interest in observing the rapidly changing social world and stimulated the search for new interpretations guided by a newly won confidence in the application of the methods of science to social phenomena.

The search for the historical origins of institutions began to take the place of the belief in their immutability and the appeal to providence for their sanction began to give way to factual inquiries into their actual operation. While William Graham Sumner, the principal disciple of Herbert Spencer in the United States, was invoking his concept of the folkways and the mores to discredit the assorted man-made utopias which were in the air and to cast doubt upon the designs for social reform which called for state intervention in the economic process, Lester F. Ward, in a spirit akin to that of the eighteenth-century perfectionists, though disciplined by the demonstrated achievements of modern science, was propounding a sociology which asserted the possibility of the purposeful improvement of the human lot through the distinctive agency of intelligence applied to the intricate web of man's relationship to his environment and his fellow men.

The high hopes of the pioneers of American social science, however, were still far from realization. There remained many scholars in important places who were skeptical of the claims made by those who had been fired by the enthusiasm which they had gathered in the German universities and in their newly established American outposts. Sometimes these ambitions were indeed extravagant; but even when they were modest enough, they had to run the gauntlet of a long-established intellectual heritage which, to say the least, cast doubt upon the possibility of a social science and the appropriateness of the methods developed in the physical and biological sciences to human affairs. To a goodly proportion of American scholars the social life of man called for other approaches, mainly the assimilation of the great ideas of the great thinkers of the past, the logical analysis of ethical and metaphysical doctrines, the cultivation of intuition, sympathy, and inspiration, the patient accumulation of chronicles depicting the past, and the refinement of literary skill. Though the new spirit of science was making itself widely felt, especially in the recently established academic social science departments in the universities and in the meetings of the social science associations and in their journals, it was still quite respectable for "Professors . . . to sit in chairs writing books about each other's books." [4] The charge of atheism, materialism, and vulgar mechanism was often invoked against the fledgling social scientists because of their methodological emphasis upon objectivity, the scrutiny of *a priori* assumptions, the questioning of authority, the search for reliable sources, the attempts at experimentation, and the great weight given to direct observation and mensuration. Because some social scientists became conspicuous as advocates of social reform or as critics of dominant policies and in their teaching and writing sometimes ran counter to established theological, economic, political, and moral orthodoxies, they not infrequently were denounced as socialists, revolutionaries, and evolutionists — occasionally with such dire consequences as deprivation of their academic positions.

Within the academic fraternity of the social sciences itself, moreover, rivalries and jealousies were not uncommon. This was especially evident in the resistance offered by the historians and economists, who had already "arrived," to the claim for independent status on the part of the sociologists. The early decades of American social science were characterized by separatism and in some institutions the development of new social science departments was effectively blocked by specialists representing other disciplines who happened to be in positions of authority.

III

By the end of the first decade of the twentieth century the proliferation of the social sciences, virtually in the form in which we
now know them, had practically been achieved. Within the several
disciplines, however, the intellectual division of labor proceeded at
a rapid pace as academic departments increased in size, as the literature grew in volume, and as methods of investigation became more
differentiated and technically more refined. From about 1910 on,
it became increasingly rare for a single professor to pretend to cover
the whole range of the social sciences, though in many smaller institutions one could still frequently find a professor of history or
economics, for instance, doubling in the role of political scientist or
sociologist.

The range and division of subject matter covered by the World
Congress of the Arts and Sciences, held in connection with the
St. Louis Exposition of 1904, at which the social sciences were given
full recognition,[5] comprised essentially the social sciences in their
present form. At that Congress, in which the outstanding social
scientists from Europe and America participated, the new ideas not
only in history, economics, and political science but also in sociology,
anthropology, psychology, and in related fields which had only
recently come into their own, were given an airing. It was the most
impressive educational and public relations enterprise of the social
sciences ever organized. There were definite indications in the
notable papers that were presented that the social scientists of
America, in contrast to their European colleagues, were following
the road of the division of labor by a rigorous differentiation of the
disciplines from one another.

Although, for the reason already indicated, this review is not
concerned with history, it should be pointed out that the developing
new specialisms in the social sciences were nowhere more clearly
reflected than in the changing character of history. The principle
that the historian, in Ranke's phrase, had the task of depicting the
past "as it actually was," and that in order to establish the facts he
must rely upon authentic sources and must include within his scope
the whole range of human experience which he must seek to under-

stand and interpret in the objective spirit of science, had already
been at least nominally accepted by the best historical scholars before the close of the nineteenth century. If there was a peculiar
justification during the first two decades of the twentieth century
to recognize the emergence of "the new history," it was not because
the standards for the professional historian mentioned above were
particularly novel. It was rather because the historian was becoming
more keenly aware of the assumptions — often concealed from
others as well as from himself — which guided his selection of facts
and formulation of hypotheses; it was because the historians had
assimilated from their fellow social scientists, the economists, political scientists, sociologists, social psychologists, cultural anthropologists, and human geographers, what each of them had recently
learned about the operation of the economic process, the functioning of political institutions, the structuring of society and the interaction of social groups, the nature and genesis of personality and the
varieties of human motivation, the range, the development, and the
impact of culture upon human conduct and the interrelations between man and his habitat. It was also because the historian had
become familiar with the methods which his fellow social scientists
were employing, such as the techniques of measurement and correlation and the varieties of procedures to be mastered in the testing
of hypotheses designed to explain the complex life of man.

The history that was developing during the first two decades of
the twentieth century was "new" in the sense that it was stimulated
and guided by the ideas, perspectives, and methods of the social
sciences to which it was becoming more closely allied. To cite a
recent report on the difference between the older "scientific" history
and the new:

At the same meeting of the American Historical Association in 1910
at which Turner read his presidential address on "Social Forces in
American History" James Harvey Robinson presented a paper on "The
Relation of History to the Newer Sciences of Man."

. . . The same year Carl Becker, in his article on "Detachment and
the Writing of History" . . . had launched the first of his major at-
tacks on "the fact" to which "objectivists" were proclaiming their

undying devotion. . . . Writing on "The Scientific Presentation of History" Lynn Thorndike made similar sharp criticisms of the methodology of the scientific school. In 1910 and 1911 appeared two economic interpretations: A. M. Simons' *Social Forces in American History*, definitely socialist, and Gustavus Myers' *History of Great American Fortunes*. In 1912 Robinson issued a collected volume of his essays on *The New History*. The same year Becker delivered his address on "Some Aspects of the Influence of Social Problems and Ideas upon the Study and Writing of History," perhaps the clearest early statement of the functional and pragmatic view. In 1913 was issued Beard's *An Economic Interpretation of the Constitution*. A bare list like this suggests how thick and fast the rebels were hurling their shafts against the older "scientific" history.[6]

Not only was historical scholarship in America acquiring greater sophistication as viewed in the light of the criteria of the maturing social sciences, but it was also undergoing an internal division of labor in the course of which what had mainly been political history was greatly expanded into cultural history and such specialized fields as economic history and intellectual history.

In the course of a recent survey concerning the interests, problems, achievements, and division of labor among the social sciences, Mr. Stuart Chase found:

The consensus of professional opinion . . . recognizes five disciplines as the hard core of social science: (1) cultural anthropology, (2) social psychology, (3) sociology, (4) economics, (5) political science. The order corresponds inversely with their age, for anthropology and psychology are the youngest of the disciplines, while political science is the oldest . . .

In addition to the Big Five, various other disciplines have been offered as candidates in the course of my study. History receives almost as many votes as political science, but usually with reservation . . . Legal science receives a number of votes, and so do educational methods, social work, demography, human geography, public administration . . .[7]

Without taking Mr. Chase's account too literally, it nevertheless seems convenient to depict briefly, in the reverse order which he suggests, the salient features of each of these disciplines as they have crystallized in the last half-century.

Political science, formerly inextricably linked with history and jurisprudence, having achieved independent status in the American universities, notably at Columbia under the leadership of John W. Burgess and W. A. Dunning, had turned from speculation concerning the mythical state of nature, the origin of the state, the social contract, the theory of sovereignty, and similar metaphysical issues to the empirical study of political parties and power groups, the actual operation of political institutions and the processes of government, to municipal and local governmental problems and international relations, to political psychology, public opinion, and leadership, to the making of citizens, to public administration, to the factors shaping public policy, and to the day-to-day administration of justice.

In 1903 Albert B. Hart published his *Actual Government* and a decade later Charles A. Beard his *Economic Interpretation of the Constitution*. The latter, describing major recent trends in political science, in 1908 declared:

It is . . . a false notion that the ancient and honorable discipline of politics has been overthrown or absorbed by the dissolution of the subject into history, economics, and sociology. Rather does it seem that solid foundations are being laid in reality in place of the shifting sands of speculation . . .

One of the most salutary results of this vast accumulation of data on politics has been to discredit the older speculative theorists and utopia makers . . .

The influence of the historical school on correct thinking in politics has been splendidly supplemented by that of the Darwinians. They have given us as the political unit not a typical man with typical faculties, but a man infinite in variety and capacity, ranging from . . . cannibals . . . to the highest type of modern citizen . . .

It is not only in possessing sound historical and evolutionary notions that the student of politics lays claim to being more scientific than his predecessors in the eighteenth century. He endeavors more and more to subject his own thinking to the very disciplines of history and evolution. He is convinced of what Professor Dunning has so amply and admirably demonstrated, that political philosophy is the product of the surrounding political system rather than of pure reason . . .

It is accordingly in the spirit of modern science that the student of politics turns to the great divisions of his subject, namely, the state, government, the limits of government action, political parties, and international relations.[8]

Among the important changes which Beard noted as distinguishing political science thought of his day from that prevailing twenty-five years earlier were "decreasing reference to the doctrine of natural rights as a basis for political practice," "increasing hestitation to ascribe political events to Providential causes," "rejection of the divine and racial theory of institutions," and "a persistent attempt to get more precise notions about causation in politics." He called attention to the "recent sane tendencies of legislative bodies to construct laws on reports of expert commissions rather than on impulse and high notions of popular prerogative, however legitimate," as signs of the recognition of the realism of academic political science, which was reinterpreting its ancient calling as "the counsel to princes" in the new American environment to mean the search for reliable knowledge to guide the making of wise decisions in a complex, dynamic, democratic society.

Economics in the early years of the twentieth century had already acquired a degree of respectability as a science scarcely equaled by any of the other social sciences. This was owing in part to the fact that it was operating on the basis of a set of presuppositions or "principles" the validity and immutability of which had largely gone unchallenged, and from which specific, universally valid propositions could presumably be deduced. It was also owing to the further fact that its subject matter lent itself to objectification and mensuration in terms of units of goods and quantities of money which gave to its generalizations a degree of precision unrivaled by the other social sciences. Finally, economics, whether in the form of the older "political economy," emphasizing the generalizations applying to the state as the economic unit, or later simply as "economics," which dealt with the operations of business enterprises and the behavior of consumers and producers as well, was in a position to command the attention of statesmen and businessmen for indispensable guidance on important practical affairs. The prestige of economics grew as the exuberantly expanding industrial and business enterprises of American capitalism during the first three decades of the century increasingly sought the counsel of economists. As Henry Rogers Seager put it, in the same series of lectures at Columbia in 1908 in which Charles A. Beard, from whom we have already quoted, participated:

> Businessmen are less prone to brush aside their arguments as "mere theory" and more ready to recognize that the social aspects of business also merit consideration. Even more gratifying is the increasing part which economists are being allowed to play in the drafting of legislation and in the administration of laws whose enactment they have helped to secure. The appointment of economists in tax commissions, industrial commissions and labor commissions has become so common as now to be taken for granted even in the United States, where it is a very recent development. In fact, the appreciation in which economic studies are held is growing so general that there seems just now danger that too much, rather than too little importance may be attached to the views of academic economists.[9]

The "new" economics of the twentieth century, however, differed markedly from its nineteenth-century classical and neoclassical predecessors. Whereas the older economics aimed primarily at the construction of a static, abstract model of universal scope from which elegant solutions to hypothetical problems, such as those of a Robinson Crusoe on his island, could be logically deduced, the newer economists rejected this scholastic approach and this static conception of the economy which differed so patently from the rapidly changing economic world in which they lived and to the problems of which the older economics could not produce relevant answers. In place of the rational, hedonistically calculating economic man of the eighteenth and nineteenth centuries, the economists of the twentieth century substituted a highly variable creature endowed with a wide range of "instincts," habits, interests, and motivations, responding to different situations as defined by his culture in a manner often quite unlike the picture of man which *a priori* speculation had drawn. This new version of human conduct had been made familiar to the economists of the twentieth century by the sociologists, anthropologists, and psychologists of their time.

Perhaps the most trenchant critique of the orthodox, abstract, static, metaphysical approach that had dominated economics came from Thorstein Veblen, employing the institutional approach. His *Theory of the Leisure Class*, published in 1899, though largely ignored until after his death in 1929, drew upon the heterodox writings of Marx, the hitherto largely neglected but rapidly growing body of ethnographic data, and recent sociological and social-psychological thinking. This original work, which not only signalized a wider scope for economic studies as well as the use of new methods, but also placed economic phenomena in the context of on-going social life as it could be observed among actual, living human beings in a changing society, was followed by others, on the rise of a managerial and engineering group divorced from the absentee owners, on the technological revolution that was making rapid headway and was creating a system of mass production dominated by the modern machine and revolutionizing the traditional meaning of work, and on the emergence of a new framework for industrial society. Had he been taken seriously by his economic colleagues, the older economics would have had to reconstruct itself much earlier than actually was the case. But Veblen had few, if any, genuine disciples and his influence upon economists was largely indirect and retarded.

A fresh and forceful impetus, however, came from quite another source, namely, the accumulation of reliable quantitative data concerning various phases of the economic process, especially on prices, which challenged critical examination and induced an increasing number of empirically minded economists to undertake analyses designed to test some of the most crucial hypotheses implicit in current economic doctrine. Foremost among the pioneers in this field of research dealing with the factors associated with economic fluctuations, was Wesley C. Mitchell, who published his epoch-making statistical study on economic trends in the United States, *Business Cycles*, in 1913. A year later Henry L. Moore applied mathematical analyses to the interrelations between prices of commodities in his

Economic Cycles and thus initiated a phase of economic studies in
the United States based upon the work of such European economists
as Walras and Pareto in which subsequent American econometri-
cians were to win great renown.

There were other signs that American economics was breaking
with the doctrinaire past, coming to grips with the actualities of
life and injecting a new spirit into the "dismal science." Aside from
manifesting increasing skepticism concerning a universal, unchanging, natural, economic order and a corresponding theory based on
axioms derived from a conception of human nature bent upon
maximizing the net balance of satisfactions over sacrifices, the exponents of the new economics substituted for this abstraction the
conception of highly variable and rapidly changing economic situations more in accord with twentieth-century American industrial
development. "Instead of imagining a realm that never was on
land or sea [the new economists] prefer whenever possible to look
directly at Main Street and see what they can make of the behavior
of the crowd." [10]

One of the most distinguishing marks of the new trend in economics was the rejection of the traditional fatalistic outlook and
the discrediting of the doctrine of the inherent automatism of competitive capitalism. Even before John Maynard Keynes revitalized
economic thought and practice by his analyses of the control aspects
in economic activity, especially through his theories of unemployment and instability which emphasized the importance of government monetary policies and levels of production, consumption, and
investment, American economists had injected a new attitude of
optimism into economic thinking. As Henry R. Seager said in 1908,
" . . . the chief reason for the economist's satisfaction is the change
in his own attitude in reference to social progress . . . The theory
of distribution that is now accepted and the practical measures
which follow from it have changed economics into a science full
of hopefulness." [11]

Even while he was still at Johns Hopkins, Richard T. Ely had
made American economists aware of the need to consider the ideas
of Marx and later, at Wisconsin, he and his colleague, John R. Com-
mons, had directed attention to the study of labor and the relations

between economics and welfare. By the end of World War I, American economists, while by no means neglecting the never-ending quest for a more realistic and more precise and adequate theory, were actively at work in the accumulation of firsthand data and the analyses of production, pricing, wages, employment, money and banking, savings, investment, consumption, standards of living, management, labor relations, technology, class stratification, market-ing, land economics, international trade, taxation, and public eco-nomic policies. They were professionally directly involved in gov-ernment and business and had succeeded in building up not merely an imposing body of data and general knowledge but had also in large measure integrated the component elements of their subject matter into a coherent discipline which had achieved greater sci-entific validity because it drew fundamental assumptions from, and checked its conclusions against, a more authentic political science, sociology, anthropology, and social psychology.

When sociology made claims for academic recognition it did so under the great handicap of lack of clarity of the term and wide difference of opinion among its proponents concerning its sub-ject matter and scope. Unlike economics and politics, which could point to specific aspects of human activity as their principal themes of intellectual preoccupation, sociology was looked upon either as too general or as too miscellaneous a collection of particulars to warrant serious consideration. This confusion was further com-plicated by the circumstance that the originator of the term "so-ciology," Auguste Comte, had used it to designate the social sci-ences as a whole, that Herbert Spencer had lent his prestige to the practice of applying the word to a general science of the social or "superorganic," that Lester F. Ward, the father of American soci-ology, by virtue of his publication of *Dynamic Sociology* in 1883, thought of sociology as the synthesis of all the separate social dis-ciplines, and that Franklin H. Giddings regarded it as the basic social science.

The variety of subject matter that found its way into sociology was conditioned in part by its heritage from philosophy and theol-ogy and in part by the growing awareness of acute social problems which were pressing for practical solution. The ascendancy of the latter interest, which combined the increasing interest of religious bodies in social reform with the nascent profession of social work and led to the emergence of "Christian sociology," might be illustrated by the content of a course on sociology given by Professor Sanborn at Cornell University which offered "practical instruction calculated to fit young men to discuss intelligently such important social questions as the best methods of dealing practically with pauperism, intemperance, crime of various degrees and among persons of different ages, insanity, idiocy, and the like." [12]

Though intensely concerned with the social problems of his day and intent upon directing sociology to enable it to furnish a scientific foundation for the more enlightened and efficient treatment of the ills of man and society, no one saw more clearly than did Albion W. Small the danger that sociology might become an "omnium gatherum" without focus or logical coherence. In his *General Sociology*, published in 1905, he suggested that the proper role of sociology was the scientific analysis of social phenomena with emphasis upon the group factor in human behavior. Although he was not himself given to empirical research, his strategic position in the academic world as Head of the Department of Sociology at the University of Chicago and Editor of the *American Journal of Sociology* enabled him to exercise a powerful influence in turning sociology from speculation concerning society in the abstract to a rigorous study of interpersonal and intergroup relations.

While "sociologists" such as H. G. Wells, under the aegis of the Fabian movement in England, were urging that sociology ought to be good intuitive literature and argued "that the creation of Utopias — and their exhaustive criticism — is the proper and distinctive method of sociology," [13] American sociologists were exploring the concrete social life about them and were forging the methods appropriate to the scientific analysis of the social processes involved in the infinite variety of men, institutions, organizations, and movements with which American society presented them. Charles H Cooley had published his penetrating study of the processes by which men acquire their essentially human traits — based in part upon the observation of the children in his own family — entitled *Human Nature and the Social Order* in 1902. William Graham

Sumner, in his *Folkways* (1907), despite his economic and political conservatism, following in the wake of social Darwinism, had applied the principle of natural selection and "survival of the fittest" to social institutions and customs and thus had injected a secular spirit of social relativism into the analysis of social practices and beliefs which, while not based upon his own observations, had followed the practice of his mentor, Herbert Spencer and the French sociologists, notably Durkheim, of exploiting the increasingly rich stores of firsthand data furnished by the ethnographers. Edward A Ross, who published his *Social Control* in 1901, had drawn upon the French social psychologists and upon the data of history and current literature. In somewhat the same way Franklin H. Giddings was proceeding in his studies at Columbia, to provide a discerning picture and a fairly systematic account of the current social order and the basic processes underlying it.

Carrol Wright of the Federal Bureau of Labor Statistics and Walter F. Willcox had brought together the available statistical data on population, migration, and the state of social welfare, furnishing bench marks for the interpretation of the changing American society and its problems, a task in which the growing number of empirically and welfare-minded economists of the first decade of the twentieth century were also busily engaged, thus furnishing the sociologists with more exact data than had hitherto been available for a more sophisticated analysis of social institutions and social problems.

As a result of the establishment of social settlements like Hull House in Chicago, Henry Street in New York, Kingsley House in Pittsburgh, and similar institutions in Boston, Philadelphia, and other large cities, opportunities were being offered for university trained students to observe the life in the slums among the poor and in the immigrant quarters. Such observers accumulated substantial bodies of social data reflecting actual life conditions. The Pittsburgh Survey (1909–1914) under the direction of Paul U. Kellogg, was a systematic effort to depict the life and problems of that great steel-producing community. It gave impetus to the further work of careful social investigation into a variety of social problems by the Russell Sage Foundation, established in 1914. By the beginning of World War I scores of detailed studies of communities, both urban and rural, and of specific aspects of social and communal life were available. It was increasingly by induction from these concrete bodies of data rather than by deduction from cosmic *a priori* principles that the science of sociology was being constructed.

While to a large extent the developing study of sociology relied upon the work of government statisticians, social workers, and social reformers (including the "muckraking" journalists who were particularly assiduous in exposing the problems of housing, health, child and woman labor, unemployment, poverty, monopolies, and political corruption), there were many indications that by the end of the First World War the emphasis had shifted from the direct concern with the practical solution of social problems and the benevolent interest in social reform to a more detached program of scientific inquiry, characterized by the development of scientific method and more long-range empirical research. This is clearly seen in the sharp decline in the number of "reform" articles in the sociological journals,[14] in the growing infrequency of the appearance of articles offering apologetics for sociology, and in the multiplication of sociological publications presenting the results of concrete research and describing methods by which valid results could be attained as distinguished from pious appeals to the scientific spirit. In brief, there was less and less talk that there ought to be a science of sociology and more and more actual effort to build one.[15]

Among the most encouraging signs of the new scientific temper in sociology was the appearance in 1915 of two publications which exercised a powerful influence in directing research in two significant fields of sociological inquiry. One of these was C. J. Galpin's *The Social Anatomy of an Agricultural Community*,[16] which, growing out of the rural life studies at the University of Wisconsin, gave new impetus and a central focus to rural sociological research which, though generously supported had hitherto been relatively sterile. The other was Robert E. Park's "The City: Suggestions for the Study of Human Behavior in the City Environment," [17] sketching a systematic program of empirical research in the urban field that bore fruit in the nineteen-twenties and early thirties in the form of a series of monographs based on sociological research into various phases of the social life of Chicago. This work not only produced a vast body of systematically organized firsthand data but also developed some of the most distinctive modern methods of research and led to the reformulation of the discipline of sociology on a logically more defensible basis.

Perhaps the most important consequence of these developments for the maturation of sociology as a coherent subject matter characterized by a distinctive body of fundamental concepts and methods was the appearance in 1921 of Parks' and Burgess' *Introduction to the Science of Sociology*,[18] which brought together in systematic fashion the most important sociological literature that had been produced up to that time, provided an organizational framework for extant sociological knowledge and furnished a new impetus for more effective sociological teaching and research. This work continued to be the model for most subsequent textbooks and inspired much of the progress in the more rigorous theoretical and research efforts that have characterized sociology up to the present.

Meanwhile, William I. Thomas and Florian Znaniecki had published their monumental five volumes on *The Polish Peasant in Europe and America*,[19] which set a new and high standard for empirical sociological research and the systematic analysis of sociological data in the light of basic sociological and socio-psychological hypotheses. In this great work its authors not only demonstrated the value of life histories, letters, and other personal documents but also shed new light on the processes through which personality is formed, the relationship between personality and culture, the nexus between personal and social organization and disorganization and the role of crises in social life and, most significantly, on the importance for their conduct of the manner in which men define the situations in which they find themselves. At about the same time, a notable new approach to the same problems, which incidentally revolutionized thinking and to some extent practice on problems of immigration and the adjustment of ethnic groups in American society, was made by the Carnegie studies in Americanization.[20] These laid bare the processes of competition, conflict, accommodation, and assimilation incident to the incorporation of aliens into American society, the impact of the influx of strange peoples and their

cultures upon social institutions, and the significance of the survival
of cultural heritages for the interpretation of the attitudes and values
of their bearers. The insights and methods of investigation developed in the course of these studies were then applied to the study
of the Negro and race relations generally with great effect.[21]

The relationship between technology and culture was explored
by William F. Ogburn in his suggestive volume on *Social Change*
(New York, 1922). This study of social change, emphasizing measurable trends and taking advantage of the statistical methods the
value of which had meanwhile been recognized in sociological research, blossomed into the comprehensive studies of *Recent Social
Trends* (New York, 1931 and subsequent years). This paralleled the
study of *Recent Economic Changes,* completed just before the great
depression of the nineteen-thirties, and held up a mirror to America
reflecting virtually all of the major aspects of the changing American society. Other studies, such as the widely read volumes on
Middletown, by Robert S. and Helen M. Lynd, were symptomatic of a maturing discipline of sociology, empirically oriented
and proceeding by means of rigorous, scientific methods.

The major fields of sociology as they have come to be defined in
the course of the research since approximately 1915 and the attempts
at ordering and systematizing the knowledge thus acquired are
(1) population and human ecology, (2) social organization, (3)
social psychology and collective behavior. The first of these has
made particularly notable progress in the last two decades in part
because demography, by virtue of the very nature of its subject
matter, lends itself readily to objective study and precise methods
of quantification. In the case of human ecology the progress is to
be attributed largely to similar factors but in addition is to be
ascribed to the unusual diligence with which sociologists have
worked and the generous support they have had in exploring rural
and urban community life in all its phases. In the study of social
organization, American sociologists have been particularly interested in the study of the family, of racial and ethnic groups, and,
more recently, in social stratification, social status, and mobility.
American sociologists have only lately shown the awareness of the
importance of social class with which their European colleagues,

because of different conditions, were preoccupied at a much earlier period. The study of social organization, however, comprises not merely the analysis of the structural aspects of social life as it crystallizes in the form of social groupings and institutions, but also its dynamic aspects, namely the processes of social interaction and changing social relations. One of the most unique points of emphasis of the study of social organization in America, due primarily to the pioneer work of Charles H. Cooley,[22] has been the "primary group," or the informal, personal, and intimate relations existing between persons as distinguished from the formal, impersonal, and instrumental associations of the larger society. The third major field of interest, namely social psychology, ranging from the study of personality and attitudes to the study of such phenomena as public opinion and social movements, while of long-standing interest, has only recently been penetrated by the methods of empirical research and will be briefly treated later in connection with the developments in psychology.

Viewed from the standpoint of concrete subject matter, as distinguished from a more systematic and abstract perspective, there have emerged many other recognized fields of sociological interest, such as urban and rural sociology, which have already been mentioned; the sociology of law, art, religion, knowledge, and education; social psychiatry; the sociology of disorganization or social pathology, including criminology; and other special subjects such as industrial relations and race relations. In addition, from a methodological point of view, social statistics, while increasingly a part of all sociological research, has become so technical a subject that some sociologists find themselves compelled to pursue it as their exclusive specialty. It is encouraging to note, however, that "theory," which once was all there was to sociology, is nowadays less and less a separable aspect of sociological inquiry.

Although psychology as a recognized discipline comprises within its scope a number of important aspects which lie outside the social sciences, such as animal psychology and physiological psychology, and although in a number of respects it has closer filiation to philosophy and medicine than to the social studies, it has in the course of the twentieth century become so closely associated with the social sciences that no account of the latter would be complete without some mention of several related developments in psychology. Most significant among these is the emergence of social psychology as a central field of psychological research, its parallel development in sociology, and the consequent close association between psychology and sociology.

As in some of the other social sciences in America, so in psychology the trend away from metaphysical speculation and armchair meditation and towards empiricism, observation, experimentation, and in general the use of scientific method, came, to a large extent, as a result of the exposure of a number of American students during the last part of the nineteenth century to the ideas of European, especially German scholars. This was notably true of psychology, where new vistas had been opened in the laboratories of men like Fechner and Wundt in Germany and where, in the early twentieth century the heterodox ideas of Pavlov and Bekhterev of Russia and Freud of Vienna began to infect the psychological thinking of American scholars. These, because of the pragmatic tradition in America with only shallow indigenous roots of social and psychological doctrines of their own, were already predisposed in favor of new approaches. Psychology, which had originally been the study of the soul and remained, until the middle of the nineteenth century, the study of the mind, relying upon introspection as its principal method, underwent revolutionary changes in the last half of the nineteenth century as a consequence of the fuller knowledge of the physiological and neurological bases of "mental" activity and the introduction of experimentation. As presented by such an outstanding figure as William James in his *Principles of Psychology* (1890), it went beyond the introspective analysis of states of consciousness and came to be concerned principally with the nature and genesis of the self, individual differences, and the processes of behavior. Under the guidance of such pioneers as J. McKeen Cattell, G. Stanley Hall, E. B. Titchener, E. L. Thorndike and John Dewey, new trails were blazed in systematic theory, methods of observation, and experimental techniques. Psychologists became greatly interested in animal, comparative, and abnormal psychology, in child study, educational methods, mental tests, and the development of personality. Some applied quantitative and statistical methods to psychic phenomena.

Two lines of development during the first two decades of the twentieth century are particularly noteworthy. One of these is the attempt to turn psychology into a rigorous observational science building upon the work of Pavlov and Bekhterev with animals and children and focusing upon the process of conditioning. This approach found its most representative expression in the work of John B. Watson.[23] The other was the exploration of the unconscious aspects of human conduct initiated by Sigmund Freud, whose significance was first recognized in the United States by G. Stanley Hall and A. A. Brill. This influence not merely transformed psychology and psychiatry by introducing a novel conception of personality and human motivation, but by its emphasis upon the nonrational, and especially the sexual aspects of human nature and the mechanisms of wish fulfillment, exercised a profound influence upon morals and the general culture.

The economists, political scientists, sociologists, and other students of social life, who had been accustomed to borrowing their theories concerning human motivation from the psychologists, could not fail to note the great variety and often contradictory hypotheses concerning the reflexes, instincts, impulses, drives, and other mainsprings of action which were offered as interpretations of human action. In the absence of any conclusive evidence for the greater plausibility of one set of basic human motives offered by one school of psychology over that offered by another, the confusion among the students of human social life as to where to turn for reliable theories to interpret human action was understandably bewildering. Hence, from the standpoint of the social sciences, the vast critical, empirical, and constructive labor of the psychologists in the last fifty and especially the last twenty-five years centering on motivation, learning, the analysis of the act, and the relationship between personality and culture was of the greatest importance. Of almost equal importance was the simultaneous turn away from a structural-atomistic view toward a functional organic or configurationistic approach.[24]

From the standpoint of the social sciences, by far the most significant development in psychology during the last fifty years is the emergence of social psychology as a more or less autonomous discipline, or more properly speaking, the fairly universal recognition by psychologists of the futility of treating mental phenomena in isolation from the social milieu. Apart from a philosphically oriented and largely speculative "folk psychology" which postulated as its unit of analysis a "collective mind," social psychology scarcely existed a generation ago. Originating in the dissatisfactions felt by sociologists and other social scientists and, indeed, psychologists as well, with generalizations concerning human behavior without reference to the specific society in which man lives and his interaction with his fellows, social psychology has developed into a general discipline basic to all of the social sciences. During the past fifty years social psychology has made rapid progress through an enormous amount of rigorous observation, experimentation, and systematic theorizing to which not only psychologists but also sociologists, anthropologists, linguists, psychiatrists, educators, and social workers have richly contributed.

As a result of these efforts we now have a more tenable and penetrating understanding of how the individual becomes a person; how he is molded by the groups with their cultures in which he participates; how his conceptions of himself and his attitudes toward others and his world arise and and are modified; and how public opinion and social movements operate. The knowledge thus obtained, while still far from adequate, has made itself felt not merely in a more sophisticated social science but in many practical fields of social life as well. Educational methods have been modernized; the rearing of children and the selection of personnel for industry, government, and the military have been significantly improved; the treatment of social deviants — the delinquent, the criminal, and the insane — has become more enlightened; advertising, propaganda, and mass persuasion has in many respects been transformed into a science and for good or for ill has become a major industry; and the average citizen has come to have at his disposal more adequate resources for understanding himself and his world and for dealing with his problems.

Closely related to these advances is the progress in psychiatry, which itself has become so closely allied to the social sciences — as distinguished from biology and medicine, out of which it grew — that a prominent psychiatrist, Dr. William C. Menninger, is quoted . as saying: "Psychiatry is a medical science, but it is also a social science. The psychiatrist, more than the physician in any other medical discipline, must concern himself with the social situation of his patients." [25]

The establishment of child guidance clinics, the development of psychiatric social work and of personal counseling, the growth of the mental hygiene movement, the wide use of social psychological and psychiatric techniques in the two world wars, the transformation of insane asylums into mental hospitals, and in general the wide interest in, and popular acceptance of, the naturalistic outlook on neurotic and psychotic symptoms in personality attest to the impact of these new ideas upon our civilization.

Anthropology in the early years of this century was still largely a "collector's paradise and a museum activity." [26] The prodigious work of Lewis H. Morgan in the middle of the nineteenth century, which was comparable to the best of Tylor in Britain or Bastian in Germany, had received more attention in Europe than in America. In 1886 Daniel C. Brinton was appointed to a chair in anthropology at the University of Pennsylvania and about the same time F. W. Putnam of the Peabody Museum assumed his professorial post at Harvard. Under their leadership, together with that of a small group of government anthropologists, notably Major Powell, interest turned to the investigation of living nonliterate peoples by trained field observers instead of the almost exclusive reliance upon the accounts of travelers, missionaries, traders, and soldiers. Symbolic of this new orientation of American anthropology was the Jesup North Pacific Expedition planned and guided by Franz Boas to explore the cultural relationships between the Indian tribes of the North Pacific Coast and the natives of Northeast Siberia. The field work on this strategic coöperative project extended from 1897 to 1902 and was followed by a number of significant monographs. Boas contributed to Columbia University a group of students who became the most distinguished figures in American anthropology, including Clark Wissler, Alfred L. Kroeber, Robert H. Lowie, and

Edward Sapir.[27] The American school of anthropology of which Boas remained the undisputed leader for more than three decades set diligently to work to exploit its accessibility to the sources of knowledge concerning the native peoples of the American continent. Through the labors of Boas and those of his many gifted students, anthropology took root in a number of the major universities and rapid strides were made particularly in anthropometrics, linguistics, and ethnology.

One of the first opportunities to make a signal scientific contribution which was also of general interest came to Boas in connection with the reconsideration of American immigration policy. In his report to the Immigration Commission on *Changes in Bodily Form of Descendants of Immigrants* (Washington, 1910) he delivered "a substantial blow to the then current ideas on the stability of physical traits" [28] and stimulated a lively interest in the scientific study of the physical, psychological, and cultural similarities of the racial and ethnic groups in America which challenged the widely current notions concerning not only the fixity of alleged pure racial types but also the dogmas concerning the superiority of the white, especially North-European stocks as claimed by the propagandists and pseudoscientific cult of racists.

Of considerable interest from the standpoint of the development of social science in general during the last half century was the critical reappraisal, in the light of the rapidly growing body of evidence gathered through firsthand field studies, of the dominant evolutionary and diffusionist interpretations of culture. For these quasi-historical notions which held either that cultural development everywhere follows uniform lines and passes through comparable if not identical stages, or accounted for cultural similarities by a common ancient heritage and borrowing through historical contact between tribes, the American anthropologists substituted more flexible hypotheses which took account of man's capacity for origination as well as for learning from others. As Goldenweiser puts it, "The residual deposit left in America by these prolonged controversies expresses itself in a marked interest by the 'moderns' in the problems of cultural contact, particularly those of acculturation."

Perhaps the most significant contribution which anthropology has made to social science and to popular intelligence centers around the concept of culture and the independence of culture from biology. Correlative with this clarification of the difference between characteristics of human beings which are transmitted through the germ plasm and those which are transmitted through the cultural heritage, that is, through communication, contact, and education, is the further contribution to our understanding of the physical as distinguished from the cultural elements in individual and group differences. There is also the more recent illumination anthropology has given of the processes by which cultures are transformed and of the impact of Western civilization upon other, especially nonliterate, peoples and cultures.

In recent years anthropology, along with sociology and psychology, has shown considerable interest in the intricate problems of the nexus between personality and culture, and through the accumulation of broadly comparative, cross-cultural data has been able to furnish correctives for untenable generalizations based upon evidence of limited cultural scope. The contemporary tendency of anthropology to deal with modern civilizations, as indicated by studies of modern communities, makes it indistinguishable from sociology. By holding up "a great mirror to man" and letting him "look at himself in this infinite variety" [29] modern anthropology not only enlarges the perspective of all who would understand social life as it is and has been among all members of the human race but also acts as a civilizing agent.

A review of the social sciences in the past half-century would be incomplete if it failed to take account of the role played by geography, or at least that part of it which is called human geography. Although geography appeared sporadically on the American academic scene throughout the last quarter of the nineteenth century, it was practised more as a physical than a social science and did not take the direction of human geography until considerably later.

To Miss Ellen Semple belongs the credit of having been the pioneer in human geography in this country. After studying with Ratzel in the early nineties she returned to America an ardent and engaging protagonist of his views, in particular as to geographic interpretations of history. By writing and lecturing she steadfastly advanced this position.[30] In 1903 the University of Chicago established the first regular geographic chair. Though Miss Semple never was regularly connected with the university, her influence, joined to the support of the physiographer Salisbury, guided the early growth of the teaching of geography at that institution . . . In 1921 President Atwood undertook the formation of a School of Geography at Clark University, and here again the support of Miss Semple has been freely given.[31]

This early emphasis on the determinative influence of habitat on ways of life and institutions subsequently shifted to a concern with man's adjustment to his natural habitat and still later to a primary interest in the interrelations between man in his group existence and his habitat. This brought human geography to a position where it was virtually identical with human ecology.[32] Meanwhile socially and culturally oriented geographic research was being energetically pursued both in government and in some of the universities where geography was accepted. Reliable atlases depicting the economic, political, social, and cultural distributions were being developed which proved of great significance not merely as contributions to scientific knowledge of the various sections of the earth but were of practical usefulness in agriculture, commerce, and administration. Less ambitious than the objectives envisaged by such writers as Ellsworth Huntington [33] and even Ellen Semple, the American geographers of recent decades have envisaged their task as that of grouping "the content, individuality, and relation of areas, in which man comes in for his due attention as part of the area, but only in so far as he is really significant by his presence and works." [34] Their aim has been to offer a reliable account of "certain repeating patterns in the forms of settlement" [35] in relation to natural and cultural features and in respect to origin and function so that the earth's surface can be viewed as a series of similar and contrasting regions. Geography conceived as human ecology aiming at a description and analysis of the spatial, temporal, physical, and technological bases and matrices of social life is properly a social science and in recent years has definitely developed into one.[36]

Only a brief comment can be given within the scope of this review on certain other significant, but in a sense peripheral developments in part attributable to and in turn impinging upon the progress of the social sciences in the twentieth century. Jurisprudence, social work, education, administration, planning, marketing, banking and finance, commerce and industrial management, labor relations, race relations, international relations, mass persuasion, and social psychiatry, to mention only some major contemporary areas of professional activity which rest in large degree upon social science knowledge and methods, are not merely arts and "applied social science," but also furnish the social scientist with much of his data and set some of his most challenging problems of research.

Thus, for instance, stimulated by such figures as Oliver Wendell Holmes, Jr., Roscoe Pound,[37] Louis D. Brandeis[38] among others, American jurisprudence, beginning with the first decade of this century, was greatly invigorated by questioning the origins and purposes or functions of the law in relation to society. Discarding the textbook maxims, teachers of law turned to the analysis of specific cases. Questioning immutable principles and metaphysical absolutes, there was a growing disposition among lawyers and jurists to inquire into the purpose of law, to assert that laws are made by men for men, and to recognize that whatever their degree of universality or antiquity, legal institutions are the product of a changing social world and must fulfill changing social ends. Referring to the social sciences in relation to the law, a lawyer wrote in 1924 in a manner that could scarcely have been anticipated a quarter century earlier:

These sciences . . . have an inspiring and profound significance to one who believes that the law is a reflection of progressing life and not an unchanging set of words, graven on tablets of stone; that it is a part of life and not apart from life; that it should meet the ever-changing needs of the present hour; and that its life is not embedded in the logic or precise technique of a game of chess, but hinges and depends upon a progressive ability to solve the novel . . . problems continually developing in a rapidly altering economic and social era.[39]

Although legal teaching, research, and practice are still far from thoroughly integrated with the social sciences and the contacts between these two fields are still far too few and superficial, there are many signs that collaboration is growing and that law is being looked upon more and more as a social science by lawyers themselves. As the Report of the Committee on Curriculum of the Association of American Law Schools (*Handbook*, December 1946, p. 61) points out, referring to the Law School of Yale University: "We take it to be self-evident that law will be most fruitful and critical when the skills and perspectives of history, economics, statistics, psychology, political science, sociology and psychiatry are fully and effectively used in the work of the law schools." [40]

The relationship between the social sciences and social work has, of course, been much closer. From the very beginning they have had intimate association. The social sciences have aided materially in getting those dealing with problems of individual maladjustment to recognize the larger social setting in which personal problems must be viewed, just as the psychiatrists have furnished a more penetrating understanding of the individual himself. Through the development of the survey technique which provided a more comprehensive view of the community within which the social worker had to deal with the problems of people in need or in trouble and within which the resources for treatment had to be found; through the settlement movement and the community organization efforts which developed rapidly especially during the First World War; through the perfection of the "case method," most dramatically symbolized by the publication of Mary Richmond's *Social Diagnosis* in 1917; and through the gradual abandonment of a moralistic point of view and its replacement by a scientific attitude, social work in all of its aspects has become a profession grounded in the social sciences. [41]

To trace even the most obvious interrelations between the social sciences and education would be a task far beyond the limits of this review. The same applies in less degree to the other peripheral social science fields mentioned earlier. Hence it will have to suffice to treat them summarily in a subsequent section on the impact of the social sciences on American civilization.

IV

Considering the personnel involved, the public acceptance achieved, the support which it attracts, the organization it has developed and the role it plays in American life, social science may be regarded as an important development in American society. There is not an aspect of the life of our time worth mentioning which is not reflected in and influenced by social science activities. Many of the most characteristic and significant advances in our mode of thought and of living and some of the most dramatic changes in our civilization are to be traced back to or have been guided by the methods and products of speculation and research carried on by social scientists. As a silently working force influencing their conceptions of themselves and their outlook on the world no less than as a major factor in shaping public policy and guiding their collective action in their communities and organized groups, the social sciences in the last half-century and especially the last quarter-century have exerted a perceptible impact upon the American people.

One could scarcely imagine such innovations as we have made in the last fifty years as the Juvenile Court; our social security system; the TVA; our methods of marketing, of dealing with industrial disputes, of selecting personnel for government, the armed forces, or business; our ways of educating and rearing the young, of dealing with crime, slums, poverty, old age, race prejudice, unemployment, and personal maladjustment, of conducting political campaigns, of planning cities and improving the life of the farmer, of waging war and making peace, of managing the complex problems of self-government in our democracy and promoting the general welfare — all these would be hard to imagine without the stimulation and contribution of the social sciences.

To demonstrate how these changes in our social life were mediated and facilitated by social science and in particular to show how the changing social scene stimulated the interest of social scientists and turned their attention to these problems would require an extensive treatise on the sociology of knowledge. Major factors in setting the problems for the social scientists of our time included the expansion and growing complexity of American society, its increasing interdependence with the rest of the world, and associated social changes. Among the social changes which especially conditioned the development of the social sciences and set the problems for social scientists were the rapidly increasing population; the turn from a rural to a predominantly urban mode of life symbolized by the emergence of scores of metropolitan centers; the acquisition by the United States of the stature of, and the need to play the role of, a world power with decisive influence in world affairs, and with increasing responsibility for dependent peoples and the maintenance of world peace and order. Other factors were the growth of giant commercial corporations and the trend toward mass-production industries calling for mass markets and large-scale advertising, threatening to develop into monopolies and bringing in their wake the mass organization of labor; the invention and utilization of a number of technological innovations enhancing man's productive capacity, increasing leisure, facilitating transportation and communication and thus accelerating and multiplying the flow of goods, the movement of people and the spread of ideas, standardizing ways of living and bringing the remotest parts of the nation and the world in contact with each other. Problems were also set by advance in methods of dealing with disease, prolonging life and eliminating pain; the tremendous expansion and extension of large-scale organizations representing the political, economic, religious, and cultural interests of every conceivable group in a heterogeneous society; the trend toward a greatly expanding apparatus of government and adminstration coincident with the need for formal and more centralized controls and the widening range of public services; declining immigration and the coincidental rise to prominence of problems of race relations. Finally, progressive secularization of life, the spread of scientific knowledge and of a naturalistic outlook, of the faith in the ability of men to improve their lot, of the claim of all to share in the benefits of civilization and to have a voice in the making of common decisions set new problems for social science.

The changing interests of the social sciences during the last half-century must be viewed also against the background of great historical events which marked our epoch — the great depression of the thirties, two world wars in which the nation played a decisive role, the rise of fascism, the revolutionary upheaval as a consequence of which democratic capitalism was confronted by totalitarian collectivism in a shrunken world, and the groping for a world organization capable of maintaining world peace and justice and directing the resources of the earth to the improvement of the lot of men throughout the world.

Even a simple listing of the many ways in which the social sciences have been challenged by these opportunities and cataclysmic events and have participated both critically and constructively in the analysis of problems and the development of programs designed to meet the expanding aspirations of Americans for improvements in their conditions of life would require many pages. There are many indications that as the methods of social science developed and as the social scientists themselves gained experience in practical affairs, their confidence in themselves and public confidence in what they had to offer grew. Fatalism and the traditional trust in *laissez faire* yielded to growing trust in planned intervention and scientifically grounded methods of dealing with social and personal problems. As Wesley Mitchell remarked, there dawned the "dazed perception that social organization . . . is more amenable to purposeful control" than had been realized.[42] This changed atmosphere is dramatically exemplified by the new role of the social scientist in economic and political affairs.

With the multiplication of business schools "young economists made themselves specialists in banking, insurance, accounting, merchandising, salesmanship, transportation, corporation finance, . . . business statistics, advertising, and the like."[43] During the First World War, with a scholar in the White House, economists were called upon to advise on war financing, allocation of resources, production, shipping and transportation, labor and consumption; and when the problems of peace loomed, on war debts, reparations, the public debt, taxation, and reconstruction. The war experience and its aftermath suggested to a number of economists the need for, and possibility of, the "larger and more comprehensive control of economic activity and development,"[44] aiming at increasing production, full employment, wider and more equitable distribution of the national income, wise use of resources, prevention of wild fluctuations, and the maximization of the national welfare. Economists began to take "a wider view of labor problems and a more constructive attitude toward them," and found their place not only, as traditionally was the case, on the side of corporate enterprise, but as counselors to labor unions as well. More abundant and more reliable data in the form of statistics, index numbers, and time series were being compiled. The revolutions in price levels brought about by the war afforded specialists new data on the relations between changes in volume of money and changes in prices, which led to a better theory of the interrelations of the factors in the economy underlying business cycles.

With the paralyzing depression of the thirties the interest of economists in the broader problems of national welfare were further stimulated. The strategic role of government in the economic life was powerfully reënforced. Problems of unemployment, relief, public works, taxation, public spending, public aid to private industry and agriculture, public debt management, intergovernmental fiscal relations, international trade, and economic planning which were pressing for solution gave impetus to new ideas which were undermining established doctrines. At this point a number of American economists turned to John Maynard Keynes, who "did more than anyone else in the twentieth century to revitalize economic theory, to stimulate discussion and research along new lines, to influence economic policy, and finally to discredit the doctrine of the inherent automatism of competitive capitalism." [45]

The Federal Reserve Bank, the Reconstruction Finance Corporation, Federal Deposit Insurance, Public Works programs, the National Housing and Home Finance agencies, the Agricultural Adjustment Administration, Farm Security, and other agencies concerned with agriculture, industry, labor, and the varied problems of economic life, in all of which social scientists played a part, were already established when America began to prepare for World War II. Although one of the most promising of the new agencies, the National Resources Planning Board, was abruptly terminated by Congress at a time when its services were most needed, local, state, and national planning to which the NRPB had given impetus and support went on under other agencies, though at a slackened pace.

The experience gained in the depression and the First World War by economists and other social scientists paved the way for their expanded functions when the Second World War came. Government research bureaus attached to the important agencies dealing with economic problems incident to the war multiplied. Economists found themselves increasingly in association with other social scientists in the common effort to solve problems of policy and administration in which sometimes they acted merely in an advisory capacity or in a fact-finding role, but at other times assumed a direct responsibility for the formulation and operation of programs. In the postwar period this widened scope for the services of economists was even further enhanced by the establishment of new agencies, many of them functioning on an international scale. The Office of Economic Advisors to the President has come to be one of the most strategic places at which economists can combine their research functions with an important influence upon national policy. In the various international agencies such as ECA and the technical assistance programs, a new level of responsibility has been assigned to economists among other social scientists.

Political scientists no less than economists have found increasing opportunity for research and for more direct participation in the formulation and carrying out of practical programs beginning in World War I, and particularly during the depression and World War II. Unlike the functions of the economists, however, their role has been more exclusively associated with public programs. One of the consequences of the greater demand for experts in political science has been the increasing emphasis put upon the study of public administration with the consequent declining interest in problems of political theory and political psychology. Even before World War I, political scientists had become active in local and state bureaus of research, but this activity was relatively insignificant when contrasted with the tremendously increased opportunities that opened to them with the enlargement of the functions of the federal government beginning with the depression and the coming into its own of the service state. The multiplication of the regulatory organs of government, the unprecedented expansion of government employment, the assumption by government itself or gov-

ernmental corporations of operations formerly carried on only by
private enterprises, the expansion of the role of the executive in the
modern state and the increasing utilization by legislative bodies of
experts to aid them in their investigative functions, presumably with
a view to wiser legislation, have given to political scientists a greatly
enlarged range of opportunities for research and for bringing their
knowledge to bear upon policies and day-to-day administration.
One of the most novel features of the last twenty years has been the
new role assigned to experts in government in the reorganization
of government itself of which the President's Committee on Administrative Management and the recent Hoover Commission are
notable examples.[46] The assumption by government of a wide range
of planning functions has further increased the importance of political science in connection with the practical affairs of state. The barriers that formerly separated politics from economics and the other
social sciences have all but disappeared as it is being recognized
that any problem of importance requires for its intelligent analysis
the closest coöperation among the various students of social life.[47]

Although the ascendancy of public administration overshadowed
other traditional areas of political science, one long-standing interest,
namely, the operation of the political process, especially the formation of political opinion and the analysis of elections, has become
a matter of such great interest that it is virtually a field by itself.
It is carried on, however, not by political scientists alone but in collaboration with sociologists, social psychologists, and statisticians.[48]
A similar tendency can be noted in the field of international relations which is no longer monopolized by jurists and political scientists but has become a field in which all social scientists have a
stake.

The development of sociology in the last few decades represents
perhaps an even more abrupt break with the past of that discipline
than is the case of recent developments in economics and political
science. The development of more reliable methods of observation
and measurement and the refinement of analytical methods has
given to sociology in our time a new stature. In virtually every area
of sociological research, ranging from population and ecology
through social organization to social psychology, a substantial body

of reliable empirical evidence has been accumulated. In the study of the family, for instance, great progress has been made in the development of methods of prediction of success or failure in marriage. In the field of delinquency and crime the factors accounting for delinquent or criminal careers are more adequately understood. Local communities both urban and rural have been subjected to comparative analysis. Social trends and the factors impinging upon our changing institutions are more adequately known. The study of personality and social movements has entered the scientific stage. New areas of practical significance, in government, in industry, and in community life have been opened up to sociological research. Sociologists are concerned with problems of population, planning, the organization of industry, labor relations, race relations, and with all of the problems involving social interaction ranging from relatively minute nuclear groups to the contact between nations and peoples on a world scale. At many points their knowledge has become indispensable not only to their colleagues in other social sciences but to the military, the planners, the psychiatrists, the social workers, the educators, the molders of public opinion, and those who in one way or another are concerned with the management of interpersonal and intergroup relations.

Virtually the same could be said about recent developments in the field of anthropology, where an important movement in applied anthropology, which seeks to make the knowledge gained from the study of simpler peoples relevant to the problems of modern society, has made important headway. Sociologists, social psychologists, and anthropologists are now found not only in such governmental agencies as the Department of Agriculture, which was among the first of the governmental departments to use their services,[49] but in virtually all main branches of government where human relations loom as an important element.

Before attempting a brief summary view of the salient and most characteristic developments in the last half-century it is appropriate to consider a few institutional aspects of social science in the setting of American life.[50]

The number of social scientists in the United States has been variously estimated, depending upon the standards of professional competence to be employed. Considering those largely employed by universities, government, and business and those professionally organized in their respective associations, there are approximately 30,000 social scientists in the United States.[51] While the facilities for training social scientists have been greatly improved, and the standards of competence have been virtually revolutionized in the last twenty years, their utilization by educational institutions, government, business, and the various organizations and agencies in American society has so enormously expanded that the demand for competently trained social scientists exceeds the supply. Although 681 Ph.D.'s were awarded at American universities to young social scientists in 1948, representing an increase of 16 per cent over the total number of degrees awarded ten years earlier, the social sciences are still not increasing their trained personnel at a rate comparable to that of the natural sciences. Apparently the natural sciences as a field of higher learning both on the undergraduate and on the graduate level are much more attractive than the social sciences.[52] The inducements in the form of scholarships and fellowships for students of social science still lag far behind those available for pursuing the natural science fields of study. The same applies to instructional facilities and university budgets. As Sibley pointed out, however, the social sciences attract at least their fair share of the best students.

The twentieth century has witnessed the development of a number of foundations, notably the Rockefeller Foundation, the Carnegie Corporation, the Russell Sage Foundation, and, just recently, the Ford Foundation, which have given to the social sciences substantial funds for research and the improvement of training. Government, especially in recent years and particularly in times of crises such as depression and war, has spent considerable sums on social science research.

Between 1938 and 1948 the total estimated national budget for research and development in the social sciences increased from $34 million to nearly $88 million. But this is a small increase as compared with the natural sciences whose budget went from $234 million to better than a billion and a quarter last year [1948]. In both branches of science the large items in these budgets were contributed by government and industry. It is only in the research disbursements of the private foundations that anything approximating equality of funds is to be seen. But since the Federal government is currently playing the dominant role, the discrepancy in distribution of public funds between the two fields cannot be overlooked. In 1938 the social sciences accounted for 31% of the Federal budget for research and development, but by 1948 its share had dropped to 6%. While this has been largely due to increased military and atomic energy expenditures, even when these items are excluded the social sciences received last year only 21% of the total.[53]

The question might be raised, of course, whether research could at present be significantly advanced if the social sciences had more funds at their disposal. While the answer to this question may be in doubt, since until very recently the social sciences had virtually no resources for research, it is most likely that over a period of time more generous support would make possible enormous improvements in research, especially in the kind of studies, so common in the natural sciences, where the same subject is attacked by a variety of research workers simultaneously from various angles, where the same question is subjected to repeated investigations, and where comparative studies are the order of the day.[54]

The development of graduate departments in the various social sciences in the universities, the organization of specialized social science societies, and the founding of specialized journals, gave great impetus to the maturation of the social sciences during the last fifty years. But as the social sciences became more differentiated they also became more estranged from one another. The pressure for academic recognition often led to exaggerated and illogical claims, fruitless interdisciplinary rivalry, the stunting of curiosity and imagination in the training of students, and the oversight of the essential unity and mutual interdependence of the social sciences. In part to counteract this growing parochialism there arose within some of the social sciences, especially political science, sociology, and economics, a movement, culminating in 1923 in the establishment of the Social Science Research Council, to foster research through collaborative effort. The already existing National Research Council in the natural sciences and a similar body in the humanities

served as a precedent, and the early support given by the foundations, especially the Laura Spelman Rockefeller Memorial, which
at the same time was offering support to a number of the leading
universities for the development of social science research, encouraged the formal organization in which by 1925 the American Statistical Association, the American Psychological Association, the
American Anthropological Association, and the American Historical Association joined the political scientists, sociologists, and
economists.

A number of projects on migration, the improvement in the collection of government statistics, research fellowships, a survey of
research methods resulting in a case book,[55] and the publication of
a comprehensive abstracting service [56] were initiated. The Council
served as an important catalytic agent in the social sciences, stimulating research, encouraging the improvement of scientific method,
and facilitating interdisciplinary communication and coöperation.

The aid which the Council was able to give to social science research through its operating and numerous advisory committees,
through research fellowships and grants-in-aid, through its stimulation of individual and group research effort in the universities,
through its good offices in mediating the securing of foundation
support for social science research and in general through its continuous efforts to facilitate interdisciplinary contact and coöperation and the encouragement of improved research organization, had
a significant effect in raising morale, in accentuating the groping
for more adequate research planning, the improvement of research
data and methods, and in general raising the level of research pro-
ductivity among social scientists.[57]

While it is hazardous to ascribe the developments in such a broad
intellectual area as the social sciences to any one factor, it is highly
probable that some of the progress that has been made in the last
two decades in the social sciences would not have been made without the aid of the Council. There were, of course, a number of other
important influences. The recognition by an increasing number of
universities of the legitimacy of supporting social science research
and the establishment of local university research councils and committees; the growing disposition of foundations to support promis-

ing research; the publication of the monumental *Encyclopaedia of the Social Sciences* [58] under the leadership of Edwin R. Seligman and Alvin Johnson; and the challenge of critical historical events of depression and war, were among the other forces which were moving the social sciences toward a more critical self-appraisal,[59] a determination to improve their methods, and a more responsible approach to social reality.

Social scientists have come into possession of data on a scale and of a degree of reliability that could scarcely have been imagined a generation ago. The United States Census and numerous other governmental and private sources of basic information reflecting conditions and trends, not to speak of the large-scale efforts to collect facts, opinions, and attitudes through polls, interviewing, questionnaires, and of the personal document variety, have given the social scientist access to materials for scientific analysis which makes possible empirical studies in place of guesswork or speculation. Such studies as the *Recent Social Trends* series, the National Resources Committee's studies of *Urbanism*, the large-scale study of race relations in the United States represented by Myrdal's *An American Dilemma* and supplementary volumes, and the recent series of studies growing out of the experience of social scientists in the Research Branch, Information and Education Division of the armed forces during the war,[60] are symptomatic of the empirical bent, of the closeness to the problems of human social life and the advanced techniques of modern social science. They are symptomatic also of the tendency to work coöperatively in the accumulation of mass data and its analysis, requiring a variety of techniques which can be mastered only by a group of workers functioning as a team.

The social sciences of today no longer conform to the pattern set by the social philosophy of a half-century ago. They are dominated by, and reflect the ascendancy of, a secular view of society which rules out providential causes and is characterized by a naturalistic approach. The dominant motif is no longer to moralize, but to understand and if possible to predict. Social scientists of today understand better than did their predecessors of a generation or so ago the assumptions with which they start and the fact that their conclusions are relative to these assumptions.

Social science literature of today is much less concerned with apologetics than that of an earlier period. It takes its existence and its importance and ultimate practical unsefulness for granted. The first impulse of the social scientist when he discovers a social problem is not immediately to propose a scheme for social improvement, but to discover the factors that are at work and among these to discern those that are amenable to alteration and deliberate intervention. The social scientist typically takes an instrumental view of his science. This, however, does not mean that he is unaware of the role that values play. Indeed, he is increasingly concerned with making these values explicit and by doing so becoming a more dispassionate analyst of what within a certain degree of probability is likely to happen, given alternative values, assumptions, and conditions. The role of the social scientist as a citizen is becoming more and more clearly differentiated from his role as a social scientist.

Change is accepted as a pervasive fact of social life. The nonrational aspects of human nature are more clearly recognized. There is greater boldness based upon achievement to venture forth to attack practical problems, a boldness which is at times not wholly warranted by the knowledge which social scientists have at their disposal. The greatly enlarged participation of social scientists in practical affairs, as advisors to government, business, labor, and philanthropy, to international organizations, and to organized groups in the community, and sometimes, though more rarely, their role as policy makers and administrators, has given to social science of our time a realism and has impressed upon social scientists a responsibility of which social scientists a half-century ago could only dream. Rigorous training in field work and in statistics, the inculcation of the respect for facts, and the urge to go to original data stand in contrast to the uncontrolled speculation and armchair theorizing of a half-century ago.

There are many more social scientists and many more advanced students of social science undergoing rigorous training than could have been anticipated in 1900 or even in 1920. There is less of a sense of self-sufficiency and less interdepartmental jealously than was evident at the beginning of the period we have reviewed. Although the position of the individual social scientists is still obviously crucial, there is a recognized need for coöperative research among the different branches of social science. Although the public relations of social science still leave much to be desired, the social sciences generally are accepted and generously supported.

Social science knowledge today reflects less the local color and the national provincialism characteristic of social science a generation ago. It is increasingly recognized that while social science knowledge must always reflect the cultural conditions, the time, the place, and the circumstances in which social reality is embedded, the quest for universally valid knowledge goes on. The prestige of objectivity is high. "Increasing concern with factual observation is breeding in us a more scientific and a less dialectical temper." [61] There is much greater methodological sophistication. At the same time, the range of accessible data and the variety of social science data have been tremendously enlarged. The social scientist of today attempts to approximate, wherever his problems and data allow, the methods of the natural sciences. He resorts to laboratories, experimentation, controlled observation, and scrupulous comparison. He seeks to measure wherever measurement improves knowledge and facilitates prediction.

The social scientist of today is better organized and has greater facilities at his disposal for effective work than his predecessors. While his knowledge is more specialized, this progressive discovery of fields marginal to his own central interest is constantly giving birth to new specialties. In the face of this fragmentation of knowledge there is a more urgent need than there ever was before for the mastery by social scientists of a minimum common broad foundation of knowledge concerning human nature and the social order and for the systematization and integration of knowledge.[62]

While social science is becoming more of a science, it is also recognized that there are many areas of social life in which the temper of the artist and the humanistic scholar is still appropriate. At the same time as social sciences are recognized to have a bearing upon the practical arts and professions, the limitations of social science, as of all scientific knowledge, become apparent. Since science deals with hypothetical situations, the answer to its problems can only be put in hypothetical terms. The man of action, however, wants certainty, and to translate the tentative and hypothetical knowledge of science into a plan for practical action requires more than knowledge — it calls for wisdom. The problems which the social scientists of today face are vast in scope. Among them are the problems of resolving conflicts within and between individuals and groups; of maintaining peace, order, and freedom; of insuring security and well-being; of enhancing the degree of participation among men in the making of common decisions and of achieving consensus; of utilizing the resources of the world for the benefit of the people of the world; of adapting ancient institutions to a changing social order and changing needs. Among these problems are some which call for quick answers which the social scientist cannot always give. The enhanced responsibility, the improved methods, the enlarged resources, and the more general acceptance of the social sciences in the last half-century augur well for the future. It should be noted, however, that, as recent tragic experience has shown, the social sciences, like all scientific knowledge, can be used for good or for ill. There are signs that as the scientific phase of social science knowledge advances, the sense of responsibility of the social scientist will keep pace. Above all, by the very nature of their subject matter, the social sciences require an atmosphere of freedom, for without freedom of inquiry they will perish and with them one of the best hopes of a happier future for mankind.

III ·

Historical Scholarship

W. STULL HOLT

I

Historical scholarship, like other branches of thought and human activity, is inevitably integrated with the society of which it is a part. There may occasionally be an individual scholar significantly out of touch with the time and place in which he is working. Thus Richard Hildreth departed so far from many of the prevailing assumptions of the middle of the nineteenth century that his major historical work received little attention, although forty years later, in the 1880's and 1890's and in a more favorable climate of opinion it was generally regarded as the outstanding example of historical scholarship by an American. Such exceptions do not invalidate the generalization that there is always a close connection between the historical scholarship of any period and the fundamental prepossessions and characteristics of the society in which the scholars are living.

This nexus is economic as well as ideological. Scholarly activity, if not a luxury, depends nevertheless upon the support which its nourishing society can or will give it. Consequently perhaps the first fact to record in a consideration of historical scholarship in the first half of the twentieth century is that the United States during those fifty years has gone through an amazing economic development and has amassed wealth unequalled by any other people during the same or any other period. The statistics showing the increase in the annual production of iron and steel, of coal, of wheat, and of manufactured goods reveal a process that literally staggers the imagination. Yet large as they are, they are surpassed by the rate of increase in the number of students attending colleges and universities. In 1900 these numbered 238,000, or approximately the ratio of one student to 323 persons in the total population. By 1950 the number of students had reached 2,500,000, and the ratio of students to total population was one to 60. Whatever may be thought of this increase in the percentage of students seeking training beyond the level of secondary education, it is a product of the increasing complexity of a civilization in which the specialist is of prime importance, of the vast increase in national wealth, and of the ideal that education to the limit of his capacities is the right of every citizen and that the diffusion of appropriate training is basic to the welfare of the nation.

Naturally scholarship in all fields has been affected by this development. Whether or not historical scholarship received a fair portion of the national investment in post-high school education or even relatively as large a share as in earlier and poorer days, there can be no doubt of the vast increase in the support given. To appreciate the truth of this one has only to compare the library resources available in 1900 with those of 1950, when there are three or four dozen libraries larger and better in quality than the best of 1900. The Harvard University library, which had just under 600,000 volumes in 1900, had expanded to over 5,000,000 by the middle of the century. Others grew at comparable rates. More significant than mere growth in size were the increasing emphasis given to university libraries as centers for research and the appearance of distinctively research libraries. While the gradual and unheralded increase of materials for research in nearly every university library had more effect on scholarship, the establishment of special research libraries dramatized the process. Among the latter the Hoover Library on War, Revolution, and Peace at Stanford University, the William L. Clements Library of American History at the University of Michigan, and the Henry E. Huntington Library at San Marino, California, deservedly received much publicity.

Perhaps the best illustration of the way in which private philanthropy and government combined to facilitate historical scholarship was the project for the reproduction of materials in foreign archives relating to American history. In 1927 Mr. John D. Rockefeller, Jr., gave half a million dollars to the Library of Congress for such a purpose. After that sum was exhausted the Library of Congress from another philanthropic fund and from moneys appropriated to it by Congress continued the project so that by 1940 there were in the Library some three million pages of manuscript documents in the shape of photostats and especially of microfilms. Thus for many subjects the scholar in the middle of the twentieth century does not have to rely on handwritten transcripts or notes nor does he have to travel from archive to archive in foreign countries, as did the scholars of the nineteenth century. In spite of these great advantages very little of this vast deposit of scholarly ore has as yet been refined into historical works.

Other benefits to historical scholarship resulting from the increased wealth in America have come from private philanthropy which that wealth made possible. These are the grants-in-aid, the fellowships, and the various subsidies which are now available and which were almost nonexistent in 1900. Literally dozens of fellowships have been endowed in the leading graduate schools of the country to encourage scholarly work and there are, of course, the larger and better known grants made by the Social Science Research Council, the American Council of Learned Societies, the Guggenheim Foundation, and many others.

But the best index of the relation between the economic development of America and historical scholarship can be found in the number of professors of history who are fed, clothed, and sheltered, not of course in the style which they would prefer or which they perhaps deserve, but at least on a scale which permits them to engage in scholarly work. Not all members of the guild have been or are scholars, yet historical scholarship throughout the first half of the twentieth century has been in the custody of this professional group. On a very few occasions the field has been successfully invaded by nonprofessionals like Senator Beveridge or the early James Truslow Adams, both of them men whose scholarly abilities have been readily acclaimed by the profession. Instances of this kind have, however, been rare. Consequently, any account of historical scholarship in America from 1900 to 1950 must be focused on the professional group upon whose ideas, vision, standards, and methods the fate of that body of knowledge depended.

In the transit of a science or an art from one civilization to another a number of stages have been distinguished. In the first the sole practitioners of the art or science in the country are aliens. During the second stage there are native practitioners who have been educated abroad. The third stage is reached when natives are educated in the field of knowledge at home in schools whose faculties are composed of aliens or natives who have been trained abroad. In the last stage marking the final transition of the art or science to the new country natives are taught by natives who have been educated at home. Perhaps a further development can be noted if the new country surpasses the old and persons from the old center of civilization must seek training and knoweldge in the new country.

By 1900 the profession of historical scholarship was in the third stage of its transit from western Europe. Forty years earlier there had been no such profession and the few historians in the country were lawyers or clergy or gentlemen with leisure to devote to their avocation of studying and writing history. Twenty years earlier the new profession emerged in the persons of eleven professors of history. Between 1880 and 1900 the profession became firmly established. There were at the beginning of the new century something over one hundred professors of history and more significantly there were a number of graduate schools for the training of new recruits. The instructors in these schools were native Americans many or most of whom had studied in Europe. They and their students, for obvious and professional reasons, had in 1884 created a national organization, the American Historical Association, and in 1895 they launched the professional journal, *The American Historical Review*.[1]

The new profession could not have been established at a more favorable time nor in a more favorable society. The phenomenal increase in the number of students from 1900 to 1950 necessitated a corresponding expansion of faculty to instruct them. At present there are approximately 7,500 professional historians, the vast majority of whom are teachers of history rather than scholars who also contribute to knowledge by writing history. The professional training of such numbers has been possible only because a considerable number of American colleges became universities where graduate work was offered and where scholarly attainments, especially in research, were the criteria for appointments and promotions. Rightly or wrongly the same training and the same standards of appointment have been employed for college teachers. Throughout the period various people have argued that the preparation for the Ph.D. degree, by requiring so much concentration on research from men who are unlikely to engage in research after leaving graduate school, has prevented the students from getting the broad scholarly knowledge essential for good college teachers. In spite of repeated protests of this nature the program of graduate training in history has retained the emphasis on research. In fact there is probably greater weight attached to research now than there was fifty years ago. At least the prevailing standards for doctoral dissertations have come to demand a much more extensive piece of research than would formerly have been accepted. There is truth in the gibe that the graduate students write books while the professors write articles. Whatever the merits of the arguments about the program for the Ph.D. degree, it is clear that long before the middle of the century Americans wishing to enter the profession of historical scholarship could receive, and regularly did receive, the necessary training in American graduate schools staffed by Americans who had themselves been educated in America. The science of history, to give it the name most used in the early years of the twentieth century, had been successfully transplanted from its European source. There is, however, little evidence that the stage has been reached where Europeans feel compelled to come to America because they recognize a superior or richer standard of historical scholarship, except, of course, in the specially favored field of the history of the United States.

If the new professional group in America has flourished and prospered since 1900, what can be said of historical scholarship whose fate was in the hands of the group? Certain results are obvious. There has been great activity, specialization, elaborate organization, a much higher level of technical scholarly standards, a few distinctive schools of interpretation, and a growing interest in basic conceptions.

Members of a professional group, in America at least, seem to feel a need for many organizations. The historians were no exception to this rule. Their rapid expansion in numbers, the tendency to narrow specialization as more thorough research has led to fragmentation of even such a subject as history, and other obvious professional considerations have led to the creation of a multiplicity of organizations. In nearly every instance one principal objective, certainly one consequence of the organization, has been the publication of a scholarly journal. The American Council of Learned Societies, itself an illustration of one type of scholarly organization, has published at five-year intervals *A List of American Learned Journals Devoted to Humanistic and Social Studies*. In that of 1945, there are listed 86 journals under History, all except a handful started in the twentieth century. In addition to these there are many others under other catagories which are essentially historical in character, like the *Journal of the History of Ideas* under Philosophy or the *Journal of Economic History* under Economics, to mention only two. The titles of these journals, each of which has a separate scholarly organization sponsoring it, illustrate the wide range of subjects in which American scholars have specialized. The following is a random selection: *Journal of Modern History, Byzantion* (The Byzantine Institute), *Speculum* (The Mediaeval Academy), *Agricultural History, The Hispanic American Historical Review, Isis* (History of Science Society), *Journal of Negro History, Journal of Southern History, Church History, Catholic Historical Review, Military Affairs, Bulletin of the Business Historical Society*, and the *Mississippi Valley Historical Review*.

In nearly every one of the American States there is a historical society which publishes a journal. The members of these societies are predominantly not professional scholars but in the vast majority of cases the journals are now edited by local representatives of the professional group and the articles published are written by professionals. The amateur local historian so typical of the nineteenth century is conspicuously absent and the scholarly value of the history published is as conspicuously increased.

Although there are many important ways in which this intensive organization of scholarly work has contributed to historical scholarship by preventing wasted effort, by raising standards, by facilitating research, and by making possible such a notable achievement as the *Dictionary of American Biography*, it must nevertheless be emphasized that great history cannot be organized into being. There are also some positive disadvantages which have been realized from the process. Some men of genuine talent have been lured into devoting their lives to organizing scholarship rather than to using it creatively. By common consent J. Franklin Jameson was among the most distinguished of American historical scholars in the first half of the twentieth century. Many would say that no American surpassed him in breadth of learning, or in scholarly wisdom. The few small pieces of historical work of his own which he published indicate what might have been had he not dedicated his abilities of a high order to organizing scholarship, to editing journals for the work of lesser minds, to publishing documents, to preparing and administering the preparation of bibliographies and other aids to scholarship.[2]

When he denied himself the real work of the historian, Jameson was acting on the theory generally accepted by the profession in the early years of the century, if not later, that the great task confronting historical scholars was to assemble as many firmly established facts as possible, leaving their use to the scholars of the future. Many seemed to think that when a sufficiently large pile of bricks should be gathered they would arrange themselves into a beautiful and useful building. Others appreciated the fact that an architect would be necessary but with too much modesty expected that the scholar of the future would be able to do what they considered beyond their capacity and dared not attempt. Fortunately for their peace of mind it did not occur to them that the future builder might use some other material than the bricks they were piling, might ask completely different questions of the past and therefore need different facts. Meanwhile prestige and scholarly reputation were to be won, since the editing of documents and similar brick piling activities conformed to the prevailing canons of the profession.

The specialization born of the more intensive standards of scholarship and so closely related to the elaborate organization of scholarship brought significant changes in the form of the history written. Prior to the twentieth century the dominant type of the best histories was the extensive treatment by one author of a large subject in many volumes. Several of these painters on huge canvases overlapped the twentieth century. A few of them whose volumes were all published after 1900 do not present real exceptions to this statement. Thus Channing had begun his huge work before the turn of the century, and it is perhaps not grossly unfair to E. Raymond Turner to suggest that his volumes on the Cabinet Council and the Privy Council, like Osgood's on the American Colonies, approximated collections of data rather than histories. The outstanding example of multivolumed scholarly history conceived and executed in the twentieth century is the work of Lawrence Gipson which has now reached the seventh of the contemplated twelve volumes. Other exceptions are the extended work of Louis Gottschalk on Lafayette of which four volumes have so far appeared and the seven volumes of Douglas Freeman on Lee and his lieutenants.

These instances constitute rare exceptions and no observers would deny that in the twentieth century, and under the monopoly of historical scholarship by the professionals, the characteristic form of historical writing has been the monograph. The reasons for the dominance of the monograph are obvious, as are its chief benefits. Yet if much was gained in terms of thorough research and of intensive and critical use of materials, much also may have been lost. Too many monographs have revealed superior scholarly abilities being wasted on inferior and insignificant subjects. One wonders even in the case of the most valuable monographic work if a still greater contribution could not have been made through the extensive form. For example consider the cases of Carl Becker and Henry Adams. Their talents were similar and preëminent. Becker was certainly the equal of Adams in his mastery of scholarly techniques; he had a comparable, incisive mind; he, too, probed deeply into human action while viewing events with philosophical calm, and his literary power equaled as well as resembled that of Adams. It is probably correct to say that Becker's miniatures, brilliant as they are, will not have the lasting qualities of the large canvas of Henry Adams nor have they made as significant a contribution to historical scholarship in America.

One result of the adoption of the monograph as the vehicle for scholarly work has been the development of coöperative histories. Events and human activities stubbornly refuse to atomize themselves into small units of monographic size. And human minds, including those of the scholars themselves, refuse to be satisfied with fragments, wanting larger syntheses than can be included in a monograph or the complete story of a theme too large to be circumscribed by a monograph. The solution which became a characteristic feature in American, as well as European, scholarship has been a coöperative work. Sometimes the coöperation takes the form of a series of volumes, each a monograph by a specialist in the particular subject or period. Unity and coherence in the entire work depend on the editor or editors who plan the project and are responsible for whatever integration is possible. The success, both scholarly and commercially, of the 26-volume *American Nation Series* of 1904–1907 encouraged other attempts. The most notable have been the Yale *Chronicles of America* (50 volumes), *The History of American Life* (13 volumes), *The Rise of Modern Europe* (20 volumes in progress), *A History of the South* (10 volumes in progress), *The Economic History of the United States* (9 volumes in progress). Since ventures of this size are expensive, they have usually been devoted to the history of the United States, as that is the field of history most likely to be bought by the American public. Sometimes the coöperative work results from the combination of separate articles by different authors in the various volumes. Such for example is Tenney Frank's *Economic Survey of the Roman Empire*, the five volumes of which contain sections written by various American and European scholars. Such also is the ten-volume work, *The American Secretaries of State and Their Diplomacy*, edited by S. F. Bemis and written by thirty-nine American scholars.

These attempts to supply histories on large themes while retaining the advantages of the monographs by specialists have not been attended by notable success. The standards of intensive research have usually been preserved in the separate parts of volumes, but the total picture has lacked unity, coherence, and proportion. Apparently in historical work the best results can be obtained only when one mind studies all the data and erects the entire structure. Perhaps this is saying that the writing of history is in some respects a work of art and like a symphony must be the creation of one man. Certainly the history of historical writing both in Europe and America shows no coöperative work equal to the achievements of individuals. The separate monographs may each be a scholarly jewel but when they are put together the resulting mosaic is a disappointing or drab affair.

The monographs of the new professional scholars in America were by specialists and for specialists. Scholarly history in the twentieth century was not read by the public to the same extent as the scholarly history of earlier periods. This fact did not disturb the scholars in the early years of the century. Indeed they saw in it cause for satisfaction. In their desire to be scientific and in their aversion to predecessors whom they scornfully labeled "literary historians" they deliberately shunned a felicitous literary style which might encourage reading by the public. The cold and unadorned style of a laboratory report fitted more closely their theory of history as a science. A case has been noted in which a scholar stated, by implication at least, that the historical work he was considering might be esteemed as good (that is, scientific) history if only it had been badly written.[3] Naturally the public, not being under professional compulsion to read the monographs or journals, did not do so.

One fact must be recorded to the credit of the historical scholars. They have at no time created and used a specialized or technical terminology. In thus refusing to follow the example of scholars in most branches of knowledge, including economics, sociology, psychology, philosophy, and education, to mention only a few, the historians denied themselves some advantages. The general public, as well as colleagues in the academic world, could not be impressed by an awesome vocabulary, incomprehensible to all save the initiated. More importantly, the historians lacking specially designed words have employed those commonly used and hence often loosely used. Words like "cause" or "fact" have, in fact, caused a lot of trouble. Offsetting these disadvantages is the one great gain. If the historians have anything of moment to say and if they can say it with even a modicum of literary art, the public will be able to understand it. Admittedly, the scholars in history at the beginning of the century were not taking advantage of this opportunity and were out of touch with the reading public.

Gradually during the twentieth century the profession became dissatisfied with this situation, against which there had always been a few protestants. The cause of the change in attitude was neither a desire for royalties, nor pressure from commercial publishers, since the latter willingly left the publication of historical monographs to the rapidly expanding university presses. To some extent the scholars began to take less seriously the theory of history as science, a theory which tended to make history dull. Greater weight can be assigned to World War I, which stimulated nationalism and which confronted members of the historical profession, some through direct personal experience, with the problem of making historical knowledge more directly useful to the American people. One conclusion quickly reached was that scholarly knowledge had been kept too largely within the small circle of scholars. The obvious remedy was to write scholarly history in a way that the public would read. An effort to do precisely that resulted in the Yale *Chronicles* series which appeared immediately after World War I. In these small volumes, footnotes and all the apparatus of scholarship disappeared, and deliberate efforts were made to present sound scholarly knowledge in an attractive literary style. In the second quarter of the century the new attitude won general acceptance, and more and more of the monographic work came to be written if not with literary art at least with greater effectiveness than formerly.

When throughout the period people lamented the gulf between scholarly knowledge and the public, one important consideration regularly escaped attention. If the general public refused to buy the scholarly history being written, a special and growing public was brought into contact with historical scholarship by a different path. These were the men and women who went to colleges and universities where most of them were likely to attend a course in history. The college population increased so rapidly that before 1950 statistics showed that about 30 per cent of the graduates from high school continued their education in an institution of higher learning. What proportion of them actually took any courses in history cannot be stated with any exactness but it must have been large enough to include a significant section of the total population. Thus through spoken history in lectures and through directed reading many more of the population probably had some contact with historical scholarship than several generations earlier when people bought scholarly histories because they were enjoyable.

The writing of textbooks loomed large among the activities of the professional scholars. In no other country could so many and such good textbooks be found, probably because in no other country were there such numbers of university students to buy them. The rewards for the author of a successful book have been large both in money and in prestige. It is an unflattering comment on the scholarly standards of the profession that the writing of textbooks should bring prestige since they so seldom contain either new knowledge or original interpretations. Yet such is the case, and more than one distinguished reputation as a scholar has been based primarily on a widely used textbook. In some cases — Channing's was one — a textbook has provided the author with funds necessary for original investigation and genuine contributions It can mean freedom from servitude in summer schools, thus enabling the author to escape that menace to productive scholarship. More often the textbook itself acts as one of the gravest dangers to historical scholarship. Every large publishing house wishes to have a textbook for every course in history given in several institutions. To increase sales a new edition or an entirely different book is brought out every few years. Consequently temptation has been constantly placed before the more promising members of the profession and they have succumbed with little resistance. Far too much of the time and energy of the profession in the twentieth century has been diverted to a needless multiplication of textbooks, leaving not enough for the production of scholarly work of the type which the future will not willingly let die.[4]

II

Professional scholars, like all historians of all times and places, subscribe to some theory or make some assumptions, avowed or unavowed, of the nature and limits of historiography. These ideas will inevitably determine the character of the history written. Although the American scholars of the nineteenth century and of the early years of the twentieth displayed a curious reluctance to consider what they were doing or what were their philosophical preconceptions, they undoubtedly subscribed to the belief that history is a science. Such a conclusion was a natural one. Science had triumphed in the thought of the nineteenth century. To be "scientific" was the great desideratum. The very word was a fetish. So great was the prestige that the word "science" carried in the academic world that such verbal monstrosities appeared as "library science" and "domestic science." Even a new church based on ideas denying the validity of the fundamental principles upon which contemporary science rested took the name "Christian Science."

Under these circumstances it was not extraordinary that the emerging vigorous professional historical group should think of themselves as scientists and their subject of study as science. The science of history meant to a small minority the establishment of laws or generalizations. This conception of historical science proved to be barren, for little or no history was written under the influence of this conception. To the vast majority of American scholars scientific history meant the search for objective facts alone, with no laws or generalizations and with a renunciation of all philosophy. To be scientific was to be objective. To be objective was to study critically the sources and to ascertain impartially the facts of history, as they actually happened ("wie es eigentlich gewesen"). This was to be done with the same detached mind and in the same manner in which, it was believed, natural scientists observed their phenomena. The objective facts, thus established by a completely neutral historian-scientist without benefit of generalization or any preconceptions, would speak for themselves. Nearly all of the scholarly history written in the United States in the late nineteenth and in the first half of the twentieth century was written under the influence of this basic conception. The high value put on facts as an end in themselves; the emphasis given to the establishment of facts; the fear of venturing any statement without a supporting document; the belief, occasionally avowed, that complete objectivity could be attained merely by honest effort; the denial of any philosophy or theory of history in the assumption that historians should, or could, be without prepossessions; and the very literary style of their writing all testify to the vast influence of the "objective facts" theory of scientific history.[5]

Not long after the turn of the century critics challenged the validity of this school of thought. With poetic justice the challenges received their fullest development in Germany, from where the conception of history as science had spread throughout western civilization, although non-Germanic thinkers, like Croce, also led in the attack. Traditionally, Americans have manifested little interest in the fundamental propositions on which their field of knowledge rested and at first only a few rare scholars even knew that the prevailing historical faith was under scrutiny. But by the fourth decade of the century the writings of Carl Becker and Charles A. Beard raised the issue before the profession and a heated controversy developed.

The critics insisted that the prevailing theory of objective scientific history was a theory and insisted on making explicit the assumptions implicit in it. The first assumption, they pointed out, is that the facts of history have existed as an object or series of objects outside the mind of the historian. The second is that the historian can know this object or series and can describe it as it objectively existed. This involves the question of documentation, the only way in which the historian can observe the facts. Yet documentation can only cover a small fraction of the events of history. This also requires the historian to divest himself of all philosophical, religious, political, economic, sexual, moral, and aesthetic interests so that he can view the facts with strict impartiality. It also presupposes that the facts can be grasped by a purely rational process. The final assumption is that the facts of history have some structural organization through inner or causal relations which any impartial historian can ascertain and on which all must agree.[6]

With remarkable ease and speed the old historical faith to which American historians had adhered for so long was abandoned. Undoubtedly the intellectual climate of opinion was hostile to absolutes in all fields of thought. Perhaps the same attitude which resulted in relativity in the physical sciences accounted for the new conception of history. Certainly the label used supports that conclusion, for the new historical faith is called historical relativism. How widely it has been accepted cannot as yet be stated, but it seems to have gained many converts. A Committee on Historiography, composed of eight scholars widely and favorably known in the profession, submitted a report in 1946 in which relativism was embraced.[7] It is too soon to discern the consequences of the new ideas concerning the nature of the foundations on which historical writing and scholarship rest. That they will be far reaching and fundamental must be expected.

Some other assumptions which affect historical scholarship have also been subjected to analysis especially during the latter part of the half century. One of these is the idea of progress which influenced powerfully the thinking of nearly all Americans, including those who wrote history, down to or past World War I. The characteristic optimism resulting from the rapid growth of the country and from the prosperity of its people combined with the interpretation put upon the science of the nineteenth century to persuade Americans that the concept of progress was valid.[8] Either the devastating impact of World War I or currents of thought from abroad, reaching historical scholarship directly by such works as Spengler's *Decline of the West*, profoundly altered this article of faith. When one writes of particular people at a particular time and place, as historians must, and when monographic treatment further limits the range of thought, demonstrations of progress are not likely to emerge. Yet professions of belief in progress can readily be found in the works of nine-teenth-century scholars, sometimes scattered profusely in the narrative as in the histories of George Bancroft and John Fiske, more often stated in a preface. Thus Edward Channing in the Preface to the first volume of his great work published in 1905 avowed his belief in history as "the story of living forces, always struggling onward and upward toward that which is better and higher in human conception." As the twentieth century advanced, belief in progress became increasingly difficult to maintain and increasingly rare in historical writing. In fact, much more typical were the sentences with which a young scholar, Robert R. Palmer, concluded his *A History of the Modern World*, published in 1950. In them he somewhat grimly clings to the hope that if our civilization fails in the current cataclysm another would rise in its place.

Among other basic ideas circumscribing historical scholarship have been nationalism, liberalism, pragmatism, democracy, capitalism, and the belief that man is primarily a rational being. Nearly all have been challenged and subjected to critical analysis rather than being taken for granted as formerly. The tremendous significance of nationalism in the modern world came to be appreciated after World War I and with greater understanding more and more history was written in those terms. Even in writing the history of their own nation American scholars have displayed a sophistication in marked contrast with the uncritical naïveté with which earlier generations had used what is now called "the Anglo-Saxon legend."

Less scholarly analysis has been given to liberalism and democracy in spite of the challenges from totalitarian ideas in the second quarter of the century. The influence of these concepts on historical scholarship has been vast. The most conservative of American historians could not escape from the liberal, democratic tradition of which they were a part. The result was that the worth and liberty of the individual person and of democracy as the proper way of organizing society were accepted as axiomatic. The same forces and ideas which produced the Progressive movement with its belief that the cure for the weaknesses of democracy is more democracy gave a Progressive coloring to the histories written in

America. This climate of opinion has lasted longer in scholarly circles than in the political sphere.

Everyone who writes or studies history must confront the problem of human behavior and must accordingly hold, either avowedly or unavowedly, basic conceptions regarding psychology. In 1900 there can be little doubt that the historians in America shared the prevailing view that man was essentially a rational being. Some psychologists, notably Freud, had already begun to stress the role of the unconscious and the irrational. Gradually the new concepts won widespread acceptance until today their use in scholarly history to explain human action evokes no surprise. This does not mean that the historical profession has deliberately considered the implications of modern psychology or mastered its findings or applied its techniques. It merely means that as a result of one of the deeply significant developments in knowledge, twentieth-century Americans often thought in the new terms. The anti-intellectualism which found encouragement in the new psychology and the emphasis which some exponents placed on sexual drives and frustrations made the theories distasteful to many who repudiated them by name but used them in practice. Surely one of the noticeable changes in any comparison of histories written at the beginning of the century and at its midpoint is the frequent explanation at the later date of human behavior as lying outside the area of conscious control.

III

When one turns from a consideration of the influence of basic concepts to look at the actual history written and studied by the recently established professional group of scholars, probably the first thing to be noted is the remarkable expansion of activity. Almost every portion of the long story of the human race has been the subject of intensive study by Americans in the twentieth century. Specialists are now available where fifty years ago there was either total ignorance or a bare minimum of knowledge. The list of organizations and journals already given indicates the change. It is true that certain areas such as India, the Balkans, Brazil, or the Byzantine Empire are thinly covered. It is also true that there has been retrogression in some fields. In 1900 a very large percentage of the few historical scholars there were had some knowledge of the history of peoples in the Holy Land in Biblical times. Today though there may be more who could be ranked as specialists, only a minute fraction of the body of scholars has any of this knowledge. In spite of outstanding contributions by twentieth-century American scholars to knowledge of the ancient world there has also been a sufficiently noticeable decline in the undergraduate study of the histories of ancient Greece and Rome to make some observers fear that scholarly knowledge of those momentous periods may atrophy or become the sterile possession of a few learned anchorites. The most distinguished professors of ancient history have, as a group, produced relatively few young scholars to take their places. Indeed there has been a tendency in even the leading universities not to replace professors in ancient history who retire or die. Undoubtedly a partial explanation lies in the fact that there has been a concomitant or earlier decline in the knowledge of the classical languages. Practically every arts college in the United States required some knowledge of Latin for admission in 1900, and some required Greek. Practically no arts college has such a requirement in 1950. A minority of the high schools of the country offer courses in Latin, which are taken by a still smaller minority of the students, and only a rare preparatory school gives instruction in Greek. (For a fuller discussion of the classics in twentieth-century America see the chapter by Walter R. Agard in this volume.)

If scholarly activity in a few areas contracted relatively or absolutely, there took place a remarkable expansion in other areas. This was particularly true of the study of American history. In 1890 when Herbert B. Adams was being promoted to a professorship in the Johns Hopkins University, after he had made his department the leading one in United States for graduate study, he recorded the contemporary position of American history in his comments about his title. "I have no ambition" wrote this teacher of F. J. Turner, C. M. Andrews, J. Franklin Jameson, and many others noted for scholarly contributions in American history, "to be known as a Professor of American History. At least five sixths of my three years' course of lectures to graduates and *all* of my undergraduate classes are in the European field . . . As 'Professor of Institutional History' I could have a fair field for comparative studies in Church and State and the Institutes of Education, without being regarded as an American provincial." [9] That Adams spoke for his generation can be seen from other evidence. Princeton University in its catalogue for the academic year 1900–1901 also listed no course in American History for its undergraduates. At Harvard in 1899–1900, of the twenty courses in history, including five offered jointly with the Divinity School, only three were on American history. At Yale in the same year the proportion was higher, since three of the eleven courses given were devoted to America. During the next fifty years American history became the most diligently cultivated field of scholarly activity. The Harvard catalogue of 1948–49 showed that eighteen of the fifty undergraduate courses in history, including six given jointly with the Divinity School, were listed as American history. Comparable shifts took place elsewhere and, of course, in the scholarly profession at large. They seem likely to continue if the doctoral dissertations in progress at universities in the United States are a guide to the work of the next generation. A list of dissertations in progress in September 1949, published by the American Historical Association, showed that 894 of a total of 1,634 were on the history of the United States.

In seeking the explanation for the greater emphasis on American history several factors can be readily identified. The relative ease of getting at source materials for American history and the labor involved in acquiring the knowledge of foreign languages essential in most of the other fields of history undoubtedly account in part for the larger number of graduate students in the former. More important has been the intensification of nationalism everywhere and especially, of course, in the United States since the Spanish-American War and since the American people became a self-conscious world power. Repeatedly from 1914 to 1950 the American people, speaking through newspapers, through national and state legislatures, and through various other media, have demanded that more American history be taught. American scholars, sharing the same impulses, have not been slow to comply.

Another partial explanation of the emphasis on American history is the much greater attention given to what is called recent history. Between 1900 and 1950 there has been a chronological as well as a geographical expansion of scholarly activity. The most significant extension in time has not been to earlier periods through archaeological or other discoveries. On the contrary, it has resulted from the inclusion of the most recent period within the jurisdiction of scholarship. The shift in emphasis can be measured by contrasting the practice in Justin Winsor's *Narrative and Critical History of America*, which is typical of the preprofessional nineteenth-century scholarship, and *The American Nation* series, which represents the ideas and interests of the twentieth-century scholarly profession. The former shows that the prevailing view considered the terminal point for the scholarly treatment of American history to be the American Revolution and the constitutional convention of 1789, or events of a full century earlier. The latter devoted four of twenty-five volumes to the forty years preceding and including the date of publication. As the twentieth century advanced, the shift of scholarly focus to recent history persisted, until by 1950 a large percentage of the work being done not only in American history but in British, Latin American, Modern European and Far Eastern history covered the immediately preceding decades, a period which an earlier generation would have regarded as not a proper field for scholarship. The editor of the *American Historical Review* stated in 1915 that in the first twenty years of that journal only eight out of nearly four hundred articles related to the history of Europe since 1815. In 1920 he reported that as a consequence of the new focus of interest produced by the World War a dozen articles on European history after 1815 had been added in the five-year period.[10] The most superficial glance at the courses offered in various institutions, at the table of contents in scholarly journals, and at the dissertations in progress shows that since 1920 more and more attention has been paid to the recent period in Europe, America, and Asia.

Both the geographical and chronological changes have been reflected in the programs of the annual meeting of the professional organization. In December 1899 the American Historical Association met in Boston. About 150 members, most of whom were not university professors, attended. There were five sessions at which fifteen scholarly papers were read, not counting the presidential address. The subjects at the five sessions were Colonization (in general), Church History, European History, Foreign Relations (chiefly of the United States), and Fields of Historical Study (military, economic, and sacred and profane). In December 1949 the American Historical Association again met in Boston. The number of members who registered was 1,173. Probably well over 90 per cent of them were present or prospective members of the academic world. There were 47 sessions with 204 participants, including chairmen and commentators as well as the authors of the papers. Approximately one-third of the sessions dealt with American history. Others were devoted to the histories of Great Britain, France, Germany, Russia, China, India, Latin-America, of the ancient, medieval, and Renaissance periods, to economic history, to military history, to the history of religion, to the history of science and to the history of education, and to methods and problems in teaching history.

There have been still further changes in scholarly focus which are worth noting. Within each area and each period the historians burst the bonds which had confined history so largely to the political activities of man. No department of history would in 1950 dream of inscribing on its walls and its publications the motto "History is Past Politics and Politics is Present History" as was done in the 1880's by the preëminent graduate school of that period.[11] Judging by the history written, history has been expanded to include all past human activities. Moreover, laudable if not always successful efforts have been made to achieve a synthesis of man's multifarious exploits. Still some fields of action have received more attention than others, an inevitable result which is magnified by the prevalence of the monograph in scholarly work.

It is, however, true that more political history has been, and still is being, written than any other type. The prevailing strength of nationalism in the United States, as well as in the rest of the world, precluded any possibility of shifting the main focus of attention from the political state. Another explanation for the scholarly emphasis on political history is that in nearly every country and in nearly every period political records have been better preserved and are therefore more easily available than the materials for man's other activities. Perhaps historians themselves by their very interest in the past may be more inclined to follow tradition than other people. Certainly it seems to have been difficult for them to shift their focus from political events. In the Editors' Introduction to *The American Nation* series published in the early years of the twentieth century an emphatic statement announced that the series would not be simply a political or constitutional history but would include as equally important social and economic history. In spite of good intentions and some obvious efforts, the twenty-six volumes which followed represented man as primarily a political being. Even in the *History of American Life* series, most of which appeared in the fourth decade of the century and which did in fact subordinate political events to economic and social activities, the history of the American people is divided into periods, and the series into volumes by political dates. Sometime there may be a series in which the boundaries of the segments will be the recurring economic crises.

Within the field of political history a number of noteworthy developments occurred. Constitutional history has been relatively neglected and the history of international relations has been greatly emphasized compared to the practice of the nineteenth century. The new position of the United States in world politics after 1898, and the two world wars after periods of severe tension among the world powers, are sufficient to account for the more intensive study of international relations. It is noteworthy that in the histories of foreign relations the more sophisticated scholarly standards that emerged during the period required multiarchival research. Prior to the twentieth century only the exceptional American historian felt the need for data from the records of all the participants in an international dispute. The same scholarly sophistication produced a change in the treatment of the internal political history not only of the United States but of any society. Less consideration has been given to laws and constitutional theory and much more to the actual operation of the political institution. This tendency can be seen by comparing earlier and later accounts of slavery in America and of the British mercantile policy in the colonial period. Military history, because of a combination of circumstances including the reluctance of the liberally minded American scholars to admit that war can be regarded as a normal activity of civilized man, did not share in the popularity of international diplomatic relations. The relative neglect of military history ended, temporarily at least, with World War II. Then the Army, Navy, and Air Force, far surpassing any previous action of the American government, paid tribute to the utility of history by recruiting staffs of historians, most of them in the higher echelons from the scholarly world. The result has been a greatly increased amount of scholarly, though official, military history.

If political history has continued in the twentieth century to be the most common variety, the most startling development was the advent of economic history to a prominence which challenged the supremacy of political history. Whatever the reasons, there can be no doubt that man's activities in producing, distributing, and consuming wealth and the interpretation of his other actions in the light of these operations assumed a new and huge importance in the thought and work of historical scholars during the twentieth century. The earlier writers had not been unaware of human toil but generally either dismissed it as unworthy of attention or treated it in terms of the laws, the policies, the restraints, or aids with which political society attempted to control economic events. It was only in the present century that the canvas supplanted the frame, that economic facts became an end in themselves. The program of the new self-conscious economic historians has been well stated by one of them:

We are trying to see the farmer farming, rather than watching him go to granger meetings, embark on populist crusades, clamor for greenbacks, or lobby for more than a hundred per cent of parity. We are realizing that the history of labor is not fully or even largely told by narrating the history of labor unions or socialist movements, that the history of banking is more than an account of banking or currency laws, that trade is more than a matter of tariffs, and that even the history of business itself can be studied in terms of the accumulation of capital, the organization and administration of the enterprise, and the development of policies of production or sale.[12]

Fired with the zeal of explorers in a new country, the same professional motives affecting all the scholars, the economic historians quickly won recognition for their field and themselves. They naturally formed their own organization, the Economic History Association, and established a scholarly journal, the *Journal of Economic History*, which is, however, only one of a number of scholarly journals devoted to economic history. Their accomplishments have been considerable in all areas and periods of history. Among them are such monuments as the works of Rostovtzeff and of Tenney Frank on the economic history of the ancient world, the studies of a group of scholars on price fluctuations in western Europe, the volumes on American manufacturing, labor, and agriculture published in a series by the Carnegie Institution of Washington, the Harvard Studies in Business History, and many others too numerous even to list, as well as a veritable flood of monographs.

Political and economic history absorbed most but by no means all of the time and energy of the scholars of the new century. An increasing amount of attention was devoted to other human activities, to thought, to amusements, to eating, to science, to religion, all frequently thrown together under the label "Social History." Whether or not social history constituted "The New History," as was claimed and denied, and whether or not the emphasis placed by some social historians on what the common man ate and wore and did tended "to reduce the chronicle of human striving to its lowest common denominator," as at least one critic asserted, there can be no doubt of its increasing popularity in scholarly circles.[13] This is true in spite of the obvious difficulties in trying to relate these disparate aspects of life or to achieve a synthesis of them. The most noteworthy achievements were those in the history of thought and science. Many of the very significant studies in the history of thought were made by professors of literature. The history of science won widespread recognition as a distinct field of specialization to which professors of philosophy contributed more frequently than scientists and as frequently as the scholars located in departments of history.

No matter what the period treated, or the area or the activity, the data must be interpreted according to some scheme of reference if the result is not to be a mere compilation of facts. In seeking the schools of historical interpretation which dominated the work of the scholars in twentieth-century America several facts stand out. The first is that in general the Americans did not subscribe to any single school of historical interpretation. A second fact is that a few years before the beginning of the century there appeared the two most distinctive and original interpretations of history yet formulated by any American scholar. Of these one had no perceptible influence on scholarship. The other founded a school of historical writing which gave its author a greater influence on American historical scholarship than that exerted by any other one man.

In 1890 there had appeared *The Influence of Sea Power upon History, 1660–1783* by Alfred Thayer Mahan, then a Captain in the United States Navy. The thesis in it and in subsequent volumes appearing within a decade was that sea power determined supremacy in international affairs. This hypothesis and the supporting histories won him various high scholarly distinctions, and such influence on the naval policies of the great powers that when he died, the resolution of the American Historical Association recording his death stated that "more than any American scholar of his day he has affected the course of world politics." [14] The times, so propitious for his influence on governmental policy, were decidely inauspicious for any influence on American historical scholarship. In fact he cannot be said to have had any discernible effect at all.

Instead of being illustrated in many volumes of his own, the thesis of Frederick Jackson Turner reached the scholarly world through an essay published in 1893. Its title, "The Significance of the Frontier in American History," indicated his belief that American history was shaped by the ever westward expanding frontier. It would be difficult to exaggerate the extent or the magnitude of the impact of Turner's interpretation on American historical scholarship. With extraordinary speed the thesis was applied to episode after episode in American history by more and more of the expanding number of scholars. The most distinctly American school of historical interpretation thus became a prominent feature of the twentieth century. There were many explanations for the unparalleled success of the thesis. The most obvious was its validity, its usefulness in bringing light and understanding. Other factors which contributed were the reaction against previous historical ideas, many of them German in origin; the appeal of the uniqueness of American history because of our frontier; the stress on what were considered highly desirable and typically American qualities such as individualism and democracy; the readiness of scholars to accept Darwinian or evolutionary ideas; the prevailing American optimism; and the ease with which scattered scholars could study the frontier in their own vicinity.

If such a concatenation of circumstances favored Turner's thesis, time would certainly bring changes. So it proved. After a generation of its unchallenged ascendancy, some scholars began to attack the frontier interpretation, or at least to demand serious modifications of it. The resulting scholarly discussion has produced a literature of its own, and though Turner remains a giant in American historiography, some of his conclusions and more of those put forward by enthusiastic disciples must be abandoned or altered.

There was another interpretation of history used in twentieth-century America even more than the Turner thesis, which in some respects could be regarded as similar. This was the economic interpretation of history. In no sense original with Americans, nor confined to the twentieth century, the explanation of events in terms of economic forces and motives became more widely used among American scholars than any other interpretation. There have been very few American scholars who have employed a strict Marxian economic determinism. Yet if little has been heard of the class struggle, there have been many who have relied chiefly on an economic interpretation and only a rare exception has failed to take some cognizance of the theory. The first startling and successful application of this school to American history was Charles A. Beard's *An Economic Interpretation of the Constitution* which appeared in 1913. From then on, economic interpretation flourished like the proverbial green bay tree, until toward the middle of the century more and more scholars repudiated it as a single explanation and insisted other forces and factors must also be taken into account.

Two other schools of historical interpretation deserve notice. One has been firmly established by extensive work, the other is barely in the process of emerging. The first has properly been called "The Imperial School of Colonial History." Either because of greater scholarly sophistication, or because the outcome of the Spanish-American War made Americans appreciate what had been missed before, or because of both, a new interpretation of the colonial period began in America around the turn of the century. The colonial period, including the Revolution, was viewed from the center of the empire instead of from the periphery, as a part of British history rather than as the origins of the United States. Since many of the younger generation of scholars were trained in the first decades of the century by men engaged in research in the colonial period this school had a wide influence, and its finest products, represented by the histories of Beer, Osgood, Andrews, and Gipson, compared favorably with the best scholarship of the period.[15]

The other interpretation cannot be said to have been formulated as a fully developed thesis. Yet it is evident that in the latter part of the half-century a number of scholars began to regard the urban movement as decisive a factor in all phases of post Civil War American history as the frontier and westward movement had been earlier. Professor A. M. Schlesinger, whose article in 1940 contains the nearest approach so far to a statement of the new thesis, has also made in *The Rise of the City, 1878–1898*, the most notable, if not entirely successful, attempt to use the urban movement as the synthesizing agency in recent American history.[16] What the ultimate result will be is still an open question but one to which an answer may soon be given.

This answer, together with all the answers to the problems confronting historical scholarship in America in the middle of the twentieth century, will depend on the wisdom as well as the learning of the members of the history departments of the universities and colleges. No analysis of the study and writing of history in twentieth-century America can exaggerate the part played by this professional group. Nor can one fail to pay tribute to the high scholarly standards which they employed in making their remarkable additions to knowledge and understanding.

Yet significant as have been the scholarly benefits resulting from the appearance in America of a class of professional historians, the transfer of historical scholarship so exclusively to their hands may in the end prove to have been unfortunate. History is concerned with life, and he who wishes to understand or interpret human activity must himself have participated in affairs and the richer his experience the better. That is what Gibbon meant when, referring to his own brief military career, he said the Captain of the Hampshire Grenadiers was of use to the historian of Rome. That is what ex-Senator Foraker of Ohio meant when he wrote in 1911 to a friend explaining his objections to William Howard Taft and Theodore Roosevelt. Neither, he said, has "ever earned a dollar except by earning a salary or writing a magazine article or in some such way. Neither one ever had any business experience. Neither ever knew what it was to meet a pay roll Saturday night — or to wrestle with a deficit." [17] This type of criticism may be applied with equal validity to the writing of history. There is always danger that the professional historians may spend too much of their lives in libraries. It is probably fortunate that so many of the group during World War I and World War II participated directly in military and other public service. Scholarly training and much learning are not adequate substitutes for experience. They can produce technicians but not the rich, wise minds from which alone great history can be expected.

IV ·

Literary Scholarship

RENÉ WELLEK

I

In 1900 a type of philological scholarship imported from Germany had triumphed in American graduate schools and in the production of American literary scholars. The decisive years were the eighties and nineties of the last century. In 1850 there were only eight graduate students in the whole of the United States, three at Harvard and three at Yale. In 1852, Daniel H. Gilman, later to become the first President of Johns Hopkins, could get no graduate instruction either at Yale or Harvard: he had difficulty in persuading one Professor to read a little German with him.[1] With the exception of a great scholar, Francis Child of Harvard, who edited the *Scottish and English Popular Ballads* (1857–58), there were no "producing" scholars in the modern languages in America, no periodicals, and no university presses.

The situation changed rapidly in the last decades of the nineteenth century. In 1876 the Johns Hopkins University was founded expressly for the providing of graduate instruction on the German model. Soon the other universities followed, expanding their graduate instruction so rapidly that by 1900 there were 5,831 graduate students (of all subjects) in the United States. In 1883 the Modern Language Association was founded. At first, it was only a small group of teachers who were interested in the discussion of questions of classroom instruction and grammar, but it grew rapidly and completely changed its character. In 1927 the Association voted to replace the original definition of its purpose as "the *study* of modern languages and literatures" by the "advancement of *research* in the modern languages and literatures"; but long before, certainly by 1900, this stress on research had become predominant. Several periodicals exclusively devoted to the publication of the results of academic scholarship in the modern languages were founded: *Publications of the Modern Language Association* in 1886, *Modern Language Notes* in 1886, the *Journal of English and Germanic Philology* in 1897, and *Modern Philology* in 1903. University presses were established, mainly after the 1890's, and several series of publications were devoted to printing doctoral dissertations. The *Yale Studies in English*, now running to well over one hundred volumes, were begun in 1898. The fabulous growth of the American university libraries and, later, the founding of research libraries such as the Folger and the Huntington libraries, both mainly devoted to English Renaissance literature, stimulated the expansion of research. Today American libraries are so well equipped and so well administered that for most purposes they are preferable to European libraries. If we look at these achievements we can understand the enthusiasm with which, at the height of the movement, its leaders contemplated its success. Here are a few passages from the presidential address of Thomas R. Price of Columbia University, delivered at the Annual Meeting of the Modern Language Association in 1901:

As teachers of the modern languages, in our survey of our own Association and of the American university system, we must all feel a certain warmth of exhilaration. The progress that our favorite studies have been making is so splendid. With that period of forty years . . . there has been a steady current of progress, so vast an improvement in our methods of instruction, so vast an increase in the magnitude of our work, in the number of pupils, in the size and qualification of our professorial force. There has been, indeed, in this wide enthusiasm for the spreading and elevation of modern language instruction, an intellectual movement that may fairly be compared with the enthusiasm in the days of the renaissance . . . In country villages I found the same ardor for our special studies as in great universities. No man that has shared in this movement can fail to feel a noble joy in such a display of energy and in such an achievement of results.[2]

Something happened to this "renaissance" in these last fifty years. The ardor, and that not only of the villagers, went out of it. By the mid-century, philological scholarship, though still entrenched in most graduate schools, was definitely on the defensive: its exclusive rule of the American universities was broken; and everywhere, especially among the younger men of the staff and the students, dissatisfaction with the system became so widespread that it seemed merely a matter of time when it could be seen as a historical phenomenon of American cultural history.

We can explain its triumph about 1900. It was not only owing to the importation of German scholarship and to the prestige of Germany at that time. It also met a contemporary intellectual and social situation. It satisfied the nostalgia for the past, especially the European past and the Middle Ages, and at the same time it met the desire for facts, for accuracy, for the imitation of the "scientific method" which had acquired such overwhelming prestige through the successes of modern technology so particularly conspicuous in the United States. The critical relativism implied in the method of studying literature through its historical antecedents, its open abdication before the task of evaluation, also fitted into the pattern of a civilization disoriented or skeptical in its judgments of values. The enormous possibilities of production, of production in quantities, and of a standardization of the products were aids to victory, for bulk in production was an industrial ideal, and the convenient grading of teachers was a practical necessity. The useless antiquarianism, the dreary factualism, the pseudoscience combined with anarchical skepticism and lack of critical taste characteristic of this scholarship must be apparent to almost everybody today. The system has become almost too easy a target for ridicule. Yet one must recognize that, out of inertia, it perpetuates itself even today, and that it has still some attractions for those who are enamored of its mechanical perfection and its tone of detachment, and for those who are merely docile and industrious.

Whatever the abuses of the system, one should recognize that they represent the decadence of a worthy ideal, that of philology conceived as a total science of a civilization, an ideal originally formulated for the study of classical antiquity and then transferred by the German romanticists to the modern languages. In the programmatic statements by leading American scholars, we actually find such ambitious formulations: for example, in Albert S. Cook's *The Higher Study of English* (1908) or in Edwin Greenlaw's *Province of Literary History* (1931). But while one may recognize that the standards and aims, professed in these books, are broad and humane, in actuality there was a divorce between theory and practice. Albert S. Cook himself published mainly editions, studies, and notes on Anglo-Saxon literature, many of them on trivial and minute points. His editions of classics of criticism (Sidney, for instance) are school-texts containing little editorial matter. His occasional critical pronouncements echo Arnold and his dubious theory of "touchstones." Edwin Greenlaw did mainly highly competent studies of the political allegory in Spenser. The gestures towards criticism, synthesis, the history of the human mind, remained mostly gestures or the private virtues of an individual who was unable to make his ideas effective institutionally.

The original conceptions and aims of a humane literary scholarship were constantly forgotten. The romantic stress on origins coming from Herder led in practice to the strange overrating of the study of Anglo-Saxon and early forms of medieval languages, specialties which were (and in some places continue to be) imposed on most American students of literature. The requirements in Anglo-Saxon grammar and the history of English phonology not only diverted energies from literary pursuits but deterred many students from completing their professional studies. The romantic concept of the evolution and the continuity of literature decayed so quickly that nothing was left of it save the superstition that works of literature could be reduced to compounds of parallels and sources. The evolutionary conception still survived after 1900 in the writings of Francis Gummere on the *Origins of Poetry* and on the *Popular Ballad*; but as the evolutionary concept had become far too strongly subservient to biological analogues, it was soon discarded and today seems completely incomprehensible, to the degree that the writing of narrative literary history has become an almost lost art. The romantic conception of original genius degenerated into the excesses of biographical gossip-mongering, the feverish interest in trivial anecdotes, or the constant assumption that a work of literature is an autobiographical document. The ideal of a general history of culture embodied in the literature led — especially among English and American scholars — to the indiscriminate expansion into miscellaneous social history. Papers on the "Origin of the Long-bow," theses on "The Military Profession in the Sixteenth Century," great works such as *Witchcraft in Old and New England* brought about a complete obliteration of boundaries and confusion of methods. The romantic ideal of the study of a national spirit led, in practice, to the isolation of the study of one national literature, to the obscuring of the unity of European literature, to the neglect of comparative literature, to the Anglomania, Germanophilia, and Francophilia of many teachers, and finally to the new provincialism of many specialists in American literature. What had been a worthy ideal in the minds of the founders, the Grimms, Boeckh, Diez, became sheer Alexandrianism, an antiquarianism without sense of direction and purpose.

The reasons for this decay are obvious: some are not American but European also; they are due to the general decay of the romantic ideal and its replacement by pseudoscientific mass-production. But the American cultural situation accelerated the decay. Teutonic racialism, the inspiration of the founders of Germanistics, was, for obvious reasons, a very artificial growth in America; and so was romantic medievalism, which has no roots in a largely Protestant and commercial society. The social and institutional reasons for the decay were also greater than in Europe. The American colleges and universities were far more isolated from their cultural surroundings than the metropolitan universities of the European continent (Paris or Prague, for instance). They thus invited to the academic ivory tower, to defending the professor's self-esteem and social status by indulgence in "mysteries" incomprehensible and useless outside of the university, useless even to the majority of the students who went out to teach composition, language, and literature in the small colleges and state universities. The separation between the practice of literature and academic scholarship also became wider with the rise of literary naturalism and American regionalism with their descent into the slums and stockyards, farms and mines, and with their distrust of Europe, the intellect, tradition, and learning in general.

Still, whatever the waste of the academic system and the shoddiness of its run-of-the-mill products may be, it would be entirely unjust to ignore the achievement, within its limits, of American philological scholarship during the last fifty years. Especially in the field of English literature, American technical scholarship became indispensable and surely outstripped comparable British scholarship, not merely quantitatively. Work in German, French, Italian, and Spanish by Americans is still frequently on a lower level of competence; and remoter fields (such as Slavic) are only beginning to be cultivated. The inferior state of studies in the non-English literatures is the result, in part, of the natural handicap with which every foreigner starts in studying a literature not his own, and in part of the preoccupation of American foreign literature teachers with the teaching of elementary language courses, but also, more deeply, of the "provincialism" of the student of foreign literatures. Most students of French and German adopted the methods and standards of the country whose literature they were studying quite uncritically. They thus developed a position of inferiority toward German and French scholarship, and were driven into a peculiar isolation in their own surroundings. Leo Spitzer, himself a prominent German *emigré*, has recently commented wisely on a situation in which departments of foreign literatures "are usually enclaves in American universities, very much to the detriment of an indigenous American development." [3] As Henry C. Hatfield [4] pointed out, studies in things German are badly handicapped by their dependence on German values and standards. This is, of course, the result of the early specialization which prevents the American student of things German or French from having a firm grasp on English and American literature and from thus achieving a coherent outlook of his own from which he can interpret the foreign literature. Especially in German studies, the highly metaphysical, frequently Hegelian, presuppositions of German *Geistesgeschichte* proved indigestible and unassimilable to American students, who at the same time were unable to replace them by anything of their own tradition.

The reaction against this philological scholarship in America is not merely of recent date. It is possible to distinguish between different motives of opposition and different movements in the revolt. In a roughly chronological order we would have to begin with the objections which came from the survivors of the older, more humane, but also more dilettantish, scholarship, of those who had preserved a continuity with the tradition of the British universities. The memoirs of men who have described their years of study around the turn of the century — Bliss Perry in *And Gladly Teach*, William Lyon Phelps in his *Autobiography*, and H. S. Canby in *Alma Mater* — voice deep discontent with the ruling methods and illustrate the evils of the system by anecdotes and sketches of classroom masters and tyrants. But they and their sympathizers were unable to offer any remedy or alternative except "appreciation," a romantic enthusiasm for the good and the beautiful, sweetness unaccompanied by light. Phelps was the first teacher to offer a course in the contemporary novel (1895–96 — promptly dropped at the insistence of his superiors who threatened him with dismissal) [5] and the first American academic scholar to write on the Russian novelists (1911); but the love of literature which Phelps and comparable teachers instilled in their students was without critical standards. Such teachers, whatever their use to undergraduates, could not contribute to literary scholarship conceived of as a body of knowledge. Some of the exponents of the philological method were able to combine their "austere" scholarship with such "appreciation." They taught graduate students bibliography and sources, "Shakespeare on the graduate level" (that is, the distinctions of quartos and folios, sources, stage conditions), and meanwhile they read poetry to undergraduates in a trembling or unctuous voice. Sentimentalism and antiquarianism are not incompatible, even philosophically.

Far more promising was the movement of the New Humanists, led by Irving Babbitt and Paul Elmer More, and later by Norman Foerster. Irving Babbitt's *Literature and the American College* (1908) and Norman Foerster's *American Scholar* (1929) are indictments of the philological scholarship still cogent today. The New Humanists had an ideal to offer which was not mere "appreciation": they had an ideal of criticism, a strict regard for tradition, an interest in philosophical ideas as they appear in literature, a new neoclassical taste reacting against romanticism. Babbitt's *Masters of Modern French Criticism* (1912) and his *Rousseau and Romanticism* (1919) are books of real critical power and acumen. Marred though they are by frequent obtuseness in the reading of texts and by lack of sensibility, they have a power of abstraction and generalization and a fervid "engagement" in ideas unknown to earlier American scholarship. The neohumanist movement, after a short period of great public attention around 1929, became quiescent. But Babbitt at Harvard, More at Princeton, Stuart Sherman at Illinois, and Foerster at North Carolina and Iowa awakened many students to the futility of much conventional scholarship and to the urgency of great ideas in literature. The reasons for the failure of the movement to capture the universities are, however, obvious: the social conservatism of the New Humanists ran counter to the temper of a nation plunged into the depression; their rigid moralism violated the nature of literature as an art; and their hostility to the contemporary arts cut them off from literature as a living institution. Babbitt's philosophical and religious principles, which appealed for corroboration to Confucian and Buddhist thought, were too exotic and too austere to become a reforming power; his literary views were too closely related to the French anti-Romanticism of men like Charles Maurras, Lasserre, and Seillière to be immediately relevant to the American literary scene. After the period of his *Shelburne Essays*, Paul Elmer More became a historian of Greek philosophy and of Christian theology; and his attempts to come to terms with modern writers such as Joyce or Eliot were unsatisfactory. Stuart Sherman went to New York, and becoming a journalist, lost distinction in emphatic gusto.

Other attempts at changing the orientation of literary study in the American university also failed — or failed, at least, to be generally effective. In the thirties the Marxist approach to literature excited widespread interest; and, outside of the Academy or on its fringes, some Marxist criticism was produced. But possibly for political reasons, it produced hardly any effect upon American academic scholarship. Granville Hicks's books, their most ambitious application in America, were neither learned nor bold enough to recommend themselves for imitation. Economic determinism and a basically political outlook were introduced into American studies only through the success of Vernon Parrington's *Main Currents of American Thought*. Here a vaguely sociological approach assumes the special form of propaganda for Jeffersonian democracy; the focus of the book is so extraliterary that American literature studies, as far as they followed him, were diverted from literary values into social history and the history of political ideas. On the whole, the sociological approach proved singularly unattractive to American literary scholarship and has produced relatively little work of real distinction.

The study of ideas in literature, of literature in relation to philosophy, is old, of course; and, in a technical sense, it was cultivated very strenuously in Germany during the last decades, in violent reaction against philological scholarship. But the German *Geistesgeschichte* had few echoes in this country, except among teachers of German: some of these were hostile, as witness Martin Schütze's brilliant attack, in *Academic Illusions* (1933), a book which offered one of the best analyses of the situation of literary scholarship, not only in Germany. As a movement, the "history of ideas," initiated by Arthur O. Lovejoy, made the strongest impression on students of literature in the United States. Lovejoy is a professional philosopher; and his method is that of a philosophical analysis of ideas with close attention to terminology and the contradictions of individual writers. He draws the rather artificial contrast between his method and the ordinary history of philosophy in that he studies "unit-ideas" rather than whole philosophical systems and gives attention to the dissemination of ideas through popular philosophers and poets. His method can be criticized for its excessive intellectualism: Lovejoy conceives of ideological change as a self-subsisting process and pays little attention to historical or psychological contexts. To him poetry is merely a document for intellectual history, and ideas in literature are "philosophical ideas in dilution." [6] Literature thus becomes the water added to philosophy, and the history of ideas imposes purely philosophical standards on works of imagination. Intellectual history is, of course, a high discipline, with exegetical value for the study of the history of literature. But it is no substitute for literary study. Among American literary scholars there are actually few historians of ideas in Lovejoy's sense: Louis Bredvold, Marjorie Nicolson, Perry Miller come to mind.

Clearly, the greatest hope for a reconstitution of literary study in America lies in the critical movement developed in the last twenty-five years outside of the Academy. It seems current to speak of the movement as the "New Criticism," a term which J. C. Ransom used on the title page of a book, published in 1941, discussing three critics — I. A. Richards, T. S. Eliot, and Yvor Winters; and these are there discussed with considerable reservations; but the term is often used now for any critic in the general tradition established by Richards and Eliot. This is unfortunate, for the phrase obscures the very great diversities and differences among the critics, giving the erroneous impression that these critics form a "school" or even a coterie. Only the four Southern critics, J. C. Ransom, Allen Tate, R. P. Warren, and Cleanth Brooks, have had close personal associations and show close coherence of outlook; and even they are far from subscribing to an unchanging position. Especially J. C. Ransom goes his own way in his later speculations. The other critics grouped with the New Critics are often quite isolated, like Yvor Winters, who has developed a coherent and impressive, but extremely doctrinaire view of the history of American and English poetry, and Kenneth Burke, who has evolved a system of critical theory so widely expanded that it has become, in intention, a whole philosophy of culture, utilizing semantics, Marxism, psychoanalysis, and anthropology. Edmund Wilson has used any and all methods in turn: his first book *Axel's Castle* (1931) was an exposition of the Symbolist Movement, which, though highly sympathetic and perceptive, concluded with a dirge on its supposed demise. He has since used Marxism and psychoanalysis quite eclectically and has declined into journalism and "Europe Without Baedeker." R. P. Blackmur, who began as an extremely close reader and analyst of texts, has been moving into statements of a general critical theory and has broadened his "practical criticism" to include moral and ideological discussions of the novels of Dostoevsky.

Still, in a general history of American criticism we can see that the new critics all react against a common preceding situation. They were all dissatisfied with the impressionistic, vaguely romantic, and

sentimental "appreciation" prevalent inside and outside of the universities; and they disapproved of the purely journalistic criticism
associated with Mencken and his praise of the American naturalistic novel; they felt uncomfortable with the New Humanist movement because of its hostility to contemporary writing and its rigidly
moralistic view of literature. Tate, Blackmur, and Winters even
contributed to a symposium attacking the neohumanist movement.[7]

In reaction against this situation they turned largely, at first at
least, to a study of poetry, especially modern poetry, concentrating
on the actual texts of the works under inspection and stressing the
peculiarity of a work of art which they conceived of as comparatively independent of its background in history, biography, and
literary tradition. In this turn to the text, this stress on the unity of
a work of art, this refusal to reduce literature to its causes can be
found what may be described as the common denominator of the
new critics. But, among them there are, at least, two groups: those
who have more and more brought to bear on literature all kinds of
knowledge — psychoanalysis in particular, Marxism, and recently
anthropology; and those who have tried to study literature primarily
as an aesthetic fact. The first group has again used the literary work
as a point of individual departure for general speculations on man
and the universe, the ego, and society; while the other group has
stayed more clearly within the precincts of literature, practicing
techniques of close analysis. But it seems a mistake to charge even
these latter critics with "aestheticism" and even "formalism." None
of them is an "aesthete": for their critical standards everywhere
imply a philosophical, political, and religious point of view. The
Southern group is preoccupied with the problem of modern urban
and commercial civilization and its impact on tradition. Even when,
in appearance, they are inspecting mainly what seem to be poetic
devices such as ambiguities and paradoxes, they aim at a discussion
of the general value, coherence, and maturity of a work of art —
values which are human and social. They refuse to confuse the
realm of art (which is not exempt from humanity) with the realms
of thought or ethics, and understand that the meaning of a work
of literature arises from its formal whole.

The antecedents and philosophical premises of the critical movement are quite various. T. S. Eliot is, of course, the great initiator; and Eliot's critical ideas have their antecedents in Babbitt at Harvard, in Hulme in England, and in Rémy de Gourmont in France. But Eliot's influence is combined with that of I. A. Richards, who yielded a method and procedure in many ways incompatible with Eliot's. While Eliot's early philosophical sympathies were with idealism (he expressed great interest in the Oxford Hegelian F. H. Bradley), Richards was a professed Benthamite, a physiological psychologist: only recently has he moved in the direction of idealism. The importance of Croce's *Aesthetic*, though not clearly traceable, must be assumed as background. However, there are no traces of the Crocean Hegelianism in the American critics nor are they interested in the problem of the development of literature, its dialectics, as the Russian formalists were; they all seem to accept Eliot's static view of literature as a timeless simultaneous order. They all react against the ruling philological scholarship to such an extent that they have lost all contact with modern linguistics. On these two points the American movement differs sharply from the analogous movements on the European Continent.

Still, it must strike every student of the cultural situation of the West as an almost mystical fact that in countries which had little or no direct contacts there arose the same kind of reaction against nineteenth-century positivistic scholarship. Of these movements the Russian formalists had the clearest, sharpest, and theoretically best developed set of doctrines. In Germany the same tendency took rather the form of an interest in stylistics and in the parallelism between the arts and literature; and the Germans were extremely influential in the Spanish-speaking countries. The Russian, German, and Spanish movements differ from the American movement by their close association with linguistics, which have yielded excellent results, especially in the study of style and metrics; and in Europe these movements have been supported by new trends in linguistics running counter to the doctrinaire behaviorism of the predominant Yale school of linguists. The Italian and German movements are closely associated with idealistic philosophies, and very conscious of their reaction against nineteenth-century positivism and naturalism, while the Russian movement has been professedly empirical and scientific. Still, whatever the differences, the assumptions and the direction of reaction against the nineteenth-century scholarship are the same.

In America the movement has been less academic and more clearly concentrated on problems of evaluation, while the Russians and Germans seem to cling, in practice, to historical relativism. Still, the American movement which arose outside of the Academy is increasingly finding its way into the American universities and colleges. Ransom's plea for "Criticism, Inc." and Blackmur's for "A Featherbed for Critics" are being fulfilled, at least, in part. Cleanth Brooks' remark, written as late as 1943, that the new critics "have next to no influence in the universities" [8] is apparently outdated. In most American universities, large and small, there is a minority, especially in the English departments, which is deeply dissatisfied with the prevailing antiquarianism, and, among the younger members of the staff, critical interests are so widespread that it seems merely a matter of time when (and not whether) the graduate teaching of literature will pass into the hands of those who have broken with the ruling methods.

But if criticism is to transform American literary scholarship in the universities successfully, it must face a number of problems which its original propounders outside of the university had no need to face. If they abandon the old philology with its definite methods and body of knowledge they will have to replace it with a new body of doctrines, a new systematic theory, a technique and methodology teachable and transmissible and applicable to any and all works of literature. In this respect, much modern American criticism is still deficient or, it could be argued, has the virtue of this deficiency. Its vocabulary differs frequently far too sharply from author to author and even from essay to essay: its assumptions are rarely thought through in their philosophical implications and historical antecedents. Many American critics (Kenneth Burke is an extreme example) use a homemade terminology demanding a considerable effort of interpretation. They seem to feel the need of reformulating basic questions over and over again, to start *ab ovo* to think on aesthetic and critical problems which have a centuries-old history. They are thus open to misunderstanding by the wider public, which again and again is puzzled and misled by the novel uses of such terms as "form," "technique," "structure," "texture," "rhythm," or "myth." Thus a measure of agreement on basic issues of theory will have to be reached sooner or later. One can defend individual terminology up to a point; but indulgence in idiosyncrasies damages the cumulative effect of criticism.

Besides, modern criticism will have to reopen questions which it has hitherto neglected or slighted for one or the other reason. Literary history is the most important of these. Literary history must not, of course, be confused with antiquarianism. It needs rewriting with the new methods and a new emphasis and must not be left to the philologist or dilettante. Surely many of the greatest critics were also great literary historians: the Schlegels, Sainte-Beuve, De Sanctis, Taine, Brunetière, Croce. They were critical historians of literature. There are suggestions for the rewriting of the history of English poetry in some of the essays of F. R. Leavis and Cleanth Brooks, but they are only suggestions. It is possible to break away from the traditional literary history, an odd mixture of anthology, biography, social history, intellectual history, and criticism and to envisage a history of the art of literature written with critical insight, according to critical standards. While some modern critics have brought to bear all kinds of other types of knowledge on the understanding of literature, they seem to have neglected the illumination which can be brought to literature from the two fields which seem the nearest to the art of words: linguistics and aesthetics, including the aesthetics of the fine arts. Linguistics is especially indispensable for a study of style, diction, and meter; and the relations of literature to music and painting have hardly begun to be studied by modern methods. Finally, it seems both inevitable and most important that the methods of modern criticism should be applied to works remote in time and space, to older and to foreign literatures. The selection of European writers which have attracted the attention of modern critics in the United States is oddly narrow and subject to the distortion of a very local and temporary perspective.

If this consolidation and expansion are to succeed, they must draw on men in the universities, and especially on the young men. Within the universities some older men had begun to concern themselves with critical problems or, at least, with problems of close formal analysis even before the new critical movement. The studies of prose style by Morris W. Croll, or of the technique of prose fiction by J. W. Beach come to mind, also the many essays and books by E. E. Stoll stressing the role of theatrical convention, and criticizing nineteenth-century Shakespearian scholarship. But frequently the excursions of older men into literary criticism met with little success. Robert K. Root's sympathetic but slight book on Alexander Pope, or Hazelton Spencer's and Hardin Craig's books on Shakespeare are not impressive as examples of sensibility and penetration. But other scholars who started with historical studies of a more or less conventional kind have absorbed and applied the ideas of modern criticism and developed them, independently, in contact with texts from the past. F. O. Matthiessen, for instance, began with careful analytical work on Elizabethan translation and then wrote of T. S. Eliot, Henry James, and the whole American Renaissance critically and sensitively. Austin Warren began with a monograph in the history of criticism, analyzed the philosophical ideas of the elder Henry James, and reached criticism in a distinguished study of the poetry of Richard Crashaw. Increasingly, the younger men in the universities are becoming critics and interested in criticism without having lost the advantages of historical learning and training. The future belongs to them.

Finally, one source of possible academic reform should not be neglected: the presence, in the United States, of some distinguished German, Spanish, and Russian *emigrés* who have themselves shared directly in the development of the new methods in Europe: Leo Spitzer, Helmut Hatzfeld, Erich Auerbach are eminently distinguished exponents of German stylistics now in this country. The late Amado Alonso is a Spanish scholar of the same school. Roman Jakobson was an original member of the Russian Formalist group. They might eventually contribute as much as other recent immigrants have done to the study of the history of art or to the reorganization of musicology in this country.

Thus, it is clear in what direction the reform of graduate study in English must move. The old Ph.D. degree must be changed radically. Its holder should be not an antiquarian specialist in a period but a "professional man of letters, a man who, in addition to English and American literature, knows literary theory, the modes of scholarship and criticism, who, without recourse to impressionism and 'appreciation,' can analyze and discuss books with his classes." The linguistic requirements should be changed by asking for a really advanced, literary knowledge of one or two of the great living languages of Europe. The thesis should be conceived of as flexibly as we can conceive of professional literary distinction. Its possible range should certainly include contemporary literature and allow the use of all the methods of literary criticism. There should be an increasing stress on training in other literatures, in aesthetics, in philosophy rather than in medieval philology. In short, a Ph.D. in literature rather than in English, French, or German philology is the ideal.[9]

But if this reform should be successful, we should also have to face the dangers with which it might be confronted and the excesses to which it might succumb. There may be something in the very nature of institutional academic life which will lead again to mechanization, ossification, to Alexandrianism in the bad sense. The danger of mere imitation and of routine repetition may become acute, though at a time fortunately still rather remote. More urgent is the danger that in getting free of the past we may also get rid of its genuine virtues. The originators and leaders of the revulsion against philological scholarship (and I mean not only the "new" critics but also the New Humanists) have all been men of education and frequently of learning, men who had a sense of the past and who, with it, possessed an amount of information easy to underrate because they were apt to underrate it themselves. In present-day America students will have to face the problem that in learning certain techniques and discussing theoretical problems they may neglect to acquire basic facts and a knowledge of a map of literature which, even though but a map, has its uses. The appallingly bad secondary education of most American students puts a burden on the colleges which they are sometimes unable or unwilling to bear. Our graduate schools, if reformed, must face the problem that we need not less scholarship, but better, more intelligent, more relevant, and more critical scholarship.

II

This general sketch of the main trends which have influenced American literary scholarship in the last fifty years and the reflections made here on its present state clearly need some more concrete documentation. It would be unjust to represent even the most conventional scholarship only by its failures and limitations. Some attempt must be made to describe the contribution of the last fifty years to the study of literature. The danger of merely presenting a list of titles is acute and to some extent unavoidable; but I shall try to give a highly selective account of American work on English and American literature, especially of the recent centuries. It will necessarily be confined almost totally to monographs, though one has to recognize that much valuable work is scattered through several hundred volumes of learned periodicals.

The labors of a literary scholar begin with the accumulation of his materials, the discovery of manuscripts, the elucidation of texts, with "philology" in the literal sense of "love of the word." In the discovery of documents, it was inevitable that Americans, arriving later to work in the history of English literature were left with the gleanings. Some of them, however, have become remarkably proficient in research for hidden documents and letters and have had the luck and ingenuity of finding many bits of unknown evidence. Leslie Hotson's discovery of the circumstances attending the death of Christopher Marlowe [10] is only the most spectacular of similar searches in the Public Record Office.

Most work of this kind, however, is inevitably rather a work of consolidation, classification, registration. Bibliographies, bibliographical guides, manuals of research have been the special strength of American literary scholarships. Numerous excellent short-title catalogues, indexes, guides to research, and handbooks were produced with immense labor.[11] There is now ample provision in American periodicals for the listing of current scholarship, and there are so many other specialized bibliographies [12] that the dangers of these accumulations of titles become more and more apparent. Bibliographies impose the view that writing and study should always be preceded by a complete knowledge of everything that has ever been written on the subject. Many timid souls are today discouraged by the sheer magnitude of this task, especially when confronted with the scholarly accumulations on writers like Chaucer and Shakespeare. The result has been that the false view, "everything has been done," has been encouraged, and students have been driven off into obscure subjects where they are spared competition. Much work and time are wasted today in tracing the antecedents and anticipations of even the most trivial opinion of supposed "authorities" in the past; and tremendous efforts are frequently made to refute older views not meriting preservation. While one must admit that occasionally something remote and important may be rescued by the bibliographer, in most cases he is only compiling an *Index librorum et recensionum mortuorum*.

From this type of bibliography or manual, which is largely a booklisting, the highly technical, "descriptive" bibliography must be distinguished. The latter is preoccupied with the physical make-up of books; it collates; it studies watermarks, colophons, type-fonts and paper-makes. It is part of Library Science, important for book collectors and sometimes of use in special questions of dating, authenticity, revisions relevant to the study of literature. There is some excellent American work of this kind.[13] Recently the "bibliographical" methods developed in England by R. B. McKerrow and W. W. Greg for the study of Elizabethan plays have also been used by American specialists; but this approach does not seem to have caught on widely, even though assertions have been made that the future of literary scholarship belongs to "bibliography."

Editions can be vehicles of almost every kind of literary scholarship: textual criticism, annotation, interpretation, literary history, and, occasionally, even literary criticism. American achievements in the editing of texts are innumerable, especially in the field of English.[14]

Everybody will recognize the value of a good text and of accurate, relevant annotation. Medieval manuscripts and corrupt Elizabethan plays need especial care. But, increasingly, misgivings have been expressed whether the efforts which have gone into the collation of variants (sometimes of quite trivial nature) or of scraps of personal and business correspondence are in any way commensurate with the results, even for the literary historian. Many documents published scarcely deserve close study, and will receive none, beyond the minute attention of the editor himself. Again, the devotion to the text originally justified in the interpretation of the Bible or the surviving great authors of classical antiquity has become an aim in itself, a technicality without wider purpose. The danger of overrating the unprinted is also acute. Long ago, Sainte-Beuve and Brunetière (not men who can be suspected of lack of historical interest and knowledge) warned against "La Fureur de l'inédit." "Fineness of taste, certainty of tact, the art of choosing, the art of composition, the imagination of style, felicity of expression, spirit and grace, eloquence and force, all that used to be called talent or even genius does not count in the eyes of a decipherer of some text or editor of unpublished documents." [15] Editing, a humble preparatory work, has, by a strange reversal of values, become the very height of scholarly achievement. Americans have exemplified the furor on a grand scale: unreadable romances, bad Elizabethan plays, trivial eighteenth-century letters put into print are frequently the sole printed claim to scholarship of many prominent academics. They have made a contribution to knowledge, but it is not impertinent to ask, "knowledge for what?." Accurate transcription, industry, and endurance are not intellectual virtues.

Bibliographies, manuals, and editions are basic procedures for the ordering and establishing of evidence. But they are only preparatory to literary history and criticism. Much American scholarship has been and still is concerned with what vaguely is called "literary history": the study of sources and influences, relationships and connections conceived as contributing ultimately to some systematic literary history. The effort of determining the sources and connections, especially of Chaucer, Spenser, and Milton, has been enormous. *The Sources and Analogues of Chaucer's Canterbury Tales* can be now conveniently surveyed in a great collection edited by W. F. Bryan and G. Dempster,[16] and much competent work on details has been done.[17] Arthurian romances have become a whole special field which, as it requires a knowledge of Celtic and Romance literatures, constantly broadens into Comparative Literature. J. D. Bruce, A. C. Brown, and Roger S. Loomis are possibly the

most distinguished students of this almost self-enclosed world; and
G. L. Kittredge made an impressive excursion into it when he
studied the (mainly Old Irish) antecedents of *Gawain and the
Green Knight*.[18]

Spenser has been the happy hunting-ground of scholars, since his
writings are full of echoes and reminiscences, parallels and imita-
tions. M. Y. Hughes's *Virgil and Spenser* is a careful study in book
form,[19] but the majority of such research is scattered in the learned
periodicals. Comparatively little has been done with Shakespeare's
sources, perhaps because the topic is considered as exhausted. Willard Farnham has stressed the medieval heritage of the Elizabethan
tragedy,[20] especially in Shakespeare.

There is a stream of studies relating Milton to the Bible, to
Lactantius, or examining his Semitic Studies and Rabbinical readings.[21] W. R. Parker's *Milton's Debt to Greek Tragedy in Samson
Agonistes* [22] is more than a mere source study: it is intelligent comparative criticism. Raymond D. Havens' *The Influence of Milton in
English Poetry* [23] is not only a formidable accumulation of parallels
but a genuine history of eighteenth-century poetry in the light of
its relation to Milton.

Such wider studies of "literary genetics" are still very rare: modern poetry is illuminated, for instance, by Henry W. Wells's *New
Poets from Old*,[24] which points (though not always accurately) to
the sources of many effects of recent poetry in Anglo-Saxon, medieval, and Elizabethan verse.

The number of source and influence studies is so great and the
conclusiveness of their evidence so various that a scrupulous sifting would be required to make these accumulations usable for
literary history. Many investigators (frequently beginners) are
handicapped by their ignorance of common antecedents and the
commonplaces of literature and cherish the pathetic belief that
forty zeros add up to more than zero. There is far too much work
which regards an author as a mere product of echoes and influences:
for example, Edward G. Ainsworth's *Poor Collins* [25] is an anthology
of annotated quotations, a mosaic of parallel passages. By far the
most famous investigation of sources by an American scholar is John
Livingston Lowes' *Road to Xanadu*,[26] a fascinating enquiry into

Coleridge's reading which preceded and shaped the making of the "Ancient Mariner" and "Kubla Khan." The learning, the detective skill, and the excellent (though overornate) exposition have given the book classic status in American literary scholarship. Still, the claim of the author to have demonstrated the workings of Coleridge's imagination is hardly fulfilled: the supposed psychology of the creative process consists only of a few easily manipulated metaphors about the deep well, the hooked atoms, and a sea-change. It would be difficult to prove; but it seems that in recent decades research into sources and influences has become more acutely conscious of the dangers of the method of parallelisms and that, with some exceptions, the standards of competence and critical awareness have been raised. The objections to source and influence studies have sometimes gone too far in rejecting the whole procedure. Literary relationships can be established by this method, and only its abuses have discredited it. Such abuses can be eliminated only by a recognition of the falsity of "atomism" in literary study. A work of art is a whole and thus comparable only as a whole.

Partly under the influence of the reaction against the old kind of philology American literary scholarship has expanded its themes and methods in all directions: *extensively*, especially in the study of the background and conditions of literature, frequently far remote from the text; and *intensively*, in an increasingly technical analysis of the artistic devices of a work of art.

Traditionally, the most obvious factor in conditioning literature is the author himself, and hence the study of his biography is assumed to be the most important explanatory device. Biography is a part of history and can be written of the most unliterary man. It has human interest; and, well done, it is an art. But biographies of literary figures are, one must recognize, frequently of very little relevance to an understanding and evaluation of the works themselves. One half of the world's literature is comprehensible without any biographical information; and the bulk of biographical knowledge about the movements, quarrels, and love affairs of authors is sheer ballast for literary study. Biographies are also vitiated by the frequent naïve assumption that works of literature are biographical documents. Surveying the main biographies of English literary figures by Americans one can easily distinguish several types: one, the patient accumulation and sifting of documents, with little attempt at imaginative reconstruction or psychological insight, still prevails among academic scholars. This, for older writers, is the method frequently necessitated by the paucity or externality of documents.[27] Other methods have been tried, beginning with eighteenth-century writers. The older leisurely lives of Fielding and Sterne by Wilbur L. Cross [28] attempt a social picture and some rather elementary criticism. C. B. Tinker has drawn a warm human picture of *Young Boswell*.[29] Joseph W. Krutch's *Samuel Johnson* [30] is that rare life which does not get lost in anecdotage but discusses ideas and art in a biographical frame. Also the standard lives of several of the great Romantic poets are of American origin. G. M. Harper's *Wordsworth* interprets the poet largely in terms of his political development; Amy Lowell's *Keats*, though valuable for its materials, is overflorid and unorganized; and Newman I. White's *Shelley*, though learned and judicious, lacks psychological *finesse* and critical power.[31] Works on Victorian and modern biography dwindle in number and importance.[32] On the whole, the recent growing emphasis on interpretation and psychological penetration seems a good thing. Ordinary biographical research often collects nothing but old gossip or trivia to which an artificial importance is given by their discoverers. It seems a perversion of values to study a work for the biography's sake, with the inevitable result that the most intimate (and hence frequently the most ephemeral and unfinished) product of a writer — his diary-jottings, his letters — become the central concern of the student of literature; for a writer appeals to posterity by his finished work and embodies in it what is deepest, best, and, ultimately, most personal in him.

Biography frequently contains the materials for the social history of literature. Long before Marxism, the study of the social backgrounds of literature was cultivated on a large scale. Many such studies move far away from the works themselves into general social history and scarcely pretend to be explanations of literature. Still rare are studies of the actual economic and social conditions of literature which show any precision. Some concrete attempts have been made to illuminate the social media of literature: in American scholarship there is a whole group of studies devoted to literary periodicals, to the Salon in English Letters, to Augustan Clubs, and the like. Full reviews of a poet's reputation and fame, though likewise contributory to the history of literary criticism, must be classified with attempts to study audiences and changes of taste.[33]

But, of course, the drama, with the theater, is the most conspicuous case of continuous institutional support for literature. Studies examining the physical condition of the theater and the fortunes of theatrical companies flourish, particularly in relation to Elizabethan drama. Gerald E. Bentley is continuing Sir E. K. Chambers' *Elizabethan Stage* with a similar work on the *Jacobean and Caroline Stage*.[34] In a boldly speculative book, T. W. Baldwin has attempted to reconstruct the *Organization and Personnel of the Shakespearean Company*,[35] and recently detailed studies of specific Elizabethan theaters [36] have gone beyond the earlier general accounts. Alfred Harbage has thrown light on Shakespeare's audience and his relations to it.[37] Others have illuminated the stage history of later times.[38]

The social study of literature (of English literature, at least) has usually been content with these traditional topics. American Marxist criticism of English literature is practically nonexistent.[39]

A very great deal of effort has been made to illuminate the general intellectual history of a period, to analyze the philosophical derivations of an author's ideas, to define the cosmological and metaphysical conceptions of older periods. Much of this type of work done today by literary scholars is simply intellectual history, even history of philosophy, history of political thought, scientific thought, and so forth, and is related to literary study only by its frequent citation of poets or imaginative writers as spokesmen of ideas. Frequently, indeed, the relation between literature and ideas is misconceived: not understanding how ideas get into literature, scholars treat literary works merely as dissertations, statements, and, inevitably, as second-rate versions of philosophical truths. Americans have avoided the grandiose philosophical constructions of many German proponents of *Geistesgeschichte*, usually confining themselves to concrete investigations of limited range, which frequently work merely with philological methods, accumulating quotations and establishing source relations. There are some exceptions. For example, Hardin Craig's *Enchanted Glass*,[40] which sketches with broad strokes, the Elizabethan view of the world, and A. O. Lovejoy's *Great Chain of Being*, with its suggestions of the parallelism between deism and classicism, are the nearest American scholarship has come to *Geistesgeschichte*.[41]

Most other work is more limited in scope and pretensions. Much has been made of Elizabethan psychology and its influence on Shakespeare's conceptions of characters; [42] of the moral ideas of the time; [43] of the philosophical patterns in Shakespeare [44] ultimately traceable to Scholasticism or Platonism; of the general conception of the nature of man.[45] The influence of cosmological and scientific conceptions in relation to literature has been studied ably by several scholars.[46] Joseph W. Beach's *Concept of Nature in Nineteenth Century Poetry* [47] is the best general survey of the romantic concept of nature, which Beach considers merely a beautiful illusion. Religious and theological questions in relation to literature begin to attract more expert attention: thus Miss Helen C. White [48] has sympathetically brought out the religious content of the metaphysical poets; and Maurice Kelley's *This Great Argument* [49] has stirred up further argument about the relation between *Paradise Lost* and Milton's theological treatise *De Doctrina Christiana*. Richard F. Jones has ably studied the whole debate about the ancients and moderns, leading, in England, up to Swift's *Battle of Books*.[50] Louis I. Bredvold, in *The Intellectual Milieu of John Dryden*,[51] has boldly surveyed wide stretches of seventeenth-century thought and improved our understanding of Dryden's conversion and personal creed.

Ricardo Quintana wrote a good general book on Swift entitled *The Mind and Art of Jonathan Swift*.[52] H. N. Fairchild [53] has examined the religious content of English poetry in the eighteenth and early nineteenth centuries from the position of high Anglicanism, classifying poets according to the temperature of their religious convictions and exhibiting their sins of sentimentalism, pantheism, and naturalism. To Tinker and Fairchild we owe studies of eighteenth-century primitivism, a theme also successfully pursued by Miss Lois Whitney.[54]

In Fairchild's and Beach's studies we move actually from a history of thought into a history of sentiment: the feeling for nature, religious feeling. This is a difficult branch of history, since sentiment, it could be argued, has hardly any history; but a book like Theodore Spencer's *Concept of Death in Elizabethan Tragedy* [55] shows that a topic of deep interest to European scholars — not only man's concept but his attitude and feeling for death or love — is well worth exploration.

Most of the studies in intellectual history, however, are occupied with the questions of sources.[56] Much of this work has been stimulating: it seems an advance over older pedantries to take the ideas of literature seriously and to study the history of philosophy rather than manuscript pedigrees, models in real life, parallels, and so on. But the philosophical approach has again tended to distract attention from the aesthetic nature of literature and to absorb the study of literature into the study of something else. Furthermore, much dilettantism is common in such studies, for literary students are rarely transformed into competent analysts of ideas with a proper grasp of the history of philosophy or even the nature of the thought of the relevant technical philosophers.

The history of criticism is a part of the history of thought which bears peculiarly close relations to the study of literature. A great deal has been done to increase our understanding, especially of its earlier phases, in recent decades. Earlier American work was usually vitiated by incomprehension of, and lack of sympathy for, the neoclassical point of view, but recent years have corrected this and even tipped the balance in the other direction. J. E. Spingarn was the most distinguished American student of the history of criticism; his *History of Literary Criticism in the Renaissance* [57] very properly pays most attention to Italy and his three-volume selection from English criticism of the seventeenth century [58] contains an important introduction analyzing intellectual and critical trends of the time. Austin Warren's book on *Alexander Pope as Critic and Humanist* [59] was one of the first to grasp and present sympathetically the assumptions of neoclassical literary theory; but since then there have been other perceptive monographs on individual critics and on concepts such as the sublime.[60] In nineteenth-century criticism

Lionel Trilling's book on Arnold,[61] which treats him in relation to our time as a living figure, is the major work, but studies of Hazlitt's and Pater's aesthetics [62] or William Irvine's *Walter Bagehot* [63] have considerable merit. Walter J. Bate's lectures *From Classic to Romantic*,[64] though somewhat abstract, are an able summary of the premises of eighteenth-century taste and of the changes accomplished by the Romantics. But there is as yet nothing on a larger scale to replace the impressionistic history of criticism written by Saintsbury half a century ago.

Strangely enough, the most neglected type of study was (and still is) the actual close analysis of a work of art and of the devices, techniques, and general formal procedures which differentiate it from a mere statement in prose. Techniques of analysis have fallen far behind those developed by historians of fine arts and of music — partly because of the suspicion of "aestheticism" and partly because of the whole interruption of the tradition of poetic analysis and theory caused by the Romantic revolt against the neoclassical system which, however narrow, had a clear frame of reference and the inherited techniques of ancient rhetoric. Among older American scholars a few (such as Fred Newton Scott, C. Mills Gayley) were interested in rhetorical theory; but only slowly has a new generation found its way back to these problems, largely under the stimulus of modern aesthetic and critical speculation.

There is some American interest in such technical questions as metrics and prose-rhythm. In 1880, Sidney Lanier wrote a pioneer book [65] setting forth a rather dubious theory of musical metrics which has found adherents in England also. Some careful American students have applied and elaborated the principles of musical metrics as developed by a Scotchman, William Thomson. John C. Pope's *Rhythm of Beowulf* [66] is a standard example. Experimental metrics using laboratory machinery was developed by an American physician, W. E. Scripture, rather eccentrically, while Wilbur L. Schramm has sketched a sober summary of the results of the method.[67] Most work on metrics is either mechanical or dilettantish. Modern critics have not shown much interest in these questions, partly because many of them minimize the effect of sound and its relation to meaning. Yvor Winters is an exception; but his theory of metrics evolves around an obscure use of the term "rhythm" and recommends a uniform, chantlike style of reading.

Stylistics has not had, in the United States, anything like the attention which it has received in Germany or Spain, where more and more the study of style appears to be the central preoccupation of modern literary scholarship, developed in close relationship with linguistics. This neglect is partly owing to the peculiar development of American linguistics, which either has remained within the confines of historical grammar or has moved into the technicalities of phonemics based on a behavioristic philosophy precluding linguists from attending to problems of meaning and artistic style. Literary scholars, unconverted to the imposed philology of the graduate schools, have thrown out linguistics altogether; and the critics, who have been struggling with some of these problems, have not yet found their way to modern linguistics. But, on occasion, careful and sensitive work has been done by means of rhetorical theories: W. K. Wimsatt has made an extremely able study of what might have seemed a well-worn topic, the prose style of Samuel Johnson; [68] and, earlier, Morris W. Croll wrote a series of studies on the history of prose style,[69] mainly in the sixteenth and seventeenth centuries, which show an extraordinary power of analysis and attempt with considerable success to go beyond the narrow topic to its implications in philosophy and the fine arts. The essay, "Baroque Style of English Prose," is a distinguished attempt to correlate literature and art, literature and philosophy. The study of poetic diction has also recently been revived: Miss Josephine Miles [70] studied poetic diction, combining statistical methods with a grasp of modern poetic theory, while W. J. Bate has written a monograph on Keats [71] which traces the evolution of his style, diction, and meter minutely. Mark van Doren's *Poetry of John Dryden* (1920) is an early general book of poetic analysis and criticism which discusses metrics and diction sensitively.[72]

One question which is actually stylistic has, however, almost monopolized the interest of modern scholars: that of imagery (metaphor in the wide sense), which easily leads to the consideration of symbolism and then of myth in literature. This is the point where the transition from form to content and their mutual implication become most obvious. Symbolism has been in the center of poetic theory since the French symbolists; and the age of Eliot, Joyce, Yeats, and Mann can hardly ignore the role of myth in poetry. An early book, drawing mainly on Elizabethan verse, is H. W. Wells's *Poetic Imagery*.[73] Its classifications are not wholly convincing, but it was an important beginning. The most elaborate study of the problems of imagery is Miss Rosemond Tuve's *Elizabethan and Metaphysical Imagery*,[74] which tries to give a historical justification of poetic practices of the age in terms of contemporary theories of rhetoric and logic. This book, learned but diffuse, is a polemic against the modern critical view of the function of imagery.

Imagery has been most successfully studied, however, by those who have not adhered to the statistical or historical methods of Miss Spurgeon and Miss Tuve. Much in the writings of the so-called "new" critics concerns imagery. Most systematic are the books of Cleanth Brooks and *This Great Stage*, a detailed examination of *King Lear*, by Robert Heilman.[75] In Austin Warren's monograph on Richard Crashaw,[76] imagery is sensitively and persuasively related to the religious implications of the poet's world. While the symbolic study of clusters of metaphors is sometimes carried on with too much perseverance in the new discussion of Shakespeare, symbolism and myth are clearly central for an understanding of such authors as Coleridge, Blake, Joyce, Eliot, and Yeats. Robert Penn Warren's brilliant essay on the *Ancient Mariner*[77] and the elaborate as well as critically sensitive book by Mark Schorer on *William Blake*[78] are the finest recent works on the Romantics. Much critical writing on the great modern English authors is preoccupied with imagery and myth: for example, F. O. Matthiessen's *Achievement of T. S. Eliot*,[79] which also tries to see Eliot within the American tradition, and Harry Levin's succinct book on Joyce,[80] which in its final chapter anticipates the "myth" criticism now considered the great desideratum of the future. One cannot, however, help feeling that the term "myth" is suffering abuse, that it is being used in a way which reduces it almost to the meaning of "theme," and that the Teutonic mysticism of Jung (disseminated also indirectly through the "archetypal patterns" of Miss Maud Bodkin) threatens to lead criticism into an arbitrary irrationalism.

The technique of the novel and of the drama have also excited interest in America. Certainly the most distinguished work
was Henry James's own Prefaces to his novels, which were collected for the first time in 1934 by Richard P. Blackmur [81] and which
since then have attracted deserved attention. James's principles have,
however, suggested the main concepts of an English book, Percy
Lubbock's *Craft of Fiction* (1921); and this, in turn, has become the
main *point d'appui* for the study of the technique of the modern
novel. In America, independently, though with his eye on Henry
James, Joseph W. Beach has analyzed fiction closely and written a
series of able studies of Hardy, James, and the twentieth-century
novel.[82] Beach's lead has been followed only recently, and then
only sporadically.

The drama is better off, since theatrical conventions and techniques are necessarily old topics in the study of Shakespeare and
the modern drama. There is older work which shows a sense of the
theater; [83] but Elmer Edgar Stoll [84] is the most distinguished advo-
cate and analyst of the role of dramatic convention. His many
studies, centering on Shakespeare but ranging widely over the history of the drama (not merely English), argue persistently against
treating drama as a source for social history and in behalf of the
decisive importance of stage conventions, stockfigures, and situations for the critical interpretation of the drama. Yet Stoll, who
has done much to expose the fallacies of historical scholarship, himself embraces an extreme historicism, assuming the only criterion
of relevance to be the reconstructed understanding of the audience
contemporary with the author. This rigidity has made Stoll unwilling to allow the accrual of meaning which later generations have
found in Shakespeare and other authors of the past.

American literary scholarship has been most deficient in one respect: the power of large-scale synthesis, the writing of literary history. Some of the longest and most impressive products of American research, devoted to the history of a genre, Karl Young's
Drama of the Medieval Church [85] and Henry C. Lancaster's *French
Dramatic Literature of the Seventeenth Century*,[86] are arsenals of
information and monuments of diligence but cannot be praised
for power of generalization and critical analysis. On a smaller scale

there have been many competent studies of literary types. Most of these [87] are little more than descriptive accounts of plays or books ordered according to certain categories but are not real histories which show the change and evolution of some theme or style. Howard Baker's *Induction to Tragedy*,[88] an account of the rise of Elizabethan tragedy, is one of the very few books of this kind which has a grasp of the problem of historical change and the evolution of genre.

The surveys of larger categories, the drama and the novel and the lyric, have been undertaken only by older men and are frequently nothing but manual-like compilations of information arranged in chronological order with some interspersed critical remarks.[89]

General histories of English literature, written in the United States, are almost all handbooks or textbooks elementary as to critical approach or firsthand research. The most recent *Literary History of England*,[90] edited by Albert C. Baugh, is the fullest and most learned American work: but it must be described as a mere bookbinder's synthesis: it contains long chapters written by five different scholars all totally different in outlook, method, and procedure. The medieval portions are on the level of an informed philological manual. The best section is George Sherburn's, on the eighteenth century — lucid, clear, and, within the limits of its descriptive method, a masterpiece of exposition, sympathetic, and well informed on questions of criticism and the history of ideas. Samuel C. Chew struggles valiantly with the copiousness of nineteenth-century and twentieth-century literature, but produces little more than impressionistic essays on individual authors — essays conservative in taste and loosely held together by much information on such topics as parliamentary history and the debate over evolution.

This most ambitious American history of English literature illustrates the impasse at which literary historiography seems to have arrived. Collaborative works will always lack the unity of historical imagination; and there seem to be no scholars in America who, being also critics, dare to compete with the great literary historians of the nineteenth century such as the Schlegels, Hettner, Taine, De Sanctis, or even Courthope. This lack of synthetic power, of true historical imagination, seems the surest sign of a profound crisis in literary scholarship. One of the main objections to the usual American scholarship is this fact that it has not produced works which can be compared to those of scholars on the Continent who have managed to combine devotion to the positivistic ideal of knowledge with critical insight and power of synthesis, men such as Wilhelm Scherer, and Gustave Lanson, Menendez Pidal, and Alexander Veselovsky.

The condition of scholarship in American literature reflects, of course, the picture presented for English studies, since American literature has been cultivated by English specialists and usually is taught in the same department with English literature. But the situation differs on essential points. The study of American literature, strangely enough, was long considered to be "below the dignity" of a scholar; and thus American literature studies missed the heyday of the philological method. The great expansion in the study of American literature after the First World War (heralded, in 1921, by the establishment of an American Literature group in the Modern Language Association and by the founding of a special professional journal, *American Literature*, in 1928) was engendered by patriotic motives, by a new consciousness of the American tradition. This interest in the literature of one's own country is normal and was long overdue, but its inception came at a moment when social and political preoccupations were so strong that American literature inevitably became largely social history or history of political ideas. American studies have been at an advantage compared to English in being more sensitive to contemporary literary and critical developments; but, on the other hand, they have had the attraction of easiness and nearness for provincial minds.

In the nineteenth century there were several close students of the American literary tradition; especially Moses C. Tyler, who illuminated the early literature as he sought for political ideas, and Charles F. Richardson and Barrett Wendell, who were more literary in their interests but genteel as critics. The programmatic book, edited by Norman Foerster, *The Reinterpretation of American Literature* (1928),[91] seems to have constituted a decisive turning-point. Since then scholarly work on American literature has vastly increased; and many institutions, especially in the Middle West, have added many Americanists to their staffs. But American literary studies are now in the same danger of factualism and antiquarianism as English studies have been for a much longer period.

In distinction from English studies, the territory is almost unoccupied (or was so a few decades ago); and much will have to be done before we have the necessary bibliographies and critical editions. The third volume of the recent *Literary History of the United States* is the most satisfactory general bibliography yet produced, but there are few special bibliographies of high technical competence. Furthermore, editing has not yet assumed either the proportions or the importance it holds in English studies. The ten-volume edition of Sidney Lanier, hardly an author of enduring importance, is the "first American author whose collected works and letters have been made available by scholars with authoritative texts, full introductions, and notes." [92] There are editions of individual writings by Melville and Whitman which live up to critical standards, and a large number of letters, diaries, and so forth has been collected by scholars and amateurs.[93] Still, there is much to be done before complete, accurate, and well-annotated editions of the major American authors will be available.

Literary biography of American authors is a flourishing genre in which dilettantism, gossip-mongering, and either naïve hero-worship or cheap debunking are rampant. But there are, in increasing number, lives of American authors which comply with demands for accuracy and fullness of documentation, though they may fall far short of the ideal in psychological insight, critical perception, and liveliness of presentation. They vary in these respects greatly; Stanley Williams' two-volume *Life of Washington Irving* [94] and Arthur Quinn's *Poe* [95] are valuable for their strict adherence to external evidence. Ralph Rusk's full *Life of Ralph Waldo Emerson* [96] uses many new documents but does not manage to animate its subject, while Odell Shepard's *Pedlar's Progress: The Life of Bronson Alcott* [97] shows the talent of a story-teller. Carl Van Doren's *Benjamin Franklin* and G. F. Whicher's *Emily Dickinson* are examples of distinguished biographies which combine research with interpretation.[98]

Most studies of older American literature are studies in the history of ideas, especially political ideas. Vernon L. Parrington's *Main Currents of American Thought*,[99] mentioned above, is unfortunately quite obtuse to literary values and deficient in historical insight into such movements as Puritanism. Herbert Schneider's *Puritan Mind* [100] was the pioneer book, and today Perry Miller's *New England Mind* [101] is recognized as one of the superb achievements in American intellectual history. Other important work on the Colonial writers has been done by Kenneth Murdock.[102] Howard M. Jones has made a wide-ranging study entitled *America and French Culture*,[103] covering chiefly the later eighteenth century. Curiously enough, the early nineteenth century has not received competent study. Harold C. Goddard's relatively old studies in *New England Transcendentalism* [104] is still the best survey. In nineteenth-century intellectual history, the best work comes from historians such as Ralph Gabriel [105] and Merle Curti [106] and philosophers such as Ralph B. Perry, who has written a distinguished study of William James; [107] and these, of course, move largely on the outskirts of actual literature. The one attempt at recent intellectual history, Oscar Cargill's *Intellectual America*,[108] is a crude and prejudiced account evincing little insight into philosophical ideas and little grasp of the European background.

The history of American criticism, a subject of considerable interest, has only recently received any systematic treatment. Norman Foerster [109] has analyzed the main nineteenth-century critics with a remarkable detachment from the New Humanist dogmas of his conclusion. W. Charvat, John P. Pritchard, and George F. DeMille have studied special periods or aspects; and Bernard Smith [110] has written a general survey from a Marxist point of view which, though crude, is useful.

American literary scholarship is still most deficient in close attention to texts, in technical analyses of artistic devices, Metrical and stylistic studies and studies of the technique of prose-fiction or the drama are practically non-existent. Only in recent years have scholars of critical bent begun to focus on close reading and analysis of texts. The initiative came from outside the academy; and in American literature, the texts examined are almost exclusively those of modern and difficult poetry. One could select essays and remarks from the writings of R. P. Blackmur, Yvor Winters, Cleanth Brooks [111] and others which are ingenious and highly perceptive. On a wider scale, F. O. Matthiessen's *American Renaissance*,[112] devoted to a study of Emerson, Thoreau, Hawthorne, Melville, and Whitman, is the major interpretative achievement. Critically it revolves around Goethe's and Coleridge's distinction between allegory and symbolism and exalts the art of Melville. In his *Henry James* [113] Matthiessen has summed up critical observation on Henry James's art: the function of imagery, the technique of his plots. But systematic work with modern means of analysis is only at the beginning; and its beginnings are scattered in critical articles not in academic theses.

The writing of literary history on a larger scale, the need for synthesis and also for popularization, has been felt in American literature more than in the history of English literature. Yet one cannot say that the attempts to write a history of American literature have been conspicuously successful, even within the limits of individual genres and categories. Quinn's volumes on the American drama and novel [114] are mere external repertories of facts interspersed with critical opinions. Horace Gregory and Marya Zaturenska's *History of Modern American Poetry* [115] is largely polemics devoted to the satisfaction of personal grudges. The detailed histories of special periods of the American novel [116] are collections of curiosities from social history; and the surveys of the modern novel by Carl Van Doren [117] or J. W. Beach [118] fall short of the best work of their authors. Alfred Kazin has written a largely expository survey of the recent American novel and criticism with an emphasis on social questions, and these are also dominant in Maxwell Geismar's much inferior volumes on the last half-century.[119] Among general histories of American literature, Parrington's is admittedly extra-literary, Hicks's [120] is a rather elementary, fervid, and benign Marxist interpretation, while Ludwig Lewisohn's [121] is a particularly elementary application of psychoanalysis. The recent volumes by Van Wyck Brooks,[122] in his youth a distinguished critic of American civilization, are a disappointing performance. They are nostalgic chronicles, collections of vignettes, mosaics of quotations and anecdotes with no sense of literary history and with little critical integrity.

The older coöperative *Cambridge History of American Literature*,[123] valuable for the information it accumulated, was badly organized, haphazard, and uneven to a degree unusual even in such enterprises. The new *Literary History of the United States*,[124] edited by Robert E. Spiller, W. Thorp, Thomas H. Johnson, and H. S. Canby, a coöperative enterprise of fifty-five writers, is much better planned, much more accurate, and much more fully informed. But ultimately it also is a collection of essays, excellent, or mediocre, in which individual studies of the great authors biographically framed, are unrelated to background chapters on social and historical trends. There is no unified or even approximately similar critical outlook in the two large volumes; and, disappointingly, little is done with the history of genres, styles, and poetic traditions which one would expect to be the central theme of any literary history. *Literary History of the United States* demonstrates the impasse which literary history has reached in our time. As conceived by the editors of these volumes (and they are not exceptional) it has no subject matter, no definite method, no focus of interest, no coherent critical standards. It is social history, intellectual history, history of sentiment, biography, anthology, and literary criticism — an *omnium gatherum*. It is the *Allerleiwissenschaft* professed by Diogenes Teufelsdrökh. The correction must be clear: it can be only through a definition of subject matter, through a development of a clear methodology, through a conception of what is meant by history and what is meant by literature.

This is also the central problem of American literary scholarship (and not only American, of course). It is time to break definitely both with the meaningless accumulation of facts, mere antiquarianism, and also with the vague expansionism which has submerged literary studies in general cultural history. There are many signs of change in this direction but much still has to be done before the reform will be accomplished. Literary study must become purposively literary. It must turn away from the engaging details of "research" and direct itself toward the large, unsolved problems of literary history and literary theory. It must receive stimulation and direction from modern criticism and contemporary literature — from participation in literature as a living institution.[125]

V ·

Classical Scholarship

WALTER R. AGARD

"Herein lies the opportunity, the call of American classical scholarship," wrote Francis W. Kelsey in 1908, "that it blend together into one both the humane and the scientific, and thus create a new type which shall be as strong in sympathy and appreciation as it is broad, exact, and thorough." [1]

Kelsey had in mind the humanistic tradition in which American classicists were trained until the middle of the nineteenth century, and the scientific methods, imported from Germany, which generally won their allegiance in the second half of the century. To study the two concepts of scholarship, to determine how far the opportunity of integrating them has been realized, and to appraise the actual and potential importance of classical scholarship in our culture, is the purpose of this essay.

I

Prior to 1860 the aims and procedures of American classical scholarship followed fairly closely those of England; the guiding thread was the education of cultured gentlemen and citizens, in which the Greek and Roman literary classics were considered to have unique value. During the Colonial period, Southern planters continued to cultivate their youthful acquaintance with Greek and Latin authors by building up good libraries and using them; [2] in New England and the Middle Atlantic states grammar schools and colleges with classical curricula gave training which later bore fruit in the speeches of statesmen and the writings of men of letters. Grammars, texts, and translations were usually imported from England, but even in this early period American teachers started to produce books of their own which had the concise and practical quality which was to characterize later American scholarship.[3] One of the chief reasons advocated for such study was that it trained men for the learned professions, especially the ministry, law, and medicine. In so training them, it put a strong classical stamp on the cultural leaders of the Colonies.

As a result of this education, much of the intellectual foundation of the new Republic was classical. Thomas Jefferson, John Adams, and James Madison had the examples of Athens, the Achaean League, and Rome in mind when they formulated the principles on which the government of the United States was built, and quoted freely from Plato, Aristotle, Demosthenes, and Polybius in support of those principles. Classical ideals of individual freedom and social responsibility influenced our statesmen as well as our poets and philosophers. Symbolic of the pervasive classical influence were the buildings erected all over the country from 1800 to 1850, decorated like Greek temples.[4] Benjamin Latrobe, the first professional American architect, expressed the conviction of many other leading Americans when he wrote to a sympathetic Jefferson, "I am a bigoted Greek."

But as the century wore on, this traditional humanism seemed less important. Commercial expansion, scientific discovery, democratic education, and closer contacts with Europe led to a lessening of the classical element in education and more devotion to the sciences, modern languages, and business and vocational subjects. And the attitude of classical scholars themselves was changing in the direction of critical and specialized research, as a result of their training in German universities. George Ticknor and Edward Everett of Harvard led the way when they went to Göttingen in 1815 for advanced study. "We [Americans] do not yet know what a Greek scholar is," wrote Ticknor. "We do not even know the process by which a man is to be made one." Everett went even further, declaring that American universities "have nothing to learn

from England, but everything to learn from Germany." He began
a custom followed by many later Americans, of translating German
editions of a Greek grammar and Greek reader for use in schools
in this country. A few years later, Cornelius Felton, professor of
Greek at Harvard, based his text of the *Iliad* on Wolf's work; and
Edward Robinson, tutor in Greek at Hamilton College, who had
studied in Halle and Berlin, prepared an *Iliad* with Latin notes
based on a German edition. Such dependent scholarship soon became the accepted procedure.[5]

   From 1850 to 1890 the ablest classical students in this country
completed their training in Germany. It is not surprising that they
were captivated by their experience in the German universities.
There they came into contact with a new type of scholar and a new
system of training: the critical analyst of language and literature and
the collector and organizer of factual material in every field of classical life; and the seminar type of instruction and coöperative research, culminating in the dissertation on a highly specialized individual project. It was a challenging and invigorating intellectual atmosphere, this *Lehr- und Lernfreiheit*, out of which came a constant
series of critical texts, grammars, commentaries, lexicons, collections
of inscriptions, and encyclopedic articles.[6] To this environment the
youthful American scholars responded with passionate enthusiasm, and on their return they introduced into American education
the methods of instruction and graduate administrative procedures
which they had learned there. One of the greatest of them, Basil
L. Gildersleeve, acknowledged the indebtedness in a warm tribute.
After remarking on the shortcomings of teachers of the classics
in the United States, their "lack of independent research, the whole-
sale conveyance of foreign work, the limited range of study, the
mechanical multiplication of textbooks, the want of honest, manly
criticism," he wrote: "For the American classical teacher who
wishes to fit himself for his work in life the only sensible course is to
familiarize himself with German methods . . . What I have done in
my long life as teacher, as grammarian, is due in large measure to the
example and inspiration of Boeckh, of C. F. Hermann, of Schneide-
win, of Ritschl, of Welcker, of Bernays." [7] Gildersleeve was not,
however, an uncritical admirer; while insisting that our scholars

must work in the scientific spirit of the Germans, he advised them
to cultivate a broad background rather than do merely specialized
exercises in research, and criticized German scholars for the "misty,
tortuous and muddy path" of their exposition.

The roster of classicists trained in Germany between 1850 and 1870
who participated with their colleagues in other fields in the creation of American universities with high standards of critical scholarship is an impressive one.[8] The outstanding representative was
Gildersleeve, who instituted at the Johns Hopkins University at
its founding in 1876 a graduate department in classical philology
constructed according to the German blueprint. During his thirty-
nine years at that university Gildersleeve won distinction as an exacting analyst of syntax, an inspiring teacher, and a humanist of
broad range. As a scholar he produced authoritative editions of
Persius, Justin Martyr, and Pindar, and (with C. W. E. Miller) a
monumental *Syntax of Classical Greek*, as well as hundreds of
articles and notes ("Brief Mention") in the *American Journal of
Philology*, which he founded in 1880. His contributions were more
than scholarly; they were pungent, witty, and exhilarating. As a
teacher, he supervised the doctoral dissertations of sixty-seven candidates, many of whom later held key positions in American universities. As a champion of the humanities he made numerous ad-
dresses and wrote many articles and books; and his personal power
and charm won friends for the classics far beyond the bounds of his
own seminar and his own university. His influence on the development of the enterprise of learning in this country can hardly be over-
estimated. He was a scholar, scientific in spirit; he was also a humanist of profound understanding, eager to have incorporated into
American life the intellectual, aesthetic, and moral values which
he found in the record of classical antiquity.

Based likewise on German practice was the establishment of
learned societies, publications, and schools of classical studies in
Athens and Rome. In 1868 the American Philological Association
was founded, "for the advancement and diffusion of philological
knowledge," with W. D. Whitney as its first president, and in 1879
the Archaeological Institute of America was founded under the
presidency of Charles E. Norton. At their sessions scholars from all

over the country gathered to discuss their researches on controversial issues. The official publications, the *Transactions of the American Philological Association* (1870 —) and the *American Journal of Archaeology* (1885 —) carried the results of American scholarship widely here and abroad, as well as summarizing the results of foreign research. Soon it was realized that centers in the heart of the classical world were also needed if American students were to have the materials for independent contributions. The American School of Classical Studies at Athens [9] was founded in 1881 and the American School of Classical Studies in Rome in 1895; they provided for more or less permanent staffs, visiting annual professors from American universities, and fellows from supporting universities and colleges in this country.

With several libraries now well equipped at home and opportunities for supplementary study abroad, Americans were prepared to make steady contributions to classical scholarship. Further opportunity for publication was made available by university presses, which encouraged the production of monographs; the Cornell Classical series began in 1887, followed by the *Harvard Studies in Classical Philology* in 1890 and many others in the early years of the following century. Commercial publishers welcomed college texts of classical authors.[10] To the laboratory of the classical library there was added the laboratory of archaeological excavation. The young American School in Athens started promptly to dig at Assos in Asia Minor (1881–83) and to explore minor sites near Athens, and then undertook a more difficult archaeological venture at the site of the Argive Heraeum. In 1896 plans were made to undertake the excavation of Old Corinth, a large-scale project comparable with the work of the Germans at Olympia and the French at Delphi. Now, as C. E. Norton put it, for the first time Americans were able "to contribute by fresh discoveries and labors of their own to the common stock of learning; they have become partners in the actual increase of knowledge; they have begun to discharge, even if as yet in comparatively small amount, their debt to the old world of learning, they are no longer mere borrowers and dependents." [11] But the American School was conceived as having a broader function than merely that of scientific research. "The School desires also, and perhaps chiefly, to encourage on the part of classical scholars archaeological study which will throw light upon their classical studies and will give life to their teaching and interpretation of literature." [12]

So toward the close of the century American classicists had become far less dependent on German equipment. Many in the next generation of students went for supplementary training to Germany, but from now on the doctorate was generally obtained from an American institution and further study was done in Greece and Italy. And a new spirit of independence was growing, a new consciousness of intellectual maturity.

II

Since that time, in line with the prevailing spirit of specialization, scholars have tended increasingly to devote themselves to intensive study of one particular phase of classical scholarship: grammar, philology, linguistics; manuscripts, papyri, inscriptions; literary interpretation; the various aspects of archaeology and art; social, political, and economic institutions; scientific, religious, and philosophical expression. Many of the broader ranges they have been content to leave to their colleagues in other countries. Meticulous spadework as well as grandiose theories were the special province of the Germans; French scholars led the way in literary and artistic appreciation; in England a wide field of humanistic applications of classical culture was ably cultivated. The leading American classical scholars, doubtless influenced by our national preoccupation with things concrete and practical, have confined themselves chiefly to careful study of certain limited areas, in which they have made steady contributions of importance; in certain fields, such as comparative philology, epigraphy, papyrology, and archaeology, they have recently won top rank.[13]

Although the turn of the century saw the zest for syntactical study rapidly diminishing, research of that sort still had the greatest appeal for some classicists. Veterans like Gildersleeve, Goodwin, and D'Ooge continued to explore the field with unabated enthusiasm, and inspired several of their most promising pupils to continue such study.[14] If the output in books was relatively small, the record shows that valuable papers on grammar and syntax have been regularly contributed to our philological journals by scholars too numerous to mention here.

Many scholars, however, came to the conclusion that the purely grammatical vein had been pretty well worked out, and turned to a more radical study of the basis and function of language and its comparative structure. William G. Hale established at Chicago courses in comparative syntax, and Charles D. Buck broadened the range to include Indo-European comparative philology. As study of the technical aspects of language developed, linguistics became a full-fledged science. Scholars of international standing in it have been Buck, R. G. Kent at Pennsylvania, Joshua Whatmough, who became professor of comparative philology at Harvard in 1926, and Edgar H. Sturtevant, who held a similar post at Yale from 1927 to 1946.[15] These men stimulated large numbers of students to do research in comparative philology and linguistics, and were prominent in the formation and rapid growth of the Linguistic Society of America, an organization which is now doing research of the utmost importance in the structure of language.

Other scholars have chosen as their specialized field the systematic examination of ancient manuscripts. Occasionally their labors have been spectacularly rewarded, as when William G. Hale revealed the importance of a hitherto neglected manuscript of Catullus in the Vatican. But in any event the fresh study of manuscripts has resulted in more accurate texts of the ancient authors, so that now several American editions yield to few, if any, European texts in excellence. The most important recent paleographical publication is the monumental *Codices Latini Antiquiores*, edited by E. A. Lowe of the Institute for Advanced Studies, a guide to Latin manuscripts prior to the ninth century, of which the volumes on the Vatican, Great Britain, Ireland, and Italy have already been published. An especially productive development has been the comprehensive study of medieval Latin manuscripts. Foremost in this work, which resulted in the foundation of the Medieval Academy of America in 1926, were C. H. Beeson and E. K. Rand.[16]

Additions have also been made in this country to the apparatus of indices and bibliographies. The outstanding center of such activity has been the University of Illinois, where William A. Oldfather organized a research group of younger colleagues and students which has made steady publication of indices and bibliographies of Apuleius, Cicero, Epictetus, and Seneca, as well as other studies, such as the edition of St. Jerome's *Vitae Patrum*. Oldfather himself was a scholar of vast range, interested and erudite in Greek and Latin history, social institutions, and archaeology. But his chief accomplishment was as researcher in carefully delimited areas, as energetic guide of graduate students, and as a stimulating force among his colleagues in classical studies all over the world.[17]

In the field of the compilation of inscriptions, an American addition to the standard German collections is the *Thesaurus Linguae Latinae Epigraphicae*, initiated by George N. Olcott at Columbia in 1912 and now being continued by scholars at that and other universities.

All of these specialized researches should be expected, of course, to bear fruit in more accurate and illuminating interpretations of classical literature, by scholars possessing, in addition to the necessary tools and techniques, insight and imagination. But that happy combination has proved all too infrequent. We have produced, for example, no thorough study of a major author comparable to such English work as Jebb's edition of Sophocles and, in Germany, Wilamowitz-Moellendorff's Euripides.[18] The closest approach has been Paul Shorey's study of Plato, which won him recognition as a leading authority in interpretation as well as the text. Like Gildersleeve, Shorey used his researches as a springboard to launch him into wide waters. Although he was instrumental in helping Edward Capps found *Classical Philology*, which published under his editorship his own and many other results of philological research for thirty years, and although his record in supervising over fifty doctoral dissertations was outstanding, he was not content with those distinctions. He stimulated his students and colleagues to an appreciation of literature and philosophy well beyond the range of any special subject; and he was a fighting as well as a practising humanist, doing everything in his power to educate the American public to an understanding of the classical tradition. It is a pity that his influence was not more pervasive. Perhaps it would have been if he had been capable of more tact in his attempts at conversion. But there can be no question of his unique authority in this country as an interpreter of classical literature.

The record of American achievement in the field of literary criticism is likewise unimpressive. There have been, to be sure, instances here and there of criticism of high quality; [19] but in general it must be said that no classical scholar in America has produced sustained literary analysis comparable to the of M. and A. Croiset in France and Gilbert Murray and C. M. Bowra in England.

It is probably in archaeology and the allied fields of epigraphy and papyrology that the American contribution to classical scholarship has been outstanding, largely as a result of the wise direction of the Archaeological Institute and the enthusiasm generated by the American Schools in Athens and Rome. Many of our ablest students have won scholarships for study in those schools, and have become devoted to an area in which original work of a practical nature could so effectively be done.[20] As a result of their efforts elementary and graduate courses in archaeology have become increasingly a part of the curricula in our colleges and universities, notably at Harvard, Johns Hopkins, Princeton, Yale, and Bryn Mawr; publication of researches has been made readily available; and scholarly textbooks have been published.[21]

As the program of the American School at Athens developed, under the able and stimulating directorship of B. H. Hill from 1906 to 1926 and the chairmanship of Edward Capps (1918–1939), the excavation of Corinth was continued, bringing to light the multifold activities of the most prosperous and populous city in ancient Greece. The finds, dating chiefly from the Graeco-Roman period, include the business area, two theaters, the fountains which served as the city's water supply, a basilica, propylaea, triumphal arch, and music hall, shops and taverns, and vast quantities of sculpture, pottery, coins and inscriptions. In a near-by Roman villa interesting mosaics were unearthed. The results of these excavations, which are still going on and being published, are of major importance in helping us reconstruct the way of life of an ancient commercial city.

In 1930 the most spectacular of all American excavations was begun, that of the ancient Athenian agora. Promoted by Edward Capps, this dig was planned with scientific exactitude by a corps of experts headed by T. Leslie Shear of Princeton. The results have been of the utmost value in many respects. In addition to the foundations and fragments of administrative buildings and temples, valuable sculpture, vases, coins, and ostraka have been unearthed and inscriptions which have provided important evidence regarding Athenian chronology and public transactions. The publication of these inscriptions, chiefly by the late Allen B. West of Cincinnati, B. D. Meritt of the Institute for Advanced Studies, and Sterling Dow of Harvard, has been of great value to historians. It is, in fact, a fair claim that the publication and interpretation of hundreds of newly-found inscriptions is the chief achievement of contemporary American classical scholars.

Another field in which American archaeologists have assumed a leading role in recent years has been that of prehistoric Greek archaeology. Notable discoveries made by Carl Blegen and his colleagues at the Helladic sites of Korakou, Zygouries, Prosymna, and Pylos, and a systematic restudy of the site of ancient Troy, have led to much more detailed knowledge of this early culture, and of its relation to the mature civilization of Greece.

Publications of these excavations and interpretations of other finds have been promptly made in the *American Journal of Archaeology* and in a supplementary series of books and monographs issued by the American School in Athens and the *Memoirs of the American Academy in Rome*. In 1932, when so much material was coming from the Agora dig and such other explorations as those by Homer A. Thompson and Dr. Kourouniotes on the Pnyx at Athens, a new publication was established, *Hesperia*, devoted chiefly to the publication of papers by members of the American School in Athens.

Other American excavations on a large scale have also been conducted, some of them in coöperation with the American School, others financed and directed independently. A dynamic promoter of such enterprises was Francis W. Kelsey of Michigan, who played a leading part in organizing expeditions to sites in Asia Minor and North Africa. The most important finds there were papyri,[22] which gave fresh information regarding ancient authors and ancient life, especially business transactions in Roman Egypt and the text of the Bible. The papyri have been steadily published under the expert direction of Campbell Bonner, A. E. R. Boak, H. C. Youtie, J. G. Winter, and H. A. Sanders, who, with their assistants, have created at the University of Michigan the leading center of papyrology in this country.[23] J. G. Winter commented as follows on the value of such studies:

The many letters preserved on papyri have given new reality to various aspects of ancient life and thought. They reveal, as nothing else has done, not only the methods by which Rome held sway over an important part of her Empire, but also the social and psychological background of the thousands who toiled to supply her with grain or served in fleet and camp to make that rule secure. They are . . . original and unimpeachable sources for that complete study of life in town and village which still remains to be written.[24]

Brief mention should be made of four other excavations. American archaeologists, under the direction of Howard C. Butler, David M. Robinson, William Buckler, and T. Leslie Shear, took the leading role in excavating Sardis, the chief city of ancient Lydia, from 1910 until work was interrupted by World War I. The finds included every variety of archaeological data. In 1932 Princeton initiated an expedition to Syrian Antioch, under the leadership of G. W. Elderkin and Richard Stillwell; it was financed by contributions raised by a committee representing Princeton University, the Baltimore and Worcester Museums, Dumbarton Oaks Research Library, and the Musées Nationaux de France. This expedition was also interrupted by a world war, but the finds, including mosaics of unusual value, have been steadily published. Another important excavation was begun in 1928 at Dura-Europos in Asia Minor, by a Yale staff including Paul V. C. Baur, A. R. Bellinger, Clark Hopkins, M. I. Rostovtzeff, and C. B. Welles. The French Academy of Inscriptions coöperated in this undertaking. The results of ten years' campaigns have filled in many gaps in our knowledge of the Hellenistic and Roman cities on the caravan route to the Orient.[25]

In 1928 excavations were begun at Olynthus, under the direction of David M. Robinson of the Johns Hopkins University, a classical scholar of encyclopedic range but primarily devoted to archaeology and epigraphy; in addition to his own research he has to his credit the training of more archaeologists than any other American teacher. Previously he had participated in the excavations at Corinth, Sinope, Cyrene, and Sardis, and directed the dig at Pisidian Antioch, but Olynthus became his major project. The only Greek city excavated in the Greek mainland, and the only one of the Hellenic period as yet excavated anywhere, it has proved an invaluable site for revealing the complete life of a prosperous mercantile center. The publication of the finds by Dr. Robinson and his associates, notably George E. Mylonas, has been prompt, accurate, and complete, covering the architectural layout in careful detail, sculpture, pottery, inscriptions, terra cottas, mosaics, and coins. Thus an entire ancient city has been brought to life again by the spade of the archaeologist.[26]

The American Academy in Rome (with which the American School of Classical Studies had been merged in 1911) has been unable to provide its students with the opportunity to engage in more than minor excavations; but students there have made studies of monuments *in situ* and in the museums of Italy, worked on inscriptions and manuscripts under expert guidance, and studied their classical literature in a congenial environment under the direction of visiting professors from the United States. A summer session is also provided for visiting teachers and students, which has resulted in the further spread of archaeological knowledge and enthusiasm in this country. The American Academy has performed another useful service in giving the young architects, painters, and sculptors who are there on fellowships the means of enriching their background by the study of ancient masterpieces of art. Many of our leading artists — and, through their work, the American public — have profited from these fellowships.

In 1921 the facilities of the American School of Athens were greatly augmented by the donation of his library by Dr. Johannes Gennadius. Containing some forty thousand items, it is a priceless record of Greek life from Byzantine times to the present, and has made the American School an international center of Byzantine and Neo-Hellenic studies. Recently, on the initiative of D. M. Robinson and Dr. Mavris, the Society for the Promotion of Byzantine and Neo-Hellenic Studies and its publication, *Byzantina Metabyzantina*, have been established to promote such studies.

Apart from actual excavations, new critical examination has been made of ancient sites. For many years B. H. Hill, W. B. Dinsmoor, L. B. Holland, G. P. Stevens, J. M. Paton, and their associates have done systematic work on the buildings on the Athenian Acropolis, correcting errors of earlier archaeologists and giving definitive answers to questions involving the history and structure of the buildings.[27] Museum collections in this country have also been carefully studied, including the rich collections at the Metropolitan Museum in New York and the Boston Museum of Fine Arts, as well as many smaller collections in cities and universities throughout the country. Curators of scholarly authority, such as Arthur Fairbanks and L. D. Caskey in Boston and G. M. A. Richter in New York, have issued catalogues of their collections, and G. H. Chase of Harvard wrote his comprehensive survey, *Greek and Roman Sculpture in American Collections*. Vases in museums here and abroad were made the subject of especially important publications,[28] and American scholars, notably J. C. Hoppin, D. M. Robinson, G. H. Chase, and Stephen B. Luce, have also published collections in this country for the international *Corpus Vasorum Antiquorum*. The results of archaeological research have been reflected in such books as R. C. Flickinger's *The Greek Theatre and Its Drama* and Margarete Bieber's *The History of the Greek and Roman Theatre*.

This is an impressive archaeological record, of which Americans may well be proud. But in art criticism our scholars have not made an impressive record; they have failed to keep pace either with the archaeologists or with their colleagues in foreign countries. There are a few exceptions, such as the pioneer Charles Eliot Norton, and, in recent years, Rhys Carpenter, formerly director of the American School in Athens. His *Esthetic Basis of Greek Art* is a stimulating analysis, and his many articles on Greek sculpture have been marked by sensitiveness to artistic values. But much more work of this sort needs to be done, in order to stimulate and guide contemporary movements in art which are based upon classical principles.

More productive in the interpretation of ancient values have been scholars who, well equipped with philological and archaeological knowledge, have chosen social and economic institutions for their major interest. Outstanding among them have been Tenney Frank of the Johns Hopkins University, who devoted his chief attention to the economic history of Rome, and M. I. Rostovtzeff of Yale, profound interpreter of Greek and Roman social and economic institutions.[29] In the field of law, Robert J. Bonner, early in life a member of the Ontario Bar, made his seminars at the University of Chicago such a center for the study of ancient legal institutions that they were popularly known as the "Bonner School of Greek Law." [30] Pupils of his, notably George M. Calhoun, have continued to make studies of Greek legal and business administration. At Chicago and, more recently, at Harvard, Werner Jaeger has trained students in the analysis of Greek statesmen and philosophers and the aristocratic view of Greek civilization which he summarized in his *Paideia: The Ideals of Greek Culture.*[31]

As far as science is concerned, no American scholar has made a survey comparable to the work of Charles Singer in England, but William A. Heidel's *Hippocratic Medicine, Its Spirit and Method* is a competent treatment of one phase of the subject. In religion, Clifford H. Moore's *Religious Thought of the Greeks from Homer to the Triumph of Christianity*, Arthur D. Nock's studies in the Hellenistic background of Christianity, and monographs by Campbell Bonner, Lily Ross Taylor, and I. M. Linforth stand out among the modest achievement of our scholars. The more technical aspects of philosophy have had virtually no contributions of importance, with the exception of Harold Cherniss' study of Aristotle on the pre-Socratic philosophers and the Platonic Academy; that area has been abdicated in favor of colleagues in departments of philosophy, many of whom are unable to read what the classical philosophers actually wrote.

From this survey it is obvious that in every branch of classical research American scholars, late in arriving on the scene, have nevertheless made valuable contributions, even if they have been more successful in factual analysis than in the broader ranges of synthesis. Now they face the sobering responsibility of undertaking for the first time a role of real leadership, particularly since facilities for scholarly output are seriously impaired in most of the rest of the world. It is their duty to do a far greater amount of research and publication; to organize a comprehensive program which will estimate the relative importance of various projects, concentrate on the most essential ones, and devote more attention to the integration and interpretation of their materials; to recruit young scholars, and see to it that library, museum, and publishing facilities are adequate.[32]

In spite of the long record of classical study and publication, a large amount of work still remains to be done. Even in syntax the broader investigation of its history needs to be undertaken. Hundreds of inscriptions and papyri are as yet unpublished, and more will be unearthed as excavations continue. Many manuscripts await more critical study, especially the largely neglected series of lesser classical authors and medieval and Renaissance commentaries; to make such manuscripts available the development of microfilm library equipment will be required. Indices and concordances to classical authors are as yet incomplete; the *Thesaurus Linguae Latinae* and the international dictionary of medieval Latin must be finished. In archaeology, digging remains to be done at Corinth, in the Athenian agora, and at several other sites, and new excavations are projected; the publication of the finds will engage the industry of scholars for decades to come. Revised editions of important texts should be made, in the light of further manuscript study and the more complete knowledge of ancient life furnished by archaeological discovery. And in social interpretation and in literary, aesthetic, and philosophical criticism American classical scholars have hardly scratched the surface. The task will demand all the ability and energy of our scholars in every specialized field.

III

Shall we have the scholars to meet such a demand? During this century there has been a sharp decline in the number of students majoring in classics in college and going on into graduate work in our universities. Greek has disappeared from the high schools, and nearly 90 per cent of the high school students who elect Latin now

study it for only two years. Consequently there is only a small proportion of students, in comparison with the number fifty years ago,
who continue in either Latin or Greek to the point where they are
trained to do specialized work.

There are doubtless many reasons for this decline — a decline
unfortunate if not tragic in the opinion of people who realize that
the United States, in defending Western civilization, must be itself
well versed in the humanistic values which are being defended.
Teachers of the classics cannot evade the charge that they themselves are partly responsible, by having failed to adjust their materials and methods of teaching to changing conditions. But other
factors in our national evolution are even more responsible: the
complexity of a population stemming from many countries in which
the classical tradition was weak or unknown; the dominant role of
science and its multiplicity of practical conveniences which engage
people's attention and devotion; the development of social studies
which deal with immediate problems of personal adjustment and
social relationships and investigate human achievement, past and
present, all over the world. Most potent of all has been the tremendous industrial and commercial expansion of this country, which
has opened unusually attractive careers to men trained in engineering and business and has resulted in a culture determined, to a
constantly greater degree, by the standards congenial to men who
have been narrowly educated. But whatever the reasons may be, the
consequences are all too plain; and the decline of humanistic studies
has become a cause of concern, not only to classical scholars, but to
other thoughtful people who realize how rich a heritage the classics
offer to warn, to guide, and perhaps to inspire the complex world
of today.

How to deal with such apathy and antagonism has been a per-
plexing problem for our teachers. They have constantly been aware
of the need of waging defensive warfare, in the face of opposition
from school administrators, competing fields of learning, and the
"practical" trend of American life. It is, to be sure, no new situation.
Throughout our history there has been apprehension on the part
of classicists, from the days when even the practical-minded Benjamin Franklin wrote, "It has been of late too much the mode to

slight the learning of the ancients." But the opposition has become much stronger in recent years.

Classicists have realized that in order to overcome this opposition they must reappraise their objectives and teaching methods, strengthen the morale within their own ranks, and propagandize among the wider public. Vigorous steps have been taken in all three respects. The Classical Investigation conducted by the American Classical League a quarter of a century ago led to a restatement of the aims of classical education and its teaching procedures to meet modern needs. As a result numerous Latin and a few elementary Greek texts were written, which have simplified the grammatical apparatus, provided more varied and interesting reading material, and presented the language as one element of a rich cultural pattern. Teaching devices were also worked out to further the study of ancient civilization. Recently an experimental project was initiated to base a two-year Latin course on Vergil, thus giving even beginners material of primary intellectual and aesthetic value.

Morale was improved by establishing regional classical associations, which united scholars in professional comradeship and established closer relations between university, college, and high school teachers: the Classical Association of the Middle West and South in 1905, the Classical Association of New England in 1906, the Classical Association of the Atlantic States in 1907, and the Classical Association of the Pacific States in 1915. In 1918 an over-all organization, the American Classical League, was formed, to provide its members with teaching aids and serve as a shock-troop unit in the war for survival; its membership is now over three thousand, and in its Junior Classical League more than five times that number are enrolled annually. Publications of a somewhat more popular sort than the learned periodicals were instituted: the *Classical Journal*, the *Classical Weekly*, and the *Classical Outlook*; they have included notes on teaching methods and papers on the value of classical studies as well as those of more specialized scholarly interest. Recently several of the regional associations have subsidized high school teachers for refresher summer study in Rome.

Since 1910 systematic campaigns have been planned to bring to the attention of the American public the values of classical study.

If Gildersleeve had in 1867 deplored the "depressing tendencies of modern civilization," especially its materialism and Philistinism, and advocated the study of the classics as the best means of combating these tendencies, if Charles Eliot Norton in 1900 saw the same danger and advised the same remedy, now, with increased energy and political acumen the indictment was couched in militant terms and the remedy was insisted upon. F. W. Kelsey fired an opening salvo in his *Latin and Greek in American Education* (1911). But the outstanding fighter was Andrew F. West, professor of Latin and Dean of the Graduate College at Princeton, leader in the formation of the American Classical League and the Classical Investigation. In *The Value of the Classics*, which he edited in 1917, he castigated the philistinism of the times, and argued, with the help of testimony from many sources, that the classics were invaluable for mental discipline, literary culture, and responsible citizenship. In the same year Paul Shorey contributed to the *Atlantic Monthly* his caustic article, "The Assault on Humanism." In 1921 G. D. Hadzsits and L. R. Harley published their *Bibliographical Monograph on the Value of the Classics*. Since that time there have been countless pamphlets and articles published, arguing for the retention of the classics in the curricula of our schools and colleges. The arguments have been amplified, but not greatly changed in substance; instead of the argument for "mental discipline" in general, it has been urged that Latin and Greek have special value as basic training in language study, and are uniquely useful in acquainting students with the roots of a majority of English words, notably scientific terms; that the process of translation trains students in critical judgment as well as the appreciation of literary form. And greater emphasis is put on the value of direct contact with the great minds of the past and the social, aesthetic, and moral content of the ancient civilizations, as basic to an understanding of Western culture. Such campaigns are doubtless important, even necessary, when the field is under constant attack; but classicists generally have come to realize that these defensive tactics are of secondary importance, and that survival depends chiefly on positive, dynamic, and broad-gauged teaching of such students as still study Latin and

Greek, and more effective means of bringing the classics themselves to the attention of the wider public, young and old, which does not and never will study the ancient languages.

IV

To make the classics generally appreciated and utilized as a vital force in American culture is more than a matter of tactics in the war for professional survival, it is part of the basic strategy of education. For its success we must go beyond the scientific specialists in various classical fields, important as they are, and again train classical humanists, interpreters of those values of ancient culture which still have meaning for our own.

This involves, first of all, incorporating in our training of teachers the broadly humanistic approach characteristic of early American classical instruction. The task will not be too difficult, for in spite of the inroads of specialization the devotion to humanistic breadth has always been preserved. As background for their specialties American classicists have studied the entire range of two ancient civilizations, including the history, social institutions, philosophy, and art, as well as the languages and literature; they have had, from the early days of the Colonies on, a strong conviction of the value of the classics in training their students for intelligent and responsible citizenship; and they have usually possessed a typically American common sense which saved them from conceiving their work in too restricted terms.[33] But to this general background they must now add more acute analysis and appraisal of those ancient social values which seem to be most useful to us as correctives of current prejudices and guides to a finer culture of our own.

In order to exert the necessary leadership in this respect, scholars must extend their teaching beyond those relatively few students who will learn the Greek and Latin languages. Forty years ago some teachers of the classics realized that there was an urgent need of making their material available to students who would remain ignorant of classical culture unless they could make the acquaintance through English translations. Since that time there have been developed courses in Greek and Roman life and thought, mythology, and literature in translation, at first often planned defensively, even apologetically, by members of the classics staff who regarded this as an anemic diet indeed to replace the solid fare they preferred to provide. But in recent years most teachers have recognized the importance of scholarly courses of this sort in the liberal education of students who would otherwise be confined to narrow fields of specialization, often in practical science and commerce.[34]

In common with other critics of our education who have deplored its vocational and overspecialized character, many classicists believe that a few fragmentary courses in liberal subjects are not a satisfactory solution of the problem of encouraging American students to seek a genuinely humane understanding of their world, one world in time as well as in space. In the programs of liberal studies inaugurated by Columbia University thirty years ago and since then adapted by several other institutions, the role of the ancient classics in humanities courses is an important one, and may grow to be even greater. More radical experiments in integrated programs have also made use of classical materials; the Experimental College of the University of Wisconsin (1927–32) based its entire first year's work on an analysis of Greek problems and values, and the "Great Books" curriculum at St. John's, Annapolis, gives a generous place to books produced in the ancient world. In all such programs, designed to provide students with a more coherent picture of the human enterprise, classical scholars should have an important role; and to plan how Greek and Roman ideas and values may most effectively be used as part of the curriculum in general education, in both high schools and colleges, is now perhaps the chief obligation of many classicists to their contemporary academic world.

But the obligation is not merely to youthful students, it is to the widest possible general public. Until recently, apart from polemics directed at the foes of Greek and Latin and articles praising the value of these studies, American scholars have done far less than their colleagues in many other countries, notably England and France, in presenting their material in persuasive and convincing form to adults. Now they have become more aware of the urgent need of doing so if the classics are to survive and be useful in helping to develop an America as culturally eminent as she is in military and industrial power. Some attempts have been made to popularize the results of classical study. In 1921 D. M. Robinson and G. D. Hadzsits inaugurated a series of some fifty volumes entitled "Our Debt to Greece and Rome," which discussed the contribution of various classical authors and cultural institutions to the civilization of Europe and America. For many years the Archaeological Institute published a popular magazine, *Art and Archaeology*, to bring the results of archaeological excavation to the attention of a wide public, and it has recently started a new one, *Archaeology*, with the same purpose in mind; lecturers sent out by the Institute have also aroused popular appreciation of the value of archaeology. On a high scholarly level the translations of the Loeb Classical Library, edited by Edward Capps until his retirement, and since 1940 by L. A. Post, have brought to the attention of an upper group of general readers accurate translations of the classical authors; the publication of this series is a notable achievement of American classical scholarship. Such books as W. C. Greene's *The Achievement of Greece* and *The Achievement of Rome*, and *The Greek Tradition*, edited by George Boas, have attempted to appraise the classical contribution to Western culture. But the popularization of scholarly work has not, on the whole, appealed greatly to American classicists, nor have they had the persuasive style of such English writers as R. W. Livingstone and Gilbert Murray, or the skill in *la haute vulgarisation* of their French colleagues. Much still remains to be done in this respect. And more translations in contemporary idiom need to be made, in order to let the classics speak vividly for themselves. But it is not enough to write books. Courses in adult education must be organized; radio facilities must be utilized; systematic study must be developed on the adult level. The organization of "Great Books" study groups is a step forward in this direction, and the enthusiastic response indicates that they are meeting, however imperfectly, a real need.

As American classical scholars face the future they have reason for confidence. They realize how much there is to be done in their specialized fields of research; they are convinced of the importance of the humanistic values which they profess; they are encouraged by the current movement toward general and adult education; and in the international coming of age of this country they foresee our drawing generously on the experience of the great ancient civilizations for guidance.

At the height of his teaching career, Gildersleeve had, with perhaps less justification, the same confidence. "Whether, then," he said, "it be for the historical unity of the race, whether it be for the influence on form either as example or precept, there is no danger that the ancient classics will be displaced from the list of studies necessary for the highest and truest culture." [35] Such confidence will be justified, if able and devoted scholars make it plain that their scholarship contributes not only to the acquisition of knowledge, but also to the guidance of men generally in understanding those values, individual and social, which the classical cultures realized, values which we need today and shall need, if we are to assume our mature responsibilities in world leadership, even more during the years to come.

VI ·

Philosophical Scholarship

ARTHUR E. MURPHY

How and to what purpose has philosophical scholarship been "in" the American civilization of the past half century? A critical listing of the chief works produced in the United States in this period, with due regard for their chronological order and doctrinal affiliations, would provide a partial and useful answer to this question. But it would miss the major point. For philosophical scholarship is an instrument of research in an inquiry whose goal is wisdom, and wisdom, or the lack of it, is "in" a civilization not as books are in a library or earrings in the ears to which they are appended, but rather as order or confusion, sanity or fanaticism are in the purposes and behavior of a growing mind. What sort of wisdom has been accessible to our civilization in this period and how has philosophy as inquiry, with its attendant works of scholarship, helped or hindered its attainment? These are large questions, but adequate answers to them would shed needed light on both our civilization and our philosophy. In this paper I propose to make a beginning at such answers.

I

Queen Victoria died in 1901 and in the same year Theodore Roosevelt became president of the United States. There was a general recognition in the thought and purpose of the time that something impressive was over and that something exciting had begun, and a conviction that, for all the grandeurs of the past and the risks of an uncertain future, it was well that it should be so. The eighteen years that followed, with their climax in America's tardy but triumphant participation in the First World War, are appropriately referred to as the progressive era. The temper of the time was liberal, experimental, and expansive. For progress meant a change that was also and essentially an improvement; it was growth in the eulogistic sense of that term, not the more depressing usage in which an ulcer is also referred to as a "growth." The distinctive genius of American civilization was that it had grown, was growing, and had within it inexhaustible resources for continued growth, for its own good and in some large, indefinite manner also for the welfare of humanity. To grow in that fashion is naturally to outgrow, and, in the forward march of progress there is much in its own day right and precious that must be left behind. But it is also and preëminently to grow up to the full exercise of powers and capacities that are felt to be fully adequate to the demands that will be made upon them. Not everybody felt this way, of course. Henry Adams had seen the dynamos in the great hall of machines at the Paris Exposition and been filled with forebodings about the moral implications of the forces that they embodied. But Adams' thought belonged to the past and future. In that Rooseveltian present he knew that he was out of place.[1]

Looking backward from the standpoint of our present time of troubles it is easy to see how unstable were the elements of this philosophy and how precarious the basis of their combination. The ideal framework was traditional. The good that progress was to realize was the good of free and conscientious individuals whose demands, when adequately understood and implemented, would harmonize in a community of interest and of understanding. And this good both God and evolution would somehow, in the long run, sanction and support. Its methods, however, were iconoclastic. The forms in which the good had so far been embodied were felt to be in various degrees abstract, outmoded, out of contact with the growing needs and forces of the time. New energies and interests clamored for release and old ideas would no longer serve for their interpretation. The underlying faith was that in the process of liberation and revision on which the twentieth century had embarked the new would be the fulfillment of the best that the old had promised, that the liberated would at last be liberals and the future not only newer and bigger but also recognizably better than the past.

For the historian of knowledge, wise, as always, after the event, this faith is readily identifiable as an "ideology" of local origin and limited plausibility. Like the bison and the bicycle, it has had its day. For those who shared in it, however, and who were trying to be wise in the midst of events, where wisdom might still make a difference, it was a program and a promise, to be made good in a continuing process in which human effort and inquiry were to play a vital part. They saw plainly enough the gaps between the facts and forces of their time and the ideals that would justify their aspirations. But they saw these discrepancies as setting problems to be solved and they believed they had the means to solve them. Their philosophy in consequence was more than a climate of opinion or conventional mannerism of thought. It was a faith seeking substantiation in knowledge and justification as wisdom in the right ordering of beliefs and values for the attainment of the good it promised. As such it had not only preferences to express but problems to solve. Philosophy as inquiry was primarily the attempt to solve these problems and scholarship the refinement of its method of research.

First, there was the problem of "advancing knowledge." The ideal here was still in principle that of the Enlightenment, of which American liberalism was the natural offspring and legitimate heir. The forward march of science and technology had already served to emancipate men's minds from fear and superstition and to place at their disposal unexampled new resources for the satisfaction of their desires. Let knowledge, therefore, grow from more to more, enlightening human purposes and increasing humanitarian understanding as it progressed. The troublesome fact was, however, that this advance had so far been markedly and even dangerously one-sided. The triumphs of science had been achieved in what the philosophers of the time liked to call "the world of description," [2] the impersonal order of measurable and predictable events. Both its methods of inquiry and the world view derivable from any easy generalization of its results were patently colored by this so far limited area of its application. What was to happen when "advancing knowledge," with the positive sciences as its model, reached the areas of experience in which ideals are not only to be described but justified, and in which a reason is not simply or primarily a correlation or a cause? The issue is by no means merely academic. For the Enlightenment had been as essentially moralistic and humanitarian in its aspirations as it was prosaic and factual in its critical procedures. If the generalization of its method meant the undermining of its ideals, it was by no means clear that the ensuing change of mind could properly be called a progress. And how, indeed, was progress to be measured in a world of facts? The problem, therefore, was how to utilize the growing resources of factual information for a just understanding of the nature and validity of human ideals. Every major philosophy of the period was, in one way or another, an attempt at its solution.

Second, the problem of the community. The ideal, again, was general, humanitarian and traditional. All men, it was held, have human dignity and equal rights. A political society is morally justified to the extent that it preserves these rights and maintains, in freedom, the conditions for their secure and mutual enjoyment. The United States was founded on this principle and its history was thought to provide, with only minor deviations, a shining example for mankind of its ever wider application. There was still hard, reforming work to be done and sinister "special interests" to be controlled, but the goal was clear and commonly accepted and the methods of political democracy were believed to be fully adequate to the task ahead. "The cure for democracy is more democracy." But here, too, the supporting facts were spotty, incomplete, and problematic. Our humanitarian ideals had been developed on a strictly national basis in separation from and in contrast to a reactionary "old world" that so far did not share them. What would happen to them when the expansive forces of American nationalism outgrew their continental limits and made explicit contact with competing nationalisms on a global scale? The Spanish-American War and its aftermath in the Philippines set the problem unmistakably. Could we retain our special and separate righteousness in this larger world? What sort of moral community was possible or desirable on a more than national basis? At home, too, there were tensions to be faced as traditional preconceptions were confronted by the growing demands of relatively underprivileged groups for a larger share in the common good and for more positive governmental action to assure it to them. How, then, were the traditional "rights" of the individual to be related to the growing claims of "the community"?

Third, the problem of the individual and his self-expression. Individualism was traditionally held to be the toughest and most enduring factor in any characteristically "American" way of looking at the world. It was in the claims of the self-reliant individual that the love of freedom had its roots, in his basic fairness and good sense that we placed our democratic trust, and by their contribution to the release and realization of his capacities for self-development that the worth of our institutions was finally to be judged. The progressive era carried on this faith and spoke its language. Yet it was in the twentieth century preëminently that the individual became a problem for the sciences, for society, and, most urgently, for himself. His goal presumably was self-expression, and the means for its attainment seemed almost endlessly various and promising. But before he could achieve such self-expression he must have a self to express. And, amid the impersonal mechanisms of the modern world, where was he to find it?

Fourth, and finally, is the Universe friendly? To the advanced thinker this query has a rather foolish sound. He would put the question more cautiously and answer it with elaborate critical indirection. Yet in one form or another it must be asked and answered whenever men try seriously to make sense of the world and of their own place and purposes within it. For if our ultimate ideals are to be more than wishful thinking there must be something real in the world that warrants and supports our confidence in them. In 1901 the signs of the times appeared to be propitious but the eternal verities had still to have their say and wise men were well aware of this. Could our changing ideas and aspirations make contact with a greater mind and purpose that both corrected and fulfilled them, with God, as the personal or superpersonal foundation of our faith? Was the trend itself, perhaps, the ultimate reality, for human purposes at least, and evolution, history and man's progressive participation in their forward movement the final truth for an enlightened mind? Or were there obdurate and alien realities behind the trend to which, in a disillusioning last analysis, we must conform our beliefs if we were not to be defeated and deceived? The part of wisdom is to "face reality" and to build one's plans and hopes upon it. But what is reality and how are we to recognize it when we face it?

These were problems for philosophers, but they were also problems for the civilization in which the philosophers shared, a civilization which must somehow broaden and clarify its preconceptions if it was to fulfill its purposes and substantiate its ideals. Their success or failure has made a difference in that civilization which it is our business, now, to try to understand.

II

The best established version of philosophical inquiry in America at the turn of the century was speculative idealism. Borrowing their method and major doctrines from what they held to be the definitive achievements of modern philosophy in Kant and Hegel, and surveying the tensions and incoherences of contemporary thought from the vantage ground that these provided, the spokesmen for this school of thought were in a position to make sense, and even system, of much that otherwise seemed out of focus and obscure. By 1900 the American idealists already had a generation of solid scholarly achievement to their credit and, in their commanding positions in the leading universities of the country, had become the teachers of the generation that was to follow. Thus, while they made relatively little direct contact with the popular thinking of the time, they set the academic standard for thoroughness and adequacy in systematic inquiry into ultimate truth with which succeeding thinkers had somehow, by conformity or rebellion, to come to terms.

The primary concern of these philosophers was the maintenance and reinforcement of the over-all ideal structure of a civilization whose traditional ideas were in process of drastic and perilously lopsided reconstruction. They claimed to stand for total against partial truth, for the central facts of life against the peripheral, for time-transcending finalities as the rational foundation of a world of change. Their message was both sobering and inspiring. They taught that our highest ideals, rightly interpreted, find their fulfillment in Reality, and that, in the end, the best that we can think or will must *be*. But only in the end and after a process of correction in which finite thought and will have been purged of one-sidedness and temporal limitation and have considerably changed their aspect in the process. If the plain man is tempted to observe that the best in this kind are but shadows there is a ready answer. Only those who have a sure and ultimate criterion can truly distinguish realities from shadows, and this the plain man too often lacks. Idealism offered such a standard and challenged the trends of current halfway thinking to justify or to modify their pretensions on its all-comprehending terms.

With the problem of advancing scientific knowledge these philosophers were well prepared to deal. The progress of impersonal inquiry carried with it, in their interpretation, no threat to the rational authority of moral and religious ideals. Quite the contrary, in fact. For such knowledge was the mind's own work, the embodiment of one of its loftiest ideals. The trouble with the agnostics, evolutionists, and empiricists who sought to limit knowledge to sequences of mere and mindless facts was not at all in what they claimed to know, which was usually informative and sometimes important. It was in what, ironically, they claimed *not* to know, that knowledge of phenomena is the work of a mind that is not itself a mere phenomenon and that, in consequence, behind the appearance of a world of matter and of evolution there stands the spiritual reality of the mind for which this world exists and whose rational structure is presupposed in every meaningful attempt to doubt or to deny it. "When me they fly, I am the wings." Emerson had said it enigmatically, but these idealists, who were transcendentalists with Ph.D.'s, were prepared to spell it out at length in sober and sometimes stodgy prose and to bring the heavy artillery of Kantian criticism and Hegelian dialectic to its support. G. H.

Howison's formidable lecture on *The Limits of Evolution* [3] put the naturalists in their "phenomenal" place with firm benevolence and Josiah Royce's demonstration that the possibility of error presupposes the actuality of absolute knowledge and hence of an Absolute Knower dazzled even William James for years. [4]

The task of philosophical scholarship, for the idealists, was to translate these epistemological profundities into usable knowledge for American civilization and to use it to steady the thinking of a generation thrown off balance by the jerky forward movement of empirical inquiry. Their lengthy analyses of "thought," mixing Kantian categories with the data of introspective psychology in a peculiarly gritty blend, make laborious reading today. But they stood for sanity and thoroughness in an age of half-baked ideas. And at its best, as in Royce's *The World and the Individual*, [5] this philosophy achieved a range and richness of articulation that has rarely been equaled in America before or since its time.

Their solution of the problem of knowledge provided a substantial basis, also, for the understanding of other and no less urgent issues. For the Mind that is the presupposition of objective knowledge proves also to be the Will that is objectified in the standards and purposes of a moral community. The growing demands of society upon the individual take on ideal meaning and are rationally examinable as just or arbitrary in so far as the life of that society can be interpreted as the institutional embodiment of shared purposes in a genuinely common good. The authority of this good is at once ideal in its claims upon the self-willed individual, and actual in the work and will of the community to which, organically and essentially, he belongs. His true or positive freedom, adequately understood, is his fulfillment of his function in this greater whole and his appropriate self-realization the attainment of moral personality within it.

Here, again, the doctrine offered had deep roots in the history of philosophy, from Plato and Aristotle through Rousseau, Kant, and Hegel to the more recent teaching of Green and Bosanquet in Britain. Yet its timeliness in the progressive era as a persuasive redefinition of individual freedom as a kind of social service was obvious. Royce's *Philosophy of Loyalty* [6] struck a note that was to reverberate in later American thought and action. The lost individual finds himself in thoroughgoing devotion to a cause and in loyalty to the community lies the whole fulfillment of the moral law.

How wide is the community thus idealized? The most potent claimant to such loyalty is the national state. Hence the idealistic "philosophy of the state" is readily usable as a rationalization of the "spiritual" pretensions of expanding nationalism. Much of its prestige in this period stemmed directly from this use. It is to the credit of the American idealists, and of Royce in particular, that they took a larger view. The national state, Royce insisted, is but one community of many. Direct participation in autonomous local groups is essential to individual self-realization, hence the need in America for a vigorous provincialism as a counterweight to the growing power of the federal government.[7] And beyond the conflicting interests of competing states stands the ideal and hope of a world community for which, in the disillusioning years of the First World War, Royce spoke with earnest eloquence.[8]

Time and "progress" have not realized this hope, and subsequent events have made us increasingly aware of the existential gap between idealized "communities" and *de facto* social forces. To interpret this as a refutation by "the facts" of essential idealistic doctrine would be to miss the most fundamental of all its teachings. The theory does not hold that in given temporal experience ideal and actuality will ever come to coincide. Its claim is that in Ultimate Reality they are essentially at one and that temporal experience borrows such reality and meaning as it has from its fragmentary reflection of this larger truth. Whether this spiritual reality is essentially many or one, a "moral republic" or a single all-inclusive Individual of which all other individuals are but "adjectives" or aspects, was a disputed issue between "Personal" and "Absolute" idealists that has not yet been settled.[9] Moral considerations seem to favor the first alternative; speculative logic the second. But that in either case it is finally what in our best moments we would wish it to be was taken to be proved. The facts of history more or less embody this great truth but, being only facts, they cannot possibly refute it. Time marched on, even then, but the Universe stood firm and the "heart" of it was friendly to the best in man.

III

How was this philosophy to be critically examined? Within its all-embracing benevolence there seemed *prima facie* to be room for all the growing forces of the time, if only each would acknowledge its own finitude and incompleteness and pay homage to the endless "more" in experience that lay outside its scope and to the final "all" for which the idealist philosopher was the authoritative spokesman. Inside this "all" there was no standpoint for criticism that did not show itself "in the end" to be a one-sided aspect of the very truth the critic sought to limit or deny. There were, however, ideas and interests outside it, but within the growing forces of the time, which found no adequate expression in its terms. From the standpoint of these interests its answers to the urgent problem for the philosophy of the period appeared at once empty and evasive.

The trouble lay, of course, in the tremendous gap between the ultimate truth of the idealist's "last analysis" and truth as we need it here and now in the process in which as finite individuals we must somehow solve our human problems. In Speculative Idealism the ultimate fulfilment of our best ideals is guaranteed, but only as they are transmuted in an absolute maximum of "Reality" transcending space and time. This is comforting, in a general way, but hardly clear. For when we try seriously to use this idealized Reality as a standard to determine which *are* our best ideals and in what way we can reasonably rely upon them now as guides for thought and conduct we get a dubious reply. The cogency we expect from them in intelligent action turns out to be quite different from the authority imputed to them as representative of Absolute Reality in its time-transcending truth. Scientific inquiry is no doubt a "mere abstraction" in comparison to this total Truth, but it supplies the most trustworthy information we can get about the order of events to which we must adjust our plans and hopes. The national state, again, as an instrument of community in existing society has much to be said for, and something to be said against, its present claims. But the state or any other human society, as the special deputy of God or Reason or the Absolute, is a candidate for a kind of reverence that its mundane performances by no means warrant. If we are genuinely to understand our human situation and reliably to distinguish truth from falsity within it, we must, like Hamlet, have grounds more relative than this.

The philosophers who took this critical position were called, and in the early days were glad to call themselves, pragmatists. William James and John Dewey were their leaders, the most influential and, in general recognition, the most "American" philosophers our civilization has produced. Their way of thinking has had its fullest empirical application in the writings of George Herbert Mead. It borrowed its guiding maxim and some of its deepest insights from the philosophy of C. S. Peirce. Its influence on American thought and practice has been broad and deep.

These men were quite as deeply concerned to understand the nature and function of human ideals as were the idealists. The difference was that they proposed to understand them in their human use and context, as arising out of the conflicts and problems of unideal experience and leading on to conduct that can confirm or correct the confidence that has been placed in them. The meaning that our ideas can be shown to have in this unfolding process is what they *really* mean; it is their primary, ultimate, and cognitively decisive meaning. The "pragmatic maxim" [10] is no mere logical or linguistic rule. It defines a philosophical position and thus sets up a standard for thought and conduct to which clear-headed and forward-looking thinkers are invited to repair. When you know the sort of conduct to which the acceptance of an idea would commit you and the empirical condition, in which expectations based upon it could, directly or indirectly, be confuted or confirmed, you have understood its intellectual import. Nothing more is needed; nothing less will suffice.

No formula can give an adequate notion of the generous enthusiams expressed in this philosophy or of the freshness and variety of its insights. For William James, the beginning and end of wisdom was to be sought in the vital connection of ideas with direct, personal, intimately lived experience. This connection must be active and dynamic, since the human individual is essentially, not merely incidentally, alive. It ought to be as wide-ranging and discerning as the free expansion of his spiritual capacities can make it. Experience in its concrete reality answers to man in the full exercise of his creative powers. Ideas may be the means by which we further this expansive process, opening our minds to new possibilities and bringing ever wider areas of life within the range of meaningful experience. Ideas may also be used, however, not as guides to experience and action but as fixed, external standards to which they must conform — as stereotypes that confine our appreciative capacities within preconceived and arbitrary limits and cut us off from the wider world beyond. This restrictive use was what James called "vicious intellectualism." [11] He was against it whenever he encountered it and for the right to self-determination of the cognitively underprivileged varieties of experience that stood outside the scope of its official sanction.

His answers to the philosophical problems of the time were the direct expressions of this guiding interest. The progress of scientific inquiry was to be welcomed wherever it brought ideas into closer contact with empirical matters of fact. "The mind" was by no means exempt from such inquiry. James's *Principles of Psychology* was a major contribution to it, bringing the findings of Darwinian biology and of direct and penetrating observation to bear on traditional ideas of "thought," "will," "emotion," and "experience" in a wonderfully illuminating way. Nothing in this dismal subject looked the same when he was through with it; old problems were seen in a fresh and richer context; new possibilities opened up ahead.[12] But scientific inquiry is only one human interest and the facts that lend themselves to formulation in its terms no more than a selection from the varieties of experience with which a truly radical empiricism must deal. And where the demand for objectivity inhibits needed faith or cuts us off from saving experiences it becomes a kind of vicious intellectualism on its own account. There James, quite consistently, was against it and for the rights of a believing attitude which, if acted on and tested in a full experience, would fortify men's spirits and enrich their lives.[13] The worth of ideas is a function of their fruitfulness in experience and for conduct and it is by their fruits that they are reasonably to be judged.

But who's to judge? The critics scented here a dangerous relativism that might dissolve all rational standards in the arbitrariness

of uncriticized subjective satisfactions. James's answer was an individualism as traditional as his pragmatism was iconoclastic. Each
individual must judge for himself and on the basis of his own experience and needs. It is assumed throughout that this will be a
responsible, self-reliant individual with a will not only to believe
but to respect the beliefs of others, to learn from experience and to
achieve his "vital" satisfaction at a level of self-respect of which a
free-born American could substantially approve. This distinctively
moral individualism is not much argued by James. It is presupposed
in his theory and exemplified in his practice. All that is needed to
justify the assumption is a world of individuals as genial and generous as William James.

The world that best meets the spiritual needs of such an individual
is an open, risky world in which his own decisive action can make
a difference for good. There are superhuman forces at work in it
for righteousness, but not so vast or all-embracing as to make man's
contribution insignificant or to settle in advance what it shall be.
There is chance in it, but chance means here primarily *a* chance, an
opportunity to get great things accomplished. His business is to
make the most of it, and of himself in the process. It was their use
in this "business" that James had in mind when he wrote of the
"cash value" of ideas.

James's pragmatism was essentially a personal attitude toward
life. In that lay both its unique value and its philosophical limitations. Little is lost and much in freshness of insight is gained by
defining truth in terms of individual satisfaction so long as the
individual to be satisfied is William James. But in the civilization
to which his philosophy was addressed such individuality could not
be taken for granted; it was, on the contrary, becoming increasingly
a problem. For the standards traditionally presupposed as the basis
for individual judgment were also the standards from whose authority, in their traditional form at least, the individual was now being
progressively emancipated. And so far no new standards had been
reliably established. In James himself moral idealism was so deeply
rooted that he could maintain as a subjective attitude and affirma-
tion the values that the current trend of thought and experience,
and his own anti-intellectualism as a part of it, rendered objectively

insecure and even delight in the insecurity as a challenge to a more adventurous faith. The resulting philosophy was a triumph of character and courage but hardly a widely applicable solution of the pressing problems of men.

John Dewey's philosophy was designed to offer such a solution. Where James's delight had been to open up new possibilities, Dewey's systematic concern was to pin them down to the context of scientific inquiry, shared experience, and social action. The modern mind, now liberated from old preconceptions, was to be put to work in the solution of urgent social problems. It must learn to behave itself accordingly. The transition in Dewey's thought from an early speculative idealism to the instrumentalism of his mature years is summed up in his doctrine that thinking comes out of something and is for the sake of something, and must be understood in this contextual involvement.[14] Its setting is the bio-social situation in which the human organism in its on-going activity is faced with problems that only intelligence can solve. Its proper method is experimental, critical, coöperative — the procedure exemplified in scientific inquiry. Ends as well as means are examinable in this process, for an end intelligently pursued is an end-in-view, a guide to operational procedures designed to meet the demands of the developing situation and to liberate individual capacities in meaningfully shared activity. Human intelligence, working experimentally within this context, is scientific in its method, progressive in its achievement, democratic in its aims. Within the sweep of its forward movement in an evolving natural world lies all that, as men or as philosophers, we know or need to know.

By abandoning the outmoded "problems of philosophers," Dewey held, we gain new resources for solving the urgent problems of our civilization.[15] The apparent conflict between advancing science and traditional ideals is eliminated when we understand that science as reliable knowledge is the only sound basis that we have for action that can give practical effect to our ideals, and that these ideals, as ends-in-view, need just the critical enlightenment that empirical knowledge of the conditions and consequences of their application can supply. "Individualism" is a case in point. Our preconceptions concerning "liberty" and "the individual" have lagged dangerously behind the forces and demands of social change. Hence we have for the most part failed to see that in an industrialized society the liberation of individual capacity as an end demands the use of organized social effort as a means, and that the attainment of effective individuality is a community project, not a merely personal performance and prerogative.[16] On the level of traditional abstractions, social planning and control are the antithesis of individual liberty. On the level of social engineering and democratic reform they are the necessary means to a genuinely liberated individuality. To shift the debate from the first level to the second is to bring our political ideals into operational connection with applied intelligence in social action, a connection from which both can profit. From that point on, our problems are empirical and practical. But it required an empirical and practical philosophy to bring the essential issues to a proper focus in this perspective. This shift in perspective was Dewey's contribution to the problems and issues of our civilization.

A characteristic instance of applied instrumentalism is Mead's account of the way in which, by "taking the role of the other" in linguistic behavior, the human organism *becomes* a self and the moral community a social achievement. Where Royce had anchored the "hope of the Great Community" in an Absolute Mind, Mead undertook to link it to an evolutionary process in which the "conversation of gestures" of a dog fight and the games of children are stages on the road to more widely effective methods of communication.[17] International-mindedness is a further stage, not yet attained but progressively attainable as the techniques of such communication are more adequately understood and put to wider social use. The ideal is much the same for the two philosophers but the contrast in methods used for its authentication is a sufficient indication of the shift in intellectual orientation for which the instrumentalist philosophy had come to stand. As time went on, it was Mead's method, not Royce's, that commended itself as usable and enlightening to "forward-looking" social inquirers.

To place Peirce's philosophy in this context is to some degree to misplace it, for in many of its larger aspects it does not belong here. In this respect Peirce's ideas are like their author, they do not really fit anywhere in the culture of the period, though they make connection with it from a variety of angles. The work of an original, eccentric, and endlessly inquiring mind, his philosophy was given to the world in fragments, and not even the prodigious multiplication of these fragments in the posthumous *Collected Papers* [18] has served as yet to make its total import clear. But its major influence on contemporary thought came through the use that James and Dewey and their followers made of it, and both its resemblance to and differences from their doctrines are illuminating.

The language and logic of Peirce's essay "How to Make Our Ideas Clear" [19] set a pattern for pragmatic thinking. Controlled or logical thinking occurs in a process aiming at the resolution of doubt, the fixation of belief. Belief is a habit of response to stimuli presented or presentable in "sensible experience." To make our ideas *logically* clear, then, we must consider the habits of response to which their acceptance would commit us and the eventualities in experience to which such response would be appropriate. Our idea of an object, thus clarified, simply is our idea of its conceivable sensible effects in their conceivable "practical" bearing on such habits. Coupled with Peirce's praise of scientific method as a self-correcting process, his respect for the laboratory habit of mind, and his repeated injunction against blocking the path of inquiry by "final" explanations that do not explain, this theory seemed to offer an account of the relation of logic to behavior which hardheaded empiricists could happily embrace.

In Peirce's own philosophy, however, all the key terms in this theory have a larger and more speculative import. The conceivable sensible effects which constitute the meaning of a concept are of a general nature. Not all of them could even conceivably be exemplified in the actual sequence of events. A habit, too, is something general, a conditional resolution to act whose significance is inexhaustible in actual behavior. Where Mead says that a "so-called" universal is just a habit of response, Peirce holds that a *habit* of response is a universal, with a distinct mode of being and efficacy of its own — the efficacy of general ideas in shaping actual occurrences to rational ends. Such "concrete reasonableness" is the work of thought objectified in the evolutionary processes of a world becoming orderly and continuous through the spread of general ideas.

The development of reason is man's proper final aim and "The creation of the universe, which did not take place during a certain busy week in the year 4004 B.C., but is going on to-day and never will be done, is this very development of Reason." [20]

This emphasis on reason as an objective and irreducible factor in evolution seemed old-fashioned to the pragmatists, who had emancipated themselves from such romantic notions, and merely speculative to the analysts who were glad to make use of Peirce's more technical contributions to logic and the theory of signs. Hence the work for which he is best known has gained currency in a form in which it is divorced from his own interpretation of it. This sometimes leads to confusions for which Peirce himself was hardly to blame. In his philosophy, logic, and the use of signs are exemplifications of "concrete reasonableness" and what he has to say about them does not make adequate sense without the larger meaning thus put into it. For better or worse his thought belongs to the rationalistic tradition in which natural evolution is not just a sequence of events but a forward movement toward ideal ends. In making the growth of *reason* man's final aim he puts his faith in that factor in human behavior which can grow in such a way that growth will also be a progress, because it is a process that justifies itself as it proceeds. It may be that a later generation will find the elements in Peirce's thought which his own time could not use the most usable and significant of all. In any case, we have not heard the last of Peirce. For a long time to come we shall be learning from him, and profiting anew from the inexhaustible fertility of his ideas.

IV

Judged by its own standards, the pragmatic philosophy has been a very considerable success. Commager's account of its influence, in *The American Mind*, is hardly an exaggeration. "Practical, democratic, individualistic, opportunistic, spontaneous, hopeful, pragmatism was wonderfully adapted to the temperament of the average American. . . . No wonder that, despite the broadsides of more formidable philosophers, pragmatism caught on until it became almost the official philosophy of America." [21] In *The Amer-*

ican Spirit Charles and Mary Beard do not hesitate to refer to it, without qualification as "the American philosophy." [22] Philip Wiener, more moderately, describes it as the form in which "American liberalism came to philosophic maturity." [23] Certainly it set the tone and pattern for such liberal thinking for a generation, and found its applications in every field from the "child centered" school to the dissenting opinions of Mr. Justice Holmes in the Supreme Court. It has determined the shape in which American liberalism has come down to us and has fashioned the intellectual tools which are still its primary instruments for solving present problems.

Yet when we turn from cultural reminiscence to contemporary fact we face a puzzling situation. What we should expect, in terms of the progressive prospectus, is creative intelligence in the vanguard of the still advancing forces of science, democracy, and social welfare. What we find is rather a liberal ideology on the defensive, radically unsure of its position and of what it has to offer that is worth defending. In the current battle of ideologies its weapons are tired words of questionable meaning and ideas that seem largely to have lost their cogency as instruments of rational discrimination. The trends and on-going forces of the time have turned against it, while it was in trends and on-going forces that it had come increasingly to place its faith. It still has a real hold on our affections, but rather as a survival from a happy past than as the spokesman for the forces in the present that can shape the future to the pattern of our hopes.

What happened to this American philosophy in the period between the wars? The answer to this question will tell us something, I think, about our philosophy and our civilization in their reciprocal relations. Nor is there much doubt any longer as to what that answer must be. The philosophy fell apart under the pressure of forces which its central ideas were incompetent to understand or to direct to "liberal" ends. Its "coöperative intelligence," an unstable combination of social gospel and scientific method, lost its moral bearings as "advancing social science" grew increasingly specialized, technical and noncommittal as to values. Its progressive faith in "on-going forces" turned in the direction of disillusionment as the course of events was found to be on the whole unfriendly to its antecedent hopes. And its liberal preconceptions, unsupported by engineering techniques and evolutionary tends, either survived, as in Dewey, as a noble nineteenth-century attitude or dissolved into expediency, accommodation, and a tolerance based less on principle than on the lack of it.

Each step in this process is identifiable and understandable. The reduction of practical reason to instrumental intelligence in the interest of liberal enlightenment presupposed a moral standpoint which its critical methods served rather to undermine than to sustain. In the interest of scientific objectivity we were asked to free our minds of moral preconceptions and learn from scientifically verifiable facts.[24] Yet it was confidently expected that these facts would teach a liberal lesson to emancipated minds, discrediting selfish, authoritarian, and reactionary ideas and pointing an evolutionary way ahead to general welfare and common good. Hence the paradoxical phenomenon of the amoral moralist, "the scholarly product of a progressive age bent on raking muck and fulfilling the promise of American life."[25] But muck can point a moral only for a mind for which that moral has a point, and only trends that have already been idealized carry with them an imperative to fulfill ideals. The promise of American life was more than a portent of big days ahead; it was a faith to be kept and justified in the keeping. The paradox of the amoral moralist as progressive reformer was that he was obliged by his critical method to state as empirical hypotheses ideas which must be understood as moral reasons by those to whom they were addressed to make the "liberal" sense required of them.

So long as the liberal's own preconceptions were not seriously challenged and the trends remained propitious this procedure worked. The role of reason could be limited to its problem-solving function inside the process which progressive tendencies and democratic aims defined. Within these limits there were no "real" problems not thus soluble, for those that did not arise and find their answer in this process were, by stipulation, unreal. We do not solve such unreal problems, Dewey said, but since Darwin we get over them.[26] And this too, for the modern mind, is evidence of progress.

But in American civilization such problems did arise, and with growing urgency, as trends and ideals seemed patently to fall apart and liberal preconceptions became, in consequence, increasingly problematic. The First World War raised such a problem for the progressives. On-going forces took us into it and instrumental intelligence helped greatly to carry it through to a victorious conclusion. But the attempt to idealize our share in it as a step forward in democracy was less successful. It had its consequences in the 1920's in a growing skepticism among the critically minded about both the democratic tendency of on-going forces and the empirical relevance of democratic ideals. Progress had materialized as prosperity in a business-centered civilization which high-minded liberals were unwilling to recognize as an adequate fulfillment of the promise of American life. Most ominous of all, from a liberal standpoint, was the growing gap between critical intelligence and popular ideals. The people, it appeared, were on the whole well satisfied with new material comforts which advancing science wonderfully helped to multiply and with outmoded ideas on which enlightened criticism made little serious impression. The reformers had labored to return the government from "the interests" to "the people" and the people had used it to enact prohibition and elect Harding. The people, then, as Mencken had frequently observed, were boobs, and the cure for democracy not more democracy but less, or none at all. Since people did not know what was good for them, salvation must be looked for from the experts — managers, technicians, social planners, engineers — who could decide "objectively" the requirements of the social system and would not be impeded by conventional scruples in their realistic determination to get things done. Thus spake the intellectuals, the "free minds" of the time, and Veblen was their prophet. But their ideology was no longer, in the old sense, that of freedom.

What, in this situation, was the enlightened liberal to do? Should he lend his critical intelligence to the support of on-going processes that were no longer moving in a liberal direction, to the "implementation" of such "technological imperatives" or the acceleration of such historical inevitabilities as the experts could discern in the moving forces of the time? That way led to technocracy, to Marxism and the class struggle, to the managerial revolution and all the other fashionable "isms" of a trend philosophy that had lost its morals. Or should he stand by his liberal principles *on principle* and as moral reasons? Mr. Dewey and his major disciples have taken the latter course. Their stand is a credit to their moral ideals but less convincing as an application of their instrumental logic. The comment of a recent philosophical historian of this phase of liberal thought on the value of their achievement is just and, in a way, ironical. "Above all, they communicated a respect for freedom and social responsibility which has all but disappeared from the earth. For all their fuzziness and their lack of logic they have been a force for the good in American intellectual life." [27]

Outside the ranks of the pragmatic faithful, the disintegration of progressive ideals was rapid. Critical intelligence, emancipated from old ideals and disillusioned about advancing trends, was left incongruously stranded in an alien world. "Critical realism" was Parrington's name for it, a realism that could lay bare the economic interests of the framers of the Constitution and a criticism with enough residual idealism behind it to regard this discovery as somehow an exposé.[28] But the criticism lacked a standard and a standpoint. In a world observed objectively and without illusions what else but economic determinism was to be expected and in such a world, why criticize? Is not indiscriminate acceptance a more "realistic" and really tolerant response? Theodore Dreiser was one of Parrington's latter-day liberals and appropriately so, for in Dreiser's lumbering volumes the mindlessness of a world apprehended without ideals found its suitable reflection in a mind that seemed to operate with a minimum of coherence or discrimination. Houston Peterson, in praising Conrad Aiken as "perhaps the characteristic poet of this confused, unphilosophic era" went even further. Aiken's, he tells us, is "the melody of chaos," his poetry a portrayal of mental disintegration and emotional helplessness in a senseless world. And Peterson comments: "Is this not a picture of our world, looked at as nearly as possible without dogmas of hope or assumptions of order? Is it not a picture of human life as nearly free as possible of moral presuppositions?" It is "the disillusioned acknowledgment of things as they appear to be at their honest worst. A greeting of chaos with gusto." [29]

For those who were too fastidious to greet chaos with gusto, but were still resolved to face the honest worst, there were, however, more discriminating alternatives. Henry Adams had been disillusioned ahead of time and the *Education*, coming into general currency as the First World War ended, seemed to speak for many sensitive minds. Adams was skeptical of the ideals embodied in his "education" because they had not fitted him for success in the modern world, and dissatisfied with the modern world because it did not conform to those ideals. His search for law in history led him eventually to the Virgin of Chartres and the dynamo as "symbols of ultimate energy." He was fascinated by both but could come to terms with neither, for he was trying to understand the Virgin as a generator of force and the dynamo as an object of worship.[30] The resulting critical disorientation of a thinker at home in neither past nor present was widely welcomed as a presage of a future in which the accelerating complexity of our civilization would still further baffle and defeat the mind of modern man.

But it was in Santayana's *Realms of Being*[31] that free minds that had lost their faith in ideals found their most impressive spiritual home. Mr. Santayana was certainly no liberal and his disillusionment with modern trends was of long standing. Since 1914 he had been as distant physically from the American continent as he had always been in spirit, and his more recent philosophical excursions into the realm of essence seemed to remove him even further from the main currents of contemporary thought. By the 1920's, however, this remoteness had come to stand in many minds for critical emancipation, and disillusionment with the modern was the latest and most fashionable substitute for wisdom. To such minds Santayana's nobly phrased philosophy was peculiarly persuasive. It offered a standpoint from which the disenchanted and hence "free" spirit could with dignity surrender the "realm of matter" to the arbitrary power and animal faith that would in any case control it and, with a respectful side glance at the unattainable immensities of the realm of truth, proceed to find its proper satisfaction in the intuition of timeless essences. The spiritual victory thus achieved was indefeasible but attenuated. For essences are the sheer aesthetic surface of experience, accepted without interpretation or belief and enjoyed in consequence without any sort of intellectual risk or moral commitment. The detachment of the free mind from the cause of freedom and of the vocabulary of critical enlightenment from the use of practical reason here reaches its appropriate conclusion.

V

Meanwhile the main work of philosophical inquiry was going forward along related but, in method and intention at least, professionally independent lines. Throughout the 1920's the initiative in its major fields of inquiry, from logic and epistemology to value theory and metaphysics, was held by realists of one school or another. The schools were many, and frequently in conflict with each other. But a common pattern in their philosophic faith and practice was still discernible. They proposed to base their thinking on knowledge of the real world as it exists in its own right and independently of men's ideas, wishes, or imaginings about it. Their chief opponents, therefore, were those idealists and pragmatists who had reduced knowledge to a mere construction of thought, whether Absolute or instrumental, and cut the "real" world to the measure of their practical concerns. As against all this and, as they believed, in harmony with the best scientific thinking of the time, the realists set out to show that genuine knowledge is a discovery of things not merely as they are thought to be but as they exist or subsist in their own right apart from any thought about them. In such knowledge, certified by the proper logical and fact-finding methods, we reach things as they are. Our mere opinions, plans, and wishes can then be based on what, as thus confronted, they are found to be.

The philosophical defense of realism was obviously a considerable undertaking. The whole epistemological tradition since Descartes, and more particularly since Kant, was dead against it. But the realists were confident, competent, clearheaded men not to be intimidated by philosophical tradition. They found their models for sound thinking rather in biology, physics, and, above all, in the great new merger of logic and pure mathematics achieved in the *Principia Mathematica* of Whitehead and Russell,[32] and they proposed to reform the methods of philosophy to meet the professionally high standards which these expert inquiries had attained. They thought of scientific method not as a social gospel for which philosophy was to be the propagandist but rather as a rigorous discipline to which its own procedures must conform and in which its conclusions must be tested if they were to rank as knowledge. Since such inquiries require professional skill and training and have usually a technical language of their own it is not to be expected that philosophy, thus pursued, will be everybody's business. Fortunately, however, the major graduate schools were now prepared to give such training and their products would, in turn, be the teachers of philosophy of tomorrow. And so, for the most part, they have become.

The methods of the realists were professional, specialized and, to the layman, esoteric. But since the work in which they were employed was not that of the specialized sciences but of philosophy, or science *as* philosophy, these methods took on in this use a new authority and scope. The analysis of knowing offered in epistemology was meant to be an ultimate analysis, to bring us to the foundations on which all valid knowledge must be built. The logical method used principles of the highest generality and what could not be said in the language it prescribed could not significantly be said at all. And the reality to which such inquiry led was *ultimate* reality, the final referent and measure of all that "in the end" is real. Thus the end products of this refined and specialized analysis were also the entities on which philosophic wisdom must rely in its efforts to reach a comprehensive understanding of the world and to order human beliefs and ideals to the realities that alone, in the last analysis, can sustain them. As the enterprise developed, this larger philosophic aim was frequently lost sight of or denied. But it is only in its terms that either the pretensions or the procedures of much of the philosophy of the period can be justly understood.

Rarely have more distinguished talents been devoted to philosophical inquiry than in the movement thus initiated. The speculative genius of Whitehead, the critical acumen of Lovejoy, the analytic skill of a whole group of logicians, were outstanding, and the average of careful, thorough work was high. Clarity, accuracy, and intellectual honesty are considerable merits in philosophy and these the realists had in good measure. That they can be put to clarifying use in legal and political philosophy the work of Morris R. Cohen bears witness.[33] And in symbolic logic, where philosophers and mathematicians worked together at the upper limits of abstraction, progress was so rapid that only the experts could keep up with it. Here the method admirably fitted the subject matter and clarity and precision were their own excuse for being.

In other fields of philosophic interest, however, the achievement has been less impressive. Instead of the piecemeal, cumulative advance that had been hoped for, there has been a series of competing schools and "isms," each with its own logical apparatus for exposing old fallacies and its own peculiar method of arriving at new but somehow final truth. Each has had original and striking things to say and each, in the process of saying them, has found itself engaged in endless controversy with the opposed finalities of competing sects. And each, in turn, has been superseded by still newer "isms" offering truths equally one-sided, controversial and, as philosophical ultimates, insecure. The debate between the new and the critical realists, and that between the defenders of "critical" and "speculative" philosophy are perhaps the most important episodes in a continuing civil war and will serve as examples.

Obviously a crucial issue for any realistic theory is its claim that we can and do have knowledge of an independently real world, usually identified as the physical world of public, spatio-temporal objects and events. To justify this claim it must be shown that known objects are genuinely independent and that we are able genuinely to know them. The American neorealists, inspired by the analytical achievements of G. E. Moore and Bertrand Russell, were intent on vindicating the directness and immediacy of the cognitive relation and, as realists, were therefore obliged to hold that the entities thus directly known are themselves "real" objects, "true parts of the physical world." [34] The trouble is that they do not seem to be. Bent sticks, pink elephants, and elliptical pennies are all indubitable data of experience but the task of finding a home for them in the public order of spatio-temporal events is arduous and its outcome paradoxical. Hence more cautious or, as they called themselves, "critical" realists banded together to insist that such data could not be the independently real objects at which realistic knowledge aims.[35] On the contrary, the datum of perceptual knowledge is one thing, its intended object another, and never the twain shall meet. Hence "epistemological dualism" as against the monistic identification of datum and object by the neorealists. But if the proper object of knowledge can *never* be presented in experience, in what sense can we really know it? In defending the transcendent reality of the object of knowledge, the critical realist cast grave doubt on its knowability. He had elaborate ways of dealing with this problem. "Representative ideas" were revived, and essences invoked to bridge the epistemological chasm which Santayana crossed more directly by a "leap of animal faith." While the dualist is thus in an embarrassing position the monist is no better off, as Lovejoy's brilliant *Revolt Against Dualism* [36] pointed out at length.

As the argument went on and subtleties multiplied on both sides, it began to lose its original point. New realism, in attempting to undo the "bifurcation of nature" and project the "perspectives" of sensory experience into the real world, seemed to compromise the stern, nonmental independence of that world and, in Whitehead's theory of prehensions, for example, to be closer to speculative idealism than to its realistic starting point. The critical realist leaned heavily on pragmatic postulates and "faith" to compensate for the inherent dubiety of a cognitive relation whose object lies essentially beyond experience.[37] When new realism ceased to be realistic and critical realism to be critical (except of its opponents) the debate began to peter out and philosophical attention shifted elsewhere.

At this point logic took over from epistemology as the basic discipline of philosophical criticism and the clarity of concepts rather than objectivity of data became the proper subject for analytic searchings of the heart. At first sight the subject seems a special and restricted one. But if its skilled analysis really is the *last* analysis for which philosophers have been searching, its authority will be great and final. For, as Wittgenstein's *Tractatus Logico-Philosophicus*,[38] the new gospel of the philosophical logicians, declared, "whatever can be said at all, can be said clearly." As the final judge and guardian of clarity, it is for logical analysis to discern the rules of language and, in their terms, to distinguish significant discourse from nonsense and what can be said from the unutterable, whereof one must be silent.

What then can meaningfully be said? The answer is, of course, from the standpoint of a purely formal or syntactical analysis, anything you please so long as you obey the rules. What rules? The rules of "language," to be sure. What language? That question the critical philosopher as logical analyst was hardly in a position to answer. The really decisive fact about a strictly formal logic, for philosophical purposes, is that it really is formal and analytic and can determine nothing as to the concrete content of the world or the truth or falsity of statements made about it. When the logicians had clearly reaffirmed this insight, as in C. I. Lewis' *Mind and the World Order*,[39] for example, they were left in a peculiar philosophical position. For they had retreated, in the interests of logical purity, to a critical standpoint too tenuous to supply a reason for any particular "language" which, for critical purposes, they wished to impose upon philosophers. The initial preference, among those chiefly influenced by Bertrand Russell, was for a language that referred exclusively to sense-data and logical relations, and to atomic facts composed of these. But this preference clearly borrowed its plausibility from the epistemological enthusiasms of new realism and was soon outmoded. Next, with logical positivism or logical empiricism, came the language of science as canonical, with some sort of verification principle which no one could precisely state as its criterion for factual significance and all forms of nonempirical (and hence nonverifiable) metaphysics as the enemy to be demolished. Whatever in philosophy could not be reduced to logic or expressed in the language of empirical science was (in this language) unsayable. So much was clear, at least, and it had the look of an important philosophical discovery.

Many of the analyses of the logic of the language of science that have come out of the inquiry thus initiated have been illuminating.[40] Particularly useful work has been done on the logic of induction. But the wider philosophical pretensions of logical positivism were logically adventitious. Its restriction of factually significant discourse to the rules of scientific inquiry was quite arbitrary from the standpoint of a strictly formal logic and its exclusive devotion to the scientific language a product less of its own hard thinking than of the professional climate of opinion of the time. Science still was marching on, especially in the graduate schools of important universities, and toughminded thinkers who had cleared their minds of "wishful thinking" naturally wanted to march with it. Why and to what end they were marching were questions that they did not need to answer because, in their own enlightened language, such questions could not significantly arise.

Then there were those who chose to follow G. E. Moore in his respect for ordinary language and its common-sense usage and to criticize philosophical statements accordingly.[41] Where philosophical puzzles had arisen out of confusions about such ordinary usage this was a clarifying procedure, but in other cases not. And, finally, as the subject broadened, more serious attention was paid to emotive meaning and to types of symbolism which could not plausibly be understood as attempts at scientific communication.[42] Even the curious locutions of the traditional philosophers, if, strictly speaking, "nonsense" might be "important nonsense," and as such entitled to careful linguistic consideration.

By this time the analysts had come a long way from the realism of the 1920's and most of them, if they had thought about the matter, would have disclaimed all connection with it. Nonetheless the pertinence of their analytical activity to philosophy grew directly out of the preconceptions of that doctrine and made little sense without them. The analysts were still the final arbiters of "language" and what could not be said clearly in their terms was ultimately without rational warrant or foundation. This was made explicit in such a work as Charles Stevenson's widely influential *Ethics and Language*.[43] Offered as an essay in linguistic or methodological clarification, this analysis identified the normative significance of such ethical predicates as good and right with their causal efficacy in influencing attitudes, and placed moral reasoning in the same general category of emotively charged discourse as advertising and propaganda. The laudable aim of such analysis was to eliminate the "occult" and the "esoteric" and to advance the cause of logical clarity and enlightenment. Its effect was to strip even "enlightenment" of its distinctive moral meaning and leave it only an emotive aura of dubious persuasive power for those who understood how drastically, for the really enlightened, its claim to rational validity had been undermined. The procedure thus reflected, with an unintended clarity, the anomalous position of critical intelligence in a community that asked for wisdom and was offered by the philosopher only a language which, in analytical elucidation, had lost its validity as moral reason.

The reaffirmation of the constructive function of philosophic reason was at this point a primary necessity and we may well be grateful to the speculative thinkers who made it and, most of all, to Whitehead. In his *Science and the Modern World* [44] and *Adventures of Ideas* [45] this critically battered subject seems to be on its feet again and about its proper business, treating of great subjects in a manner appropriately comprehensive and profound. Even those who cannot follow the intricacies of Whitehead's metaphysics are likely to be impressed by the imaginative scope of its elaboration and heartened by the generous observations on education, aesthetics, and liberal religion to which it leads. In this philosophy the modern mind seems at last to be freed from the constricting limitations of currently dominant abstractions. We see further and appreciate more with the ideas that Whitehead supplies us than we did before. This is what we expect of a philosophy and here, as almost nowhere else in recent thought, we find it.

This, however, is but half the story. In Whitehead's philosophy these genial insights are linked inextricably with a speculative hypothesis about the nature of the actual entities which are the finally real things of which the world is made and they derive their philosophical authority from this connection.[46] This hypothesis is a solution to the problem set by realistic metaphysics — to find or to construct a set of entities such that everything that is truly predicable of anything at all shall be referable to these final acutalities in some aspect or dimension of their being. Since *their* reality is "in the end," the source of all the reality there is, the metaphysician must get into them, as Noah took into the Ark, everything that is necessary to populate a world and he must get out of them all this, and a standard of human values too. Whitehead holds that actual entities thus constituted are the final reasons. Our knowledge of them is then at once the end product of an extremely intricate speculative inquiry and the beginning of wisdom.

More specifically, the speculative requirements for final actuality are existential generality, aesthetic immediacy or "concreteness" and normative finality. This is a large order and there is dazzling brilliance in the way that Whitehead proceeds to fill it. The most general concepts of recent physics are generalized to meet the even larger specifications of a world of organic processes in which mind as well as matter is to have its place. The abstractness of the sciences is corrected by filling in this schema with the content of immediate experience, so that the events described externally by the laws of physics are discovered, in their intrinsic nature, to have feelings and pursue ideals. The primordial locus of such ideals is a God whose decision among values is at once the ultimate irrationality, the final standard for human valuations and a persuasive influence for harmony and beauty in an essentially creative world.

The cultural dividend of this imposing theory is speculative information about ultimate "actual entities" presented as a measure and justification of the ideals of civilized life. Reality is process, so the conservative is working against the nature of things and the liberal, in the long run, on its side. Everything that exists has feelings and so "the basis of democracy is the common fact of value-experience as constituting the essential nature of each pulsation of actuality." [47] Aesthetic immediacy is existentially ubiquitous, as the romantic poets felt, and we should give a larger place in our society to the appreciation of beauty.

There is much to be said for and against this theory as a metaphysical construction and in due course the Ph.D. candidates in our universities will say it. We are here concerned with it as a sound basis for a wisdom that can justify itself in common understanding. For this purpose it remains, in Whitehead's philosophy, both precarious and obscure. If the case for human reason really does rest ultimately on actual entities as thus discerned we must conclude that its foundations are "speculative" indeed. The concepts borrowed from the sciences become more rather than less abstract when generalized in this sweeping fashion. Aesthetic experience, for all its concrete value in human life, seems, as a source of ontological information, to tell us more about the feelings of human subjects, than about the value-experiences of remote events in physical space-time. And the values that the whole procedure serves to vindicate are questionably related to the "reality" described. For Whitehead, they are chiefly those which Victorian liberalism, romantic poetry, and a generous mind had taught him to honor from his youth up. A later historian of ideas may well observe that the chief contribution of this philosophy to the culture of its time was the fact that it enabled its author to express some elements of nineteenth-century sanity in a form so technically sophisticated that a post-Einsteinian generation was not ashamed to acknowledge them as wisdom.

In recent years the return to metaphysics in American philosophy has become a major "movement," with a newly established *Review of Metaphysics* as its spokesman. In leading graduate schools the positivistic scruples of the 1930's have been swept aside and elaborately articulated systems of ultimate Reality are once more the accredited subject matter of professional discussion. Since the systems thus produced are as diverse in content as they are alike in their claim to present the final truth about the world, there is every reason to expect that these discussions will be prolonged and arduous. There will, no doubt, be much to learn from them. But the basic problem set by the development of Whitehead's philosophy remains unsolved. A "reality" that can meet the peculiar requirements of combined ontological, epistemological, and axiological primacy is one thing. A reality that will provide a trustworthy basis for judgment in the criticism of ideals in coöperative human understanding is another. It is on the assumption of their ultimate coincidence that the claim of speculative generalization to provide the final reasons for our thought and conduct rests. As the language of such speculation grows more esoteric and its pronouncements more oracular, the problematic nature of this claim is increasingly apparent. If this is the best that philosophic reason can do for us, it is not surprising that practical men have turned to the irrational for more usable answers to their deepest questions.

VI

Here, once more, though hardly by intention, the doctrines of the schools made contact with the popular philosophizing of the time. In the past two decades irrationalism in practice has become a dominant intellectual force in our society and increasingly it has devised the tools to rationalize and justify its procedures. We reach the limits of reason in theory when we come upon a "final" truth that falls outside the scope of rational inquiry but whose acceptance is nonetheless essential to the ordering and direction of our thought. The irrational in practice is the arbitrary, the ultimate commitment or command which must be accepted in unquestioning submission before any reason can be asked for or supplied. We face it whenever the ideals that serve as customary reasons in the criticism of conduct and mediation of social conflicts are challenged in fact, while *de jure* they remain our final reasons for which no further reason can be given. Their defense as final truth then appears essential to the preservation of group morale, and it would seem to be the business of philosophy, which deals professionally in final truth, to supply it.

In American civilization this point was reached in practical urgency in the early 1930's. The liberal preconceptions of progress and prosperity had been questioned by the intellectuals for a generation; with the coming of depression they were exposed as deeply questionable to the common man as well. In Europe democracy was superseded in country after country by one form or another of totalitarian state and the escape from freedom assumed the proportions of a mass movement. And America was finding out, reluctantly but unmistakably, that it could not isolate itself economically, politically, or ideologically from these subversive forces. In terms of effective social pressures we were confronted with a new and alien world, and must somehow come to terms with it. Could our inherited ideals of freedom justify themselves in this disturbing situation? Were there foundations for the democratic faith that still stood firm? These were the questions which conscientious men now had to face. The working philosophy of recent years has been largely determined by the answers they have given to them.

The most obvious recourse was to our tradition and the ideals bound up with it as the proper moral foundation for our political faith and practice. This tradition was liberal, of course, and in its recent or instrumentalist form seemed hardly usable for the justification of ideals. But its roots were deep. Behind the twentieth century was the eighteenth and Thomas Jefferson, and behind the eighteenth the thirteenth and Saint Thomas Aquinas, and behind that Greek philosophy and, most fundamental of all, the abiding spiritual inspiration of the Judeo-Christian faith. Here, surely, was the "forgotten foundation" of our liberal ideas, and a return to it the basic answer to our present moral problems. But how, and in what form was this tradition to be reappropriated? A characteristic answer was that of Chancellor Hutchins of the University of Chicago and his associates in a widely influential movement of educational reform.[48] The basic principles of our tradition are embedded in great books and a general, liberal education based on intensive study of a judicious selection of such books (for convenience the number was set at one hundred) should disclose the eternal principles of metaphysical and moral truth by which present judgment can properly be guided. The campaign for such liberal education took on, in advanced educational circles, the aspect of a new crusade.

As a means of purveying generalized culture to the throngs now crowding the colleges this doctrine clearly had its uses. As a philosophy, however, it lacked substance. It offered the literary remains of ancient wisdom as eternal truth, and traditional preconceptions as metaphysical first principles. But its tradition was a one-sided selection from the total wisdom of the past, guided as much by distaste for contemporary ideas as by respect for "perennial philosophy" and its principles, divorced from the faiths that had inspired them and suspended in the upper air of academic culture were thin to the point of transparency. A generation genuinely concerned to support and defend its ideals required foundations more concrete than this.

Meanwhile, in political affairs the New Deal carried forward the program and, in the person of Franklin D. Roosevelt, embodied the generous enthusiasm of the progressive era in a politically more sophisticated form. At the height of its power it seemed not so much to have solved the harder problems of political liberalism as to have postponed them indefinitely by a process of endless improvisation. Ideologically, however, it was from the start a makeshift and with continued economic instability and the growing threat of foreign war, was under increasing pressure from both Left and Right.

On the left were the Marxists, whose doctrine gained wide currency in "enlightened" circles in the 1930's.[49] Their philosophy was familiar and the incoherences of dialectical materialism and the labor theory of value had long since been exposed. It had, however, prophesied capitalist crisis, class struggle, and increasing international conflict, all of which seemed now to be upon us. And in Soviet Russia it offered something that, when viewed with eyes of love, might be accepted by the faithful, as it was by Beatrice and Sidney Webb, as at least the crude beginning of a new civilization.[50] Its decisive contribution to the intellectual struggles of the time was its version of the theory and practice of ideological conflict. The Marxists were tireless in "unmasking" the ideals of their opponents as at once projections of class bias and tools for protecting the authority of the ruling class to which such ideals were politically and economically useful. And they were skillful in using the resentments and hopes of the underprivileged, elaborately rationalized in *Das Kapital*, as weapons in attacking the morale of "liberal" society. Their partisanship was absolute. Only those who would commit themselves unquestioningly to the discipline of the Communist Party in the class struggle could expect to understand its reasons, and only in a Utopia to which totalitarian dictatorship was the historically inevitable prelude could its professed ideals be justified. For those prepared to make the initial sacrifice, however, the reward was high. At its ideological limit the converted could stop thinking and start fighting with undivided minds and the ultimate assurance that both history and proletarian righteousness were on their side. And there were many converts.

The Fascists and Nazis took over the practice of ideology without much regard for theory and made it serve their own destructive ends. "Race" and "nation" are at least as potent words as "class" for arousing and sustaining group animosities and, with a monopoly of propaganda in the totalitarian state, can be made tremendous instruments of ideological manipulation in the struggle for political power. Ideals, as Hitler wrote, are great forces in the world for those who know how to use them without "liberal" illusions in this struggle. For all its moral imbecility, *Mein Kampf* is an instructive textbook in the techniques of such use.

A very different doctrine, but equally appropriate to the pressures and anxieties of the time was the philosophy based on the doctrines of Saint Thomas Aquinas and powerfully represented in American universities through the writings and teaching of the French philosophers Etienne Gilson and Jacques Maritain. The major ideas of this philosophy were, of course, not new. That fact, indeed, was a major source of their contemporary persuasiveness. Here, rather, was a coherent, integrated scheme of thought which antedated the quarrels and confusions of modern culture and promised to survive that culture's probable collapse as a bulwark of spiritual order in a morally disintegrating world. In the field of historical scholarship the new understanding of medieval philosophy in the development of Western thought that grew out of the research of Gilson and his associates was an outstanding contribution.[51] And scholastic "realism," asserting the priority of Being to Thought in ontology and epistemology, emerged as an "ism" to be reckoned with in the textbooks of secular philosophy.[52]

In one essential respect, however, this doctrine agreed with its current ideological antagonists and differed sharply from the liberalism with which American philosophy had so far been linked. Its metaphysical doctrine was based on propositions about the nature of Being which were held to be rationally evident to those qualified to understand them. In fact, however, most secular philosophers since the seventeenth century have not seen them to be true and do not see them now. How is this difficulty to be dealt with? The answer given by Gilson was explicit.[53] Human reason in unregenerate man is wounded and requires the controlling guidance of faith properly to perform its function. This faith is Christian and Catholic. It is faith in a supernatural revelation of whose meaning the Church is the finally authoritative interpreter. In our divided world this faith is one of many and the validity of the dogmas in which it has been formulated is a contested issue in contemporary debate.

It is, however, to be accepted by faith and on authority, not as probable or debatable but as final truth. At its limits questioning must cease and on its foundation only can right reason build.

This philosophy clearly is not "liberal" in the manner of Locke and the Enlightenment and is not meant to be.[54] It meets the dogmatism of Marxist Communism with a dogma no less absolute. For just that reason it has seemed to many to provide the only really sure foundation for the moral values on which the democratic ideology is based. In recent years its influence in the United States has grown remarkably.

Caught between the competing absolutes now mobilized for total ideological war, the practicing liberal was in a difficult position. "Confused" and "sentimental" were among the kinder adjectives applied to him by partisans on both Left and Right. He, too, had ideals to which he was profoundly loyal and meant to defend them. But he could not forget that the ideals he was defending were those of freedom and that the American commitment was to the building of a community in which those ideals would be progressively embodied in processes of political behavior. He was glad to see the democratic faith preached with fervor by all the spiritual authorities that could properly be brought to its support. But he believed that men should practice what they preached and was not yet convinced that to curtail the actual exercise of freedom for the sake of ideological conformity was a sound method of demonstrating the moral cogency of freedom as an ideal. But if there was a philosophy that would say plainly what he meant and sustain it at the bar of public reason it was not easily come by in America in 1950 nor widely known.

In such a world of embattled ideologies what larger wisdom was possible? Perhaps this at least, the recognition that such in the last analysis and stripped of "liberal" illusions really is the kind of world that we are in, that human nature is essentially incapable of transcending its existential limitations of bias, ignorance, and pride and that true salvation is to be looked for only in a reality that transcends our ideologically tainted comprehension and is therefore incomprehensible in human terms. As powerfully presented by Reinhold Niebuhr, this insight is the authentic spiritual dividend of much contemporary experience.[55] It combines a realistic recognition of human sin and ignorance with a religious refusal to accept this tragic situation as final truth for faith, and hence finds the true meaning of life in its relation to a spiritual reality which can be the fulfillment because it is also the negation of our human meanings and ideals. In setting its transcendent truth beyond the animosities of ideological partisanship and pride this philosophy achieves at times a notable generosity of understanding. Nor is it without some consolation for sinful man. It rationalizes his irrationality by generalizing it as essential human nature and normalizes moral failure by exhibiting it as the destiny of man in history. We are thus enabled to acknowledge our sins without expecting ever wholly to escape them and to have faith in a final salvation whose incomprehensible meaning is confirmed precisely in our incapacity to understand it and for which, in consequence, there is a wealth of confirmation. And it links all this with our traditional faith by expressing it in the prophetic language of Christian eschatology, a language which, though recognized as "mythical" in this use is nonetheless in its associations deeply reassuring. The doctrine fits the spiritual tensions of the time, and it was not surprising that in the 1940's earnest young people came to look to Niebuhr or, back of him, to Kierkegaard,[56] as their progressive parents once looked to Dewey for a deeper understanding of the "problems of men."

VII

Looking back across the half-century, the pattern of the relation of American philosophy to its parent civilization is plain enough. We began with high hopes, with a liberal faith in ideals that were accepted as a promise and a program, and with philosophies that sought to justify and exemplify these ideals in the purposes and practice of our common life. In the period between wars this undertaking fell apart under the pressure of conflicting ideologies and untoward events and our ideals were left stranded in a world to which they seemed to critical minds to be increasingly irrelevant. Disoriented thinkers then turned to the fractured aspects of our culture to find in atoms of certainty, or in the literary survivals of traditional culture, or in the unquestioned authority of a party, state, or church the final foundations of a philosophic truth which the processes of common understanding could no longer be relied upon to supply. A whole generation of philosophers might well have said with T. S. Eliot, "These fragments I have shored against my ruins." But the support thus offered was essentially partial and extrinsic and the fragments were confirmed as final truth only for those committed in advance to such acceptance. If this was indeed the last word of human reason in its search for wisdom, then the irrationalists seemed correct in claiming that its search so far had failed.

Fortunately, however, the latest deliverances of contemporary anxiety need not be the final word of philosophical understanding. In 1950 the immediate problems for American civilization and American philosophy were formidable indeed. One world war was over and another seemed perilously near. How and in what form our institutions and ideals would survive the strain that now was put upon them no one knew. And yet, below the clamor of competing Absolutes there was great strength in this civilization and a continuing half-articulate faith and purpose that had still the capacity to grow. And there was still a real chance that, as Peirce believed, reason would grow with them, fashioning from the chaotic resources of contemporary experience ideas adequate to the work of human understanding. A philosophy with the wit and courage to play its proper part in this great undertaking would justify its claim to wisdom, as alone it rightly could be justified, in the process.

There was abundant evidence, meanwhile, that the professional philosophers had not relaxed their efforts and were becoming somewhat clearer in their aims. Brand Blanshard's *The Nature of Thought* [57] was a finely sustained defense of reason in the idealistic manner. C. I. Lewis' *An Analysis of Knowledge and Valuation* [58] was no less thorough in its efforts to rescue value theory from both transcendentalism and cynicism by exhibiting valuation as a form of empirical knowledge. In *The Meeting of East and West*, F. S. C. Northrop [59] undertook with great zeal and imagination to unify the ideologies of the world on the basis of a somewhat meager epistemology. And in *Philosophical Analysis: A Collection of*

Essays [60] the philosophic analysts were still expertly sharpening their linguistic tools.

But the basic problems grew in urgency. How can the idea of community be broadened to meet the requirements of a world society without losing its roots in local loyalties and traditional values? How can individual freedom, as actualized in responsible choice and judgment, maintain its claim to final value in a world of impersonal forces and organized group pressures? How can specialized knowledge find its fulfillment in practical wisdom and critical intelligence be brought into harmony with effective moral purposes? How can ideals be used, without special pleading and without illusion, to bring us into needed contact with realities we should never have discerned without them? These are still the basic questions that our civilization puts to our philosophy. The future of American philosophy and, in some measure, also, of American civilization, will depend on the answers that we give to them.

NOTES

Notes

I. The Setting and the Problems

MERLE CURTI

1. Max Lerner, "Science and American Power," *American Scholar*, 15:439–49 (Autumn 1946); Guy Stanton Ford, *Science and Civilization* (University of Minnesota Press, 1933), *passim*.

2. For convenient summaries see Dixon Ryan Fox, *A Quarter Century of Learning, 1904–1929* (Columbia University Press, 1931); Stuart Chase, *The Proper Study of Mankind* (Harper & Brothers, 1948).

3. Mortimer Graves, "A Memorandum on Regional Studies," *Journal of Higher Education*, 14:431–34 (November 1943); Maurice W. Rosenbaum, "Slavonic Studies in America," *Journal of Higher Education*, 14:9–14 (January 1943); *American Scholar*, 11:29 (Winter 1941–43); Tremaine MacDowell, *American Studies* (University of Minnesota Press, 1949).

4. Theodore M. Greene and others, *Liberal Education Re-Examined* (Harper & Brothers, 1943), pp. 13 ff.; Norman Foerster, *The American Scholar* (University of North Carolina Press, 1929), pp. 2 ff.; Charles Breasted, *Pioneer to the Past. The Story of James Henry Breasted* (Charles Scribner's Sons, 1943), pp. 354 ff., 225 ff.

5. Stuart Rice, ed., *Methods in the Social Sciences* (University of Chicago Press, 1931); Howard W. Odum, "The Social Sciences" in Loren C. MacKinney, Nicholson B. Adams, and Harry K. Russell, eds., *A State University Surveys the Humanities* (University of North Carolina Press, 1945).

6. David G. Ryans, "Farewell to Scholarship," *School and Society*, 43:297–99 (February 29, 1936); Edwin G. Conklin in *American Scholar*, 11:22 (Winter 1941–42); *ibid.*, 11:18 (Winter 1941–42).

7. Merle Curti, *The Growth of American Thought* (Harper & Brothers, 1943), pp. 589 ff.

8. Waldo G. Leland, *The International Role of Scholarship* (Brown University Press, 1940); *Bulletin* of the American Association of University Professors, 3:19 (February 1917); I. L. Kandel, *U. S. Activities in International Cultural Relations* (American Council on Education Studies, series I, September 1945).

9. *The Emergency Committee in Aid of Displaced Foreign Scholars Report as of Jan. 31, 1942*; *Bulletin* of the AAUP, vol. 19, n. 6 (October 1933); Harold Fields, *The Refugee in the United States* (Oxford University Press, 1938).

10. Wilson Gee, *Social Science Research Organization in American Universities* (D. Appleton-Century, 1934) and Frederick Ogg, *Research in the Humanistic and Social Sciences* (The Century Co., 1927).

11. Social Science Research Council *Bulletins, passim*; American Council of Learned Societies, *Bulletins, passim*; Hugh Carter, "Research Interests of American Sociologists," *Social Forces*, vol. 6, no. 2 (December 1927); Waldo G. Leland, "Methods of Promoting Research from the Point of View of Societies, Academies, and Councils," American Philosophical Society, *Proceedings*, 77:613–16 (April 1937).

12. Frederick Keppel, *Philanthropy and Learning* (Columbia University Press, 1936), *passim*; and reports of the Rockefeller Foundation, Carnegie Corporation, Carnegie Institution of Washington, etc.

13. W. H. Cowley, "Cooperation in American Research," *American Scholar*, 1:324–26 (July 1932). Howard Mumford Jones, "The Gay Science," *American Scholar*, 14:393–404 (Autumn 1945).

14. Frederick Keppel, *Philanthropy and Learning*, pp. 22–23; E. C. Lindeman, *Wealth and Culture* (Harcourt, Brace, 1936), *passim*; and Ernest V. Hollis, *Philanthropic Foundations and Higher Education* (Columbia University Press, 1938).

15. See Alfred E. Cohn's thoughtful evaluation, *Minerva's Progress. Tradition and Dissent in American Culture* (Harcourt, Brace, 1946).

16. Z. C. Dickinson, "Bureaus for Economic and Business Research in American Universities," *Economic Journal*, 35:398–415 (September 1925); T. Swann Harding, "How Business Leans on Government," *American Scholar*, 3:206–15 (Spring 1934).

17. John H. Teeter, "Federal Aid to Research," *Journal of Higher Education*, 16:455–59 (December 1945); A. F. Woods, *Conditions Determining the Nature of the Research Work Undertaken by State Governmental Agencies* (Papers presented at the Annual Meeting of the Division of State Relations, National Research Council, May 27, 1926); Charles D. Walcott, "Relations of the National Government to Higher Education and Research," *Science*, n.s. 13:1001–15 (June 28, 1901); Sanford Schwarz, *Research in International Economies by Federal Agencies* (Columbia University Press, 1941).

18. Merle Curti and Vernon Carstensen, *The University of Wisconsin; A History* (2 vols., University of Wisconsin Press, 1949), I: chs. 10–11; Lotus D. Coffman, *The State University: Its Work and Problems* (University of Minnesota Press, 1934).

19. *American Scholar*, 8:248–50 (Spring 1939); Grace Overmyer, *Government and the Arts* (W. W. Norton & Co., 1939); Jacob Baker, *Government Aid during the Depression to Professional, Technical, and Other Service*

Workers (Washington, 1936). The American Council of Learned Societies has in manuscript a comprehensive evaluation of the Federal Arts Projects.

20. Jacques Barzun, "The Scholar as an Institution," *Journal of Higher Education*, 18:393–400 (November 1947); James Forrestal, "The University in Public Service," *Journal of Higher Education*, 18:6 (January 1947); Claude C. Bowman, *The College Professor in America* (University of Pennsylvania Press, 1938), pp. 145 ff.; M. Baum, "Scholar, Scholarship, and the War," *School and Society*, 56:477–82 (November 21, 1942).

21. John Herman Randall, Jr., "On the Importance of Being Unprincipled," *The American Scholar*, 7:134–43 (Spring 1938); Richard H. Heindel, "The Discussion of Federal Research Problems in Congress and the 1943 Appropriations," (Mimeograph Mss., July 31, 1942).

22. Howard Mumford Jones, *Education and World Tragedy* (Harvard University Press, 1946, pp. 131 ff.

23. Douglas Bush, "Scholars and Others," *Sewanee Review* 36:475–85 (October 1928); Carl Joachim Friedrich, "The Selection of Professors," *Atlantic Monthly*, 161:110–14 (January 1938); Thomas E. Benner, "Professional Responsibilities of the Graduate School," *Journal of Higher Education*, 15:135–40 (March 1944); James B. Conant, "The Advancement of Learning in the Postwar World," American Philosophical Society *Proceedings*, vol. 87, no. 4 (1944); Walter A. Jessup, "A Future for Graduate Education," *Thirty-ninth Annual Report of the Carnegie Foundation for the Advancement of Teaching*, (1944); Ernest V. Hollis, *Improving Ph.D. Programs* (American Council on Education, 1945).

24. Robert M. Hutchins, *The Higher Learning in America* (Yale University Press, 1936), pp. 89 ff.; Harry D. Gideonse, *The Higher Learning in a Democracy. A Reply to President Hutchins' Critique of the American University* (Farrar and Rinehart, 1937).

25. William S. Dix, *The Amateur Spirit in Scholarship* (Western Reserve University, 1942); Robert Binkley, "New Tools, New Recruits, for the Republic of Letters" (Joint Committee on Materials for Research, Mimeograph).

26. *American Scholar*, 7:374 (Summer 1938); Charles Breasted, *Pioneer to the Past. The Story of James Henry Breasted*, pp. 232–33; William B. Bizzell, *The Relations of Learning* (University of Oklahoma Press, 1934), pp. 34 ff.; Jacob Zeitlen and Homer Woodbridge, *Life and Letters of Stuart P. Sherman* (2 vols., Farrar and Rinehart, 1929), II, 463.

27. Alfred Cohn, *Minerva's Progress, passim*; Alexander Meikeljohn, *Freedom and the College* (The Century Co., 1923); *passim*; and Albert Jay Nock, *The Theory of Eductaion in the United States* (Harcourt, Brace, 1932).

28. Marjorie H. Nicolson, "The American Scholar, 1932–1946," *American Scholar*, 15:11–12 (Winter 1945–46).

29. William Albert Nitze, "Modern Language Scholarship: An Enquiry," *Publications of the Modern Language Association*, pp. 38: appendix lxvi–lxxxiv (1923); Robert D. French, "Modern Scholarship and the American

Tradition," *New England Quarterly*, 3:94–107 (January 1931); William A. Neilson, "The American Scholar Today," *American Scholar*, 5:149–163 (Spring 1936); Martin Schutze, *Academic Illusions in the Field of Letters and the Arts* (University of Chicago Press, 1933); *passim*; Stith Thompson, "The Use and Abuse of Books. Literary Scholarship during the Past Century," *American Scholar*, 9:85–96 (Winter 1939–40); A. Lawrence Lowell, *At War with Academic Traditions in America* (Harvard University Press, 1934), pp. 124–25.

30. Andrew F. West, *The Graduate College of Princeton. Some Reflections on the Humanizing of Learning* (Princeton University Press, 1913; Abraham Flexner, *I Remember* (Simon & Schuster, 1942), p. 356.

31. Howard Mumford Jones, "The Gay Science," *American Scholar*, 14:393–404 (Autumn 1945), p. 397; Theodore M. Greene and others, *Liberal Education Re-Examined* (Harper & Bros., 1943), pp. 13 ff.; Norman Foerster, *The American Scholar. A Study in Litterae Inhumaniores* (University of North Carolina Press, 1929); Edward Bliss Reed, ed., *The Commonwealth Fellows and their Impressions of America* (New York: The Commonwealth Fund, 1932), pp. 110 ff.

32. Hans Zinsser, *In Defense of Scholarship* (Providence, 1929), p. 4.

33. *Bulletin* of the AAUP, vol. 5, no. 3 (March 1919); vol. 10, no. 5 (May 1924); vol. 10, no. 6 (October 1924); vol. 14, no. 2 (February 1928); Albert H. Lybyer, "Scholars in the Horseless Age," *American Scholar*, 1:194–200 (April 1932); Claude C. Bowman, *The College Professor in America*, pp. 63 ff.

34. Crane Brinton, "The New History," *American Scholar*, 8:144–57 (Spring 1939); Jacques Barzun, "The Scholar Is an Institution," *Journal of Higher Education*, 18:393–400 (November 1947).

35. George William Curtis, *The Public Duty of Educated Men* (J. Munsell, Albany, 1878); Nicholas Murray Butler, *Scholarship and Service* (Charles Scribner's Sons, 1921); David Starr Jordan, *The Voice of the Scholar* (San Francisco: Paul Elder & Co., 1903); Charles Kendall Adams, *The Present Obligations of the Scholar* (Madison, 1899).

36. Wilson's Princeton Inaugural, "Princeton for the Nation's Service," *Public Papers of Woodrow Wilson* (Harper & Brothers, 1925), 1:443–61.

37. Claude C. Bowman, *The College Professor in America*, pp. 146 ff.; "The Demobilized Professors, by One of Them," *Atlantic Monthly*, 123:537 ff. (April 1919).

38. Paul V. Harper, ed., *The Russia I Believe In. The Memoirs of Samuel N. Harper* (University of Chicago Press, 1945), p. 208; Robert Morss Lovett, *All Our Years* (Viking Press, 1948).

39. Claude Bowman, *The College Professor in America*, pp. 157 ff.

40. *Bulletin* of the AAUP, vol. 19, no. 2 (January 1936); vol. 22, no. 3 (March 1936); vol. 22, no. 6 (October 1936).

41. Quoted in Bowman, *The College Professor in America*, p. 163.

42. Bowman, *The College Professor in America*, pp. 92 ff.; Charles Breasted,

Pioneer to the Past. The Story of James Henry Breasted, pp. 227 ff.; Randolph Bourne, *Education and Living* (The Century Co., 1917), pp. 216 ff.; John Erskine, *The Memory of Certain Persons* (J. B. Lippincott, 1947), pp. 252–53; Ludwig Lewisohn, *Up Stream* (Boni and Liveright, 1922), p. 168.

43. *Bulletin* of the AAUP, vol. 22, no. 2 (February 1936); Robert F. Wagner, "The Scholar's Place in Public Life," *American Scholar*, 1:144–47 (April 1932); Charles A. Beard, "The Scholar in an Age of Conflicts," *School and Society*, 43:278–283 (February 29, 1936).

44. *Bulletin* of the AAUP, vol. 2, no. 1 (March 1916). I am indebted to Professor John Stalker of the University of Hawaii for collecting materials on academic freedom.

45. Report of Committee A, *Bulletin* of the AAUP, 1:23–29 (1915).

46. See the two articles by A. M. Withers, "Professors and their Associations," *Journal of Higher Education*, 11:125 ff. (March 1940); and "Academic Tenure Investigations," *Educational Forum*, 11:89–92 (November 1946).

47. Report of Committee A, *Bulletin* of the AAUP, 4:30–41 (February–March 1918).

48. Report of Committee A, *Bulletin* of the AAUP, 28:83 (February 1942).

49. Report of Committee A, *Bulletin* of the AAUP, 30:13 (February 1944).

50. Report of the Committee on Freedom of Teaching in Science, *Bulletin* of the AAUP, 11:95 (January 1925).

51. Report of Committee M, *Bulletin* of the AAUP, 13:554 (December 1927).

52. Resolution, *Bulletin* of the AAUP, 17:140 (February 1931).

53. Resolution, *Bulletin* of the AAUP, 27:627 (December 1941).

54. Report of Committee A, *Bulletin* of the AAUP, 22:106 (February 1936).

55. *Ibid.*

56. Resolution, *Bulletin* of the AAUP, 19:358–59 (October 1933).

57. Nicholas Murray Butler, *Scholarship and Service* (Charles Scribner's Sons, 1921), p. 115.

58. Statement reprinted from the National Catholic Educational Association on Academic Freedom in *Bulletin* of the AAUP, 22:366–67 (October 1936). See also *The Great Encyclical Letters of Pope Leo the Thirteenth* (New York: Benziger Brothers, 1903), p. 153; and Sister M. Angelicia Guinan, M.A., *Freedom and Authority in Education* (The Catholic University of America, 1936).

59. James B. Macelwane, S.J., "The Place of the Association in a Catholic University," *Bulletin* of the AAUP, 26:367–68 (June 1940).

60. Archibald MacLeish, *The Irresponsibles; A Declaration* (Duell, Sloane and Pearce, 1940).

61. Robert K. Lynd, *Knowledge for What? The Place of Social Science in American Culture* (Princeton University Press, 1939).

62. M. Baum, "Scholar, Scholarship, and the War," *School and Society*, 56:477–82 (November 21, 1942).

63. Claude C. Bowman, *The College Professor in America*, pp. 157 ff.; James Forrestal, "The University in Public Service," *Journal of Higher Education*, 18:6, 56 (January 1947).

64. Walter Lippmann, "The Scholar in a Troubled World," *Atlantic Monthly*, 150:148–52 (August 1932).

65. Carl Becker, *Every Man His Own Historian* (F. S. Crofts & Co., 1935), pp. 233 ff.; Charles A. Beard, "Written History as an Act of Faith," *American Historical Review*, 39:219–31 (January 1934); Beard, "The Scholar in an Age of Conflicts," *School and Society*, 43:278–83 (February 29, 1936). This general position was cogently stated in a remark that Santayana recalls having made to President Eliot, *The Middle Span* (Charles Scribner's Sons, 1945), p. 156.

66. Curti and Carstensen, *The University of Wisconsin; a History*, II, 87–88, 549–50.

67. Robert M. Hutchins, *The Higher Learning in America*, pp. 90, 109–10; Theodore M. Greene, "In Praise of Reflective Commitment," *American Scholar*, 11:62–63 (Winter 1941–42); Fred B. Millett, *The Rebirth of Liberal Education* (Harcourt, Brace, 1945) and Henry M. Wriston, *The Nature of a Liberal College* (Lawrence College Press, 1937).

68. Walter M. Horton, "The New Orthodoxy," *American Scholar*, 7:3–11 (Winter 1938).

II. The Social Sciences

LOUIS WIRTH

1. Frederick J. Teggart, *Theory of History* (Yale University Press, 1925), p. 71.

2. Walter Bagehot, *Physics and Politics* (London: Henry S. King & Co., 1872).

3. Albion W. Small, "Fifty Years of Sociology in the United States (1865–1915)," *American Journal of Sociology*, Index to Vols. I–LII (1895–1947), (University of Chicago Press, n.d.).

4. Stuart Chase, *The Proper Study of Mankind* (Harper & Brothers, 1948), p. 43.

5. Howard J. Rogers, ed., *Proceedings of the Congress of Arts and Science* (Cambridge: Riverside Press, 1906), V.

6. John Herman Randall, Jr., and George Haines, "Controlling Assumptions in the Practice of American Historians," in *Theory and Practice in Historical Study, A Report of the Committee on Historiography* (New York: Social Science Research Council, 1946), ch. 2, pp. 50–51.

7. Stuart Chase, *The Proper Study of Mankind*, pp. 48–49.

8. Charles A. Beard, "Politics" in *Lectures on Science, Philosophy and Art* (Columbia University Press, 1908), pp. 6–15.

9. Henry R. Seager, "Economics" in *Lectures on Science, Philosophy and Art* (Columbia University Press, 1908), pp. 25–26.

10. Wesley C. Mitchell, "Economics" in *A Quarter Century of Learning* (Columbia University Press, 1929), p. 45.

11. Henry R. Seager, "Economics," p. 26.

12. Albion W. Small, "Fifty Years of Sociology in the United States," *American Journal of Sociology*, 21:733 (1915).

13. H. G. Wells, "The So-Called Science of Sociology" in *Sociological Papers* (London, n.d., probably 1903), III.

14. Ethel Shanas, "The American Journal of Sociology Through Fifty Years," *American Journal of Sociology*, 50:522–532 (May 1945).

15. As late as 1909 Albion W. Small found it necessary to defend sociology against assorted critics from various quarters by writing an apologetic article, "The Vindication of Sociology," *American Journal of Sociology*, 15:1–15 (1909).

16. Agricultural Experiment Station of the University of Wisconsin, Research Bulletin 34 (University of Wisconsin Press, 1915).

17. *American Journal of Sociology*, 20:577–612 (1914–1915). Reprinted as ch. 1 in Robert E. Park, Ernest W. Burgess, and Roderick D. McKenzie, *The City* (University of Chicago Press, 1925).

18. Robert E. Park and Ernest W. Burgess, *Introduction to the Science of Sociology* (University of Chicago Press, 1921).

19. William I. Thomas and Florian Znaniecki, *The Polish Peasant in Europe and America* (5 vols., The University of Chicago Press, 1918–1920).

20. Including such volumes as Robert E. Park and Herbert A. Miller, *Old World Traits Transplanted* (Harper & Brothers, 1921); Robert E. Park, *The Immigrant Press and Its Control* (Harper & Brothers, 1922); Sophonisba P. Breckinridge, *New Homes for Old* (Harper & Brothers, 1921); and others.

21. See, for instance, Charles S. Johnson, *The Negro in Chicago* (Henry Holt & Co., 1930).

22. Charles H. Cooley, *Social Organization: A Study of the Larger Mind* (Charles Scribner's Sons, 1909).

23. John B. Watson, *Psychology from the Standpoint of a Behaviorist* (Philadelphia: J. B. Lippincott, 1919); and *Behaviorism* (New York: W. W. Norton & Company, Inc., 1925).

24. For a summary and critical appraisal of these developments, see Philip L. Harriman, ed., *Encyclopedia of Psychology* (New York: Philosophical Library, 1946), pp. 523–537, 885–890. See also James W. Woodward, "Social Psychology" in Georges Gurvitch and Wilbert E. Moore, eds., *Twentieth Century Sociology*, (New York: Philosophical Library, 1945), pp. 219–247.

25. Stuart Chase, *The Proper Study of Mankind*, p. 50.

26. Clark Wissler, in Edward C. Hayes, ed., *Recent Developments in the Social Sciences* (Philadelphia: J. B. Lippincott, 1927).

27. Alexander Goldenweiser, "Recent Trends in American Anthropology," *American Anthropologist*, vol. 43, no. 2, pt. 1, 151–163 (April–June 1941).

28. *Ibid.*, p. 154.

29. Clyde Kluckhohn, *Mirror for Man* (New York: Whittlesey House, 1949).

30. "In this country Miss Semple has made a careful appraisal of geographic influences in American history, which is the most significant exposition of that theme in our literature. It was an epoch-making study that made important corrections to current historical views (*American History and Its Geographic Conditions*, 1903). She undertook a translation of Ratzel's *Anthropogeographie*, but produced finally an original contribution to general human geography (*Influences of Geographic Environment*, 1911)." Quoted from Carl O. Sauer, "Recent Developments in Cultural Geography," in Edward C. Hayes, ed., *Recent Developments in the Social Sciences* (Philadelphia: J. B. Lippincott, 1927).

31. *Ibid.*, p. 158.

32. As indicated by Harlan H. Barrows in his presidential address to the Association of American Geographers in 1922.

33. See Ellsworth Huntington, *Pulse of Asia* (Boston, 1907), *Civilization and Climate* (Yale University Press, 1915), and *The Character of Races* (New York, 1924) among his numerous other works.

34. Sauer, "Recent Developments in Cultural Geography," p. 186.

35. *Ibid.*

36. See Jean Brunhes, "Human Geography" in Harry E. Barnes, *et al.*, eds., *The History and Prospects of the Social Sciences* (A. A. Knopf, 1925); C. E. Hartshorne, "The Nature of Geography," *Annals* of the Association of American Geographers 29:123 and *passim* (1946). See also C. Langdon White and George T. Renner, *Human Geography: An Ecological Study of Society* (Appleton-Century-Crofts, 1948).

37. Roscoe Pound, "The Social Sciences and Scientific Method in the Administration of Justice," *Annals of the American Academy of Political and Social Science*, pp. 110–115 (May 1933).

38. The notable brief "Fatigue and Efficiency" prepared in 1910 in connection with the women's ten-hour law case (Muller *vs.* Oregon) by Brandeis, in association with Josephine E. Goldmark was one of the most impressive legal documents using social science data to call attention to the social implications of legislation.

39. I. M. Wormser, "Sociology and the Law," *Annual Review of the Law School of New York University*, p. 11 (April 1924).

40. Esther Lucille Brown, *Lawyers, Law Schools and the Public Service* (New York: Russell Sage Foundation, 1948), pp. 121–134.

41. On the professional development of social work in the United States

see, for instance, Esther Lucille Brown, *Social Work as a Profession* (New York: Russell Sage Foundation, 1942); the publications of the American Association of Social Workers and of the American Association of Schools of Social Work; and particularly *The Social Service Review* published by the Graduate School of Social Service Administration of the University of Chicago.

42. Wesley C. Mitchell, "Economics," p. 36.

43. *Ibid.*, p. 36.

44. Allen G. Gruchy, *Modern Economic Thought* (Prentice-Hall, 1947), p. 7.

45. Lyle C. Fitch, "Review of *The New Economics*, Seymour Harris, Ed." in *Political Science Quarterly*, 63:299 (1948).

46. *The President's Committee on Administrative Management in the Government of the United States* (Washington: U. S. Government Printing Office, 1937). See also the numerous reports of the so-called "Task Forces" working under the Commission of which former President Hoover was Chairman.

47. Charles E. Merriam, "Government and Intelligence," *Ethics*, 54:263 (July 1944). See also Joseph E. McLean, "Areas for Postwar Research," *American Political Science Review*, 39:741 (1945), summarizing reports by the Committee on Government and the Committee on Public Administration of the Social Science Research Council. See also John M. Gaus, William Anderson, *et al.*, "Research in Public Administration, 1934–45," (Chicago Public Administration Service, 1945), summarizing the work of the Public Administration Committee and the Committee on Government of the Social Science Research Council.

48. See, for instance, the report to the Committee on Analysis of Pre-election Polls and Forecasts, *The Pre-Election Polls of 1948*, Social Science Research Council Bulletin 60 (New York, 1949) which analyzed the factors accounting for the failure of the forecasts of the 1948 Presidential election.

49. Conrad Taeuber, "Some Recent Developments in Sociological Work in the Department of Agriculture," *American Sociological Review* 10:169–175 (1945); Carl C. Taylor, "The Social Responsibilities of the Social Sciences," *American Sociological Review* 11:384–392 (1946); Philip M. Hauser, "Wartime Developments in Census Statistics," *American Sociological Review* 10:160–169 (1945).

50. Since the writer of this report has a professional predisposition to dwell more fully than is warranted on sociological development, a temptation which must be inhibited at all costs, the reader is referred to some of the summary accounts which record the important advances of sociology in the last fifty years, notably the following: Georges Gurvitch and Wilbert E. Moore (editors), *Twentieth Century Sociology* (New York, 1945), and the special semicentennial issue of the *American Journal of Sociology*, vol. 50, no. 6, (May 1945). See also Index to the *American Journal of Sociology* I–LII, for reference to a reprint of Albion W. Small's "Fifty Years of Sociology in the

United States, 1865–1915"; and a survey entitled "Developments of Sociology since 1915," by Louis Wirth.

51. John W. Riley, Jr., "The Status of the Social Sciences," a memorandum with special reference to methods and their utilization, personnel and research funds, prepared for the study of the Ford Foundation on policy and program, p. iii (June 1949).

52. *Ibid.*, p. iv. See also Elbridge Sibley, *The Recruitment, Selection, and Training of Social Scientists* (New York: Social Science Research Council, 1948.)

53. Riley, The Status of the Social Sciences," p. v. See National Resources Committee, "Research a National Resource," (Washington, 1939) upon which Riley's figures for 1938 are based.

54. See Elbridge Sibley, *Support for Independent Scholarship and Research* (New York: Social Science Research Council, 1951), reporting a recent investigation of the flow of resources for research into the social sciences, especially research enterprises carried on by individuals as distinguished from organized group-research.

55. Stuart A. Rice, *Methods in Social Science: A Case Book*, compiled under the direction of the Committee on Scientific Method in the Social Sciences of the Social Science Research Council, (Chicago, 1931).

56. *Social Science Abstracts* (Menasha, Wis.) began publication in 1929 and terminated in 1932.

57. *Report on the History and Policies of the Social Science Research Council*, prepared by Louis Wirth for the Committee on Review of Council Policy (New York: Social Science Research Council, August, 1937).

58. *Encyclopedia of the Social Sciences* (Macmillan Co., 1931).

59. One of the most unique undertakings of the Social Science Research Council was the sponsorship of a series of critical evaluations of research publications in several social sciences which had been voted by representatives of the respective disciplines as the most important achievements in their field. The six works selected for analysis were Frederick C. Mills, *The Behavior of Prices* (New York: National Bureau of Economic Research, Inc., 1927); William I. Thomas and Florian Znaniecki, *The Polish Peasant in Europe and America* (University of Chicago Press, 1918); Walter P. Webb, *The Great Plains* (Boston: Ginn & Company, 1931); Adolf A. Berle, Jr., and Gardiner C. Means, *The Modern Corporation and Private Property* (New York, 1932); Franz Boas, *Primitive Art* (Harvard University Press, 1927); and John Dickinson, *Administrative Justice and the Supremacy of Law in the United States* (Harvard University Press, 1927). The Council also undertook critical summaries of research methods such as *The Use of Personal Documents in Psychological Science; The Use of Personal Documents in History, Anthropology and Sociology.*

60. Samuel C. Stouffer *et al.*, *The American Soldier* (4 vols., Princeton University Press, 1949–1950).

61. Wesley C. Mitchell, "Economics," p. 51.

62. See the symposium in Louis Wirth, ed., *1126: A Decade of Social Science Research* (The University of Chicago Press, 1940).

III. Historical Scholarship

W. STULL HOLT

1. H. Hale Bellot, "Some Aspects of the Recent History of American Historiography," *Transactions of the Royal Historical Society*, Fourth Series, 28:120–148 (1946). W. Stull Holt, ed., *Historical Scholarship in the United States, 1876–1901: As Revealed in the Correspondence of Herbert B. Adams* (The Johns Hopkins Press, 1938).

2. A memoir describing his life and achievements was published in the journal he edited for so many years. "John Franklin Jameson," *American Historical Review*, 43: 243–252 (January 1938).

3. The comment is that of John Spencer Bassett on Francis Parkman in *The Middle Group of American Historians* (Macmillan, 1917), p. ix. Bassett wrote "While he [Parkman] wrote with that full appreciation of style which was characteristic of Bancroft and the literary historians, his industry, his research among documents, and especially his detachment seem to place him among the men of to-day." Carl Becker in a delightful and penetrating essay, "Labelling the Historians," quoted this sentence and observed "If Parkman had only written badly, no one could question his scientific standing." *Everyman His Own Historian* (F. S. Crofts & Co., 1935), p. 135.

4. Next to nothing has been written on the history of the writing of textbooks. Almost the only valuable account, although restricted to one important example, can be found in Eric F. Goldman, *John Bach McMaster* (University of Pennsylvania Press, 1943).

5. Some of these points are elaborated in W. Stull Holt, "The Idea of Scientific History in America," *Journal of the History of Ideas*, 1:352–362 (June 1940). An excellent, if somewhat illogically arranged, bibliography of the literature bearing on this and several subsequent paragraphs is in *Theory and Practice in Historical Study: A Report of the Committee on Historiography*, Social Science Research Council Bulletin 54 (1946).

6. Charles A. Beard, "That Noble Dream," *American Historical Review*, 41:74–87 (October 1935).

7. The title of the report is given in note 5 above. The philosophy of history accepted by the Committee can be found in the Propositions presented as those on which the branch of knowledge known as history rests. See also, Charles W. Cole, "The Relativity of History," *Political Science Quarterly*, 48:161–171 (June 1933).

8. Some of the reasons for the widespread American belief in progress are discussed in the Introduction by Charles A. Beard to the American edition of J. B. Bury, *The Idea of Progress* (Macmillan, 1932).

9. Holt, *Historical Scholarship in the United States*, pp. 145–146.

10. J. Franklin Jameson, "The American Historical Review, 1895–1920," *American Historical Review*, 26:17 (October 1920).

11. Herbert B. Adams of the Johns Hopkins University adopted this statement of the English historian, Edward A. Freeman.

12. Herbert Heaton, "The Economic Impact on History," in J. R. Strayer, ed., *The Interpretation of History*. (Princeton University Press, 1943), pp. 111–112. See also his "Recent Developments in Economic History," *American Historical Review*, 47:727–746 (July 1942).

13. The classic statement of *The New History* is the book with that title by James Harvey Robinson which was published in 1912. Caustic and penetrating criticisms are in Wilbur Cortez Abbott, "Some 'New' History and Historians," *Proceedings of the Massachusetts Historical Society*, 64:3–35 (1931), and Crane Brinton, "The New History: Twenty-five years Later," *Journal of Social Philosophy*, 1:134–147 (January 1936).

14. *Annual Report of the American Historical Association for the Year 1914*, I, 53.

15. There is a chapter on "The Imperial School of Colonial History" in Michael Kraus, *A History of American History* (New York: Farrar & Rinehart, Inc., 1937). See also, Lawrence H. Gipson, "Charles McLean Andrews and the Re-orientation of the Study of American Colonial History," *Pennsylvania Magazine of History and Biography*, 59:209–222 (July 1935), and Max Savelle, "The Imperial School of American Colonial Historians," *Indiana Magazine of History*, 45:123–134 (June 1949).

16. Arthur M. Schlesinger, "The City in American History," *Mississippi Valley Historical Review*, 27:43–66 (June 1940). The book, published in 1933, is Volume X of *A History of American Life* edited by Schlesinger and Dixon Ryan Fox. See also, William Diamond, "On the Dangers of an Urban Interpretation" in Eric F. Goldman, ed., *Historiography and Urbanization* (The Johns Hopkins Press, 1941).

17. Gibbon's comment is, of course, in his famous autobiography. That of Senator Foraker was in a letter to A. W. Jones, December 9, 1911. MSS. Foraker Papers, Library of Congress.

IV. Literary Scholarship

RENÉ WELLEK

1. Daniel C. Gilman, *The Launching of a University* (Dodd, Mead, 1906), p. 8.

2. *Publications of the Modern Language Association*, 16:77–91 (1901).

3. *Deutsche Monatshefte*, 48:477 (1946).

4. "Studies of German Literature in the United States" in *Modern Language Review*, 43:353–392 (1948).

5. William L. Phelps, *Autobiography with Letters* (Oxford University Press, 1939), p. 301.

6. Arthur O. Lovejoy, *The Great Chain of Being* (Harvard University Press, 1936), p. 17.

7. Clinton H. Grattan, ed., *The Critique of Humanism* (New York: Brewer and Warren, 1930).

8. *Sewanee Review*, 51:59 (1943).

9. The quotations are from René Wellek and Austin Warren, *Theory of Literature* (Harcourt, Brace, 1949), pp. 292–293, 294.

10. J. Leslie Hotson, *The Death of Christopher Marlowe* (Harvard University Press, 1925).

11. Distinguished examples are: Donald G. Wing, *Short-title Catalog of Books Printed in England . . . 1640–1700* (2 vols., New York: The Index Society, 1945, 1949, 1952); Carleton F. Brown and Rossell H. Robbins, *The Index of Middle English Verse* (Columbia University Press, 1943); John E. Wells, *A Manual of the Writings in Middle English, 1050–1400* (Yale University Press, 1916), 7 supplements; Eleanor P. Hammond, *Chaucer: A Bibliographical Manual* (Macmillan, 1908), continuations by Dudley D. Griffith and W. E. Martin; Frederic I. Carpenter, *A Reference Guide to Edmund Spenser* (University of Chicago Press, 1923), continuation by Dorothy F. Atkinson, (Johns Hopkins Press, 1937); Robert D. French, *A Chaucer Handbook* (F. S. Crofts, 1927; new edition, 1947); Harriet S. V. Jones, *A Spenser Handbook* (F. S. Crofts, 1930); James H. Hanford, *A Milton Handbook* (F. S. Crofts, 1926; new edition, 1948); William C. DeVane, *A Browning Handbook*, (F. S. Crofts, 1935); Ernest Bernbaum, *Guide Through the Romantic Movement* (New York, 1930; new edition, Ronald Press, 1949).

12. Clark S. Northup, *A Register of the Bibliographies of the English Language and Literature* (Yale University Press, 1925).

13. For example: Reginald H. Griffiths, *Alexander Pope: A Bibliography* (2 parts, University of Texas, 1922–1927); Francis R. Johnson, *A Critical Bibliography of the Works of Edmund Spenser* (The Johns Hopkins Press,

1933); Allen T. Hazen and J. P. Kirby, *A Bibliography of the Strawberry Hill Press* (Yale University Press, 1948).

14. Some distinguished editions are: George P. Krapp and E. v. K. Dobbie, *The Anglo-Saxon Poetic Records* (6 vols., Columbia University Press, 1930 ff.); John M. Manly and Edith Rickert, eds., *The Text of the Canterbury Tales* (8 vols., University of Chicago Press, 1940); Robert K. Root, ed., *Troilus and Criseyde* (Princeton University Press, 1926); Fred N. Robinson, ed., *Chaucer's Complete Works* (Cambridge edition, Houghton Mifflin, 1933); Richard L. Greene, *The Early English Carols* (Oxford: The Clarendon Press, 1935); Horace H. Furness, *et al.*, eds., *The New Variorum Shakespeare* (23 vols. to date, J. B. Lippincott, 1871 ff.); George L. Kittredge, ed., *The Complete Works of William Shakespeare* (Ginn and Company, 1936), and individual editions of ten plays; Thomas M. Parrott and Hardin Craig, *The Tragedy of Hamlet* (Princeton University Press, 1938); C. F. Tucker Brooke, ed., *The Works of Christopher Marlowe* (Oxford: The Clarendon Press, 1910) and *The Shakespeare Apocrypha* (Oxford: The Clarendon Press, 1908); Thomas M. Parrott, ed., *The Plays and Poems of George Chapman* (2 vols., E. P. Dutton and Co., 1910–1914), the Poems actually edited later by Miss Phillis B. Bartlett (New York: Oxford University Press, 1941); Edwin Greenlaw, Charles G. Osgood, and Frederick M. Padelford, eds., *Spenser's Works* (10 vols., The Johns Hopkins Press, 1932–1949); Lily Campbell, ed., *The Mirror for Magistrates* (Cambridge, Eng.: The University Press, 1938); John W. Hebel, ed., *The Works of Michael Drayton* (Tercentenary edition, 4 vols., Oxford: Shakespeare Head Press, 1931–1935), the fifth volume added after Hebel's death by K. Tillotson and Bernard H. Newdigate (1941); a long series of the Elizabethan poetical miscellanies, edited by Hyder E. Rollins and published by the Harvard University Press; Frank A. Patterson, ed., *The Works of John Milton* (18 vols., Columbia University Press, 1931–1938), 3 supplements and 2 volumes of Index (1940); W. S. Lewis *et al.*, eds., *Horace Walpole's Correspondence* (14 vols. to date, Yale University Press, 1937 —), some 35 vols. to follow; Chauncey B. Tinker, ed., *The Letters of James Boswell* (2 vols., Oxford: The Clarendon Press, 1924); Lewis P. Curtis, ed., *The Letters of Laurence Sterne* (Oxford: The Clarendon Press, 1935); J. DeLancey Ferguson, ed., *The Letters of Robert Burns* (2 vols., Oxford: The Clarendon Press, 1931); Geoffrey Scott and Frederick A. Pottle, eds., *Private Papers of James Boswell . . .* (18 vols., Mount Vernon, New York: W. E. Rudge, priv. print., 1928–1934), also a new series beginning with Boswell's *London Journal* (ed. F. Pottle, McGraw-Hill, 1950); Frederick B. Kaye, ed., Bernard de Mandeville's *The Fables of the Bees* (2 vols., Oxford: The Clarendon Press, 1924); Thomas M. Raysor, ed., Coleridge's *Shakespearean Criticism* (2 vols., Harvard University Press, 1930).

15. Brunetière Ferdinand, *Nouvelles Questions de Critique* (Paris: Calmann Lévy, 1898), p. 28. Originally published in 1883.

16. William F. Bryan and Germaine Dempster, *Sources and Analogues of Chaucer's Canterbury Tales* (University of Chicago Press, 1941).

17. Edgar F. Shannon, *Chaucer and the Roman Poets* (Harvard University Press, 1929); J. Burke Severs, *The Literary Relationships of Chaucer's Clerkes Tale* (Yale University Press, 1942).

18. James D. Bruce, *The Evolution of Arthurian Romance* (2 vols., Gottingen, 1923); Arthur C. L. Brown, *Iwain* (Harvard University Press, 1903) and *The Origin of the Grail Legend* (Harvard University Press, 1943); Roger S. Loomis, *Celtic Myth and Arthurian Romance* (Columbia University Press, 1927) and *Arthurian Tradition and Chrétien du Troyes* (Columbia University Press, 1949); George L. Kittredge, *A Study of Gawain and the Green Knight* (Harvard University Press, 1916).

19. Merritt Y. Hughes, *Virgil and Spenser* (University of California Press, 1929).

20. Willard Farnham, *Medieval Heritage of the Elizabethan Tragedy* (University of California Press, 1936).

21. Lists and descriptions, e. g., in James H. Hanford, *Milton Handbook*.

22. William R. Parker, *Milton's Debt to Greek Tragedy in Samson Agonistes* (The Johns Hopkins Press, 1937).

23. Raymond D. Havens, *The Influence of Milton in English Poetry* (Harvard University Press, 1922).

24. Henry W. Wells, *New Poets from Old* (Columbia University Press, 1940).

25. Edward G. Ainsworth, *Poor Collins: His Life, His Art, and His Influence* (Cornell University Press, 1937).

26. John Livingston Lowes, *Road to Xanadu* (Harvard University Press, 1927); Arthur H. Nethercot, *Road to Tryermaine* (University of Chicago Press, 1939) is a similar attempt to trace the sources of Coleridge's *Christabel*.

27. Some recent examples: Charles T. Prouty, *George Gascoigne, Elizabethan Courtier, Soldier, and Poet* (Columbia University Press, 1942); John Bakeless, *The Tragical History of Christopher Marlowe* (2 vols., Harvard University Press, 1942); Alexander C. Judson, *The Life of Edmund Spenser* (The Johns Hopkins Press, 1945); Joseph Q. Adams, *A Life of William Shakespeare* (Houghton Mifflin, 1923); Arthur H. Nethercot, *Abraham Cowley, The Muse's Hannibal* (Oxford University Press, 1931); John C. Hodges, *William Congreve the Man* (New York: Modern Language Association of America, 1941); George Sherburn, *The Early Career of Alexander Pope* (Oxford: The Clarendon Press, 1934).

28. Wilbur L. Cross, *The History of Henry Fielding* (3 vols., Yale University Press, 1919) and *The Life and Times of Laurence Sterne* (2 vols., Yale University Press, 1925).

29. Chauncey B. Tinker, *Young Boswell* (The Atlantic Monthly Press, 1922).

30. Joseph W. Krutch, *Samuel Johnson* (Henry Holt and Company, 1944).

31. George M. Harper, *William Wordsworth: His Life, Works and Influence* (2 vols., Charles Scribner's Sons, 1916; new edition, 1929); Amy Lowell, *John Keats* (2 vols., Houghton Mifflin, 1925); Newman I. White, *Shelley* (2 vols., A. A. Knopf, 1940).

32. Examples of distinction are: Emery Neff, *Carlyle and Mill*, (Columbia University Press, 1924) and *Carlyle* (W. W. Norton, 1932); Gordon Haight, *George Eliot and John Chapman* (Yale University Press, 1940); Richmond Beatty, *Lord Macaulay, Victorian Liberal* (University of Oklahoma Press, 1938); Alfred M. Terhune, *The Life of Edward Fitzgerald* (Yale University Press, 1947).

33. For example: Frederic T. Blanchard, *Fielding the Novelist* (Yale University Press, 1927); James T. Hillhouse, *The Waverly Novels and Their Critics* (University of Minnesota Press, 1936); Samuel C. Chew, *Byron in England: His Fame and After-Fame* (London: J. Murray, 1924).

34. Gerald E. Bentley, *Jacobean and Caroline Stage* (2 vols., Oxford: The Clarendon Press, 1941).

35. Thomas W. Baldwin, *Organization and Personnel of the Shakespearean Company* (Princeton University Press, 1927).

36. John C. Adams, *The Globe Playhouse, Its Design and Equipment* (Harvard University Press, 1942); George F. Reynolds, *The Staging of Elizabethan Plays at the Red Bull Theatre* (New York: Modern Language Association of America, 1940).

37. Alfred Harbage, *Shakespeare's Audience* (Columbia University Press, 1941).

38. For example: Arthur C. Sprague, *Shakespeare and the Actors: The Stage Business in his Plays* (Harvard University Press, 1944); Alfred Harbage, *Cavalier Drama* (New York: Modern Language Association of America, 1936); Hazelton Spencer, *Shakespeare Improved* (Harvard University Press, 1928); George C. D. Odell, *Shakespeare from Betterton to Irving* (2 vols., Charles Scribner's Sons, 1920).

39. An exception is Granville Hicks' *Figures of Transition* (Macmillan, 1939), a mildly unconventional study of Hardy, Morris, and others.

40. Hardin Craig, *The Enchanted Glass: The Elizabethan Mind in Literature*, (New York: Oxford University Press, 1936).

41. Arthur O. Lovejoy, *The Great Chain of Being* (Harvard University Press, 1936) and "The Parallel of Deism and Classicism" in *Essays in the History of Ideas* (Johns Hopkins Press, 1948).

42. For example: Lily Campbell, *Shakespeare's Tragic Heroes; Slaves of Passion* (Cambridge, Eng.: The University Press, 1930).

43. For example: Roy W. Battenhouse, *Marlowe's Tamburlaine: A Study in Renaissance Moral Philosophy* (Vanderbilt University Press, 1941).

44. Walter C. Curry, *Shakespeare's Philosophical Patterns* (Louisiana State University Press, 1937).

45. Theodore Spencer, *Shakespeare and the Nature of Man* (Macmillan, 1943).

46. For example: Charles Coffin, *John Donne and the New Philosophy* (Columbia University Press, 1937); Marjorie Nicolson, *Newton Demands the Muse* (Princeton University Press, 1946).

47. Joseph W. Beach, *Concept of Nature in Nineteenth Century Poetry* (Macmillan, 1936).

48. Helen C. White, *Metaphysical Poets: A Study in Religious Experience* (Macmillan, 1936).

49. Maurice Kelley, *This Great Argument* (Princeton University Press, 1941).

50. Richard F. Jones, *Ancients and Moderns* (Washington University Press, 1936).

51. Louis I. Bredvold, *The Intellectual Milieu of John Dryden* (University of Michigan Press, 1934).

52. Ricardo Quintana, *The Mind and Art of Jonathan Swift* (New York: Oxford University Press, 1936).

53. Hoxie N. Fairchild, *Religious Trends in English Poetry* (3 vols., Columbia University Press, 1939, 1942, 1949).

54. Chauncey B. Tinker, *Nature's Simple Plan* (Princeton University Press, 1922); Hoxie N. Fairchild, *The Noble Savage* (Columbia University Press, 1928); Lois Whitney, *Primitivism and the Idea of Progress* (Johns Hopkins Press, 1934).

55. Theodore Spencer, *Concept of Death in Elizabethan Tragedy* (Harvard University Press, 1922).

56. For example: Kenneth McLean, *John Locke and English Literature of the Eighteenth Century* (Yale University Press, 1936). Arthur Beatty, *William Wordsworth: His Doctrine and Art in Their Historical Relations* (University of Wisconsin Press, 1922); Newton P. Stallknecht, *Strange Seas of Thought* (Duke University Press, 1945), on Wordsworth; Charles F. Harrold, *Carlyle and German Thought, 1819–34* (Yale University Press, 1934).

57. Joel E. Spingarn, *A History of Literary Criticism in the Renaissance* (Columbia University Press, 1908).

58. Joel E. Spingarn, *Critical Essays of the Seventeenth Century* (3 vols., Oxford: The Clarendon Press, 1908-1909).

59. Austin Warren, *Alexander Pope as Critic and Humanist* (Princeton University Press, 1929).

60. Clarence D. Thorpe, *The Aesthetic Theory of Thomas Hobbes* (University of Michigan Press, 1940); Helen W. Randall, *The Critical Theory of Lord Kames* (Smith College, 1944); Clarence C. Green, *The Neo-Classical Theory of Tragedy in England during the Eighteenth Century* (Harvard University Press, 1934); Samuel H. Monk, *The Sublime* (Modern Language Association of America, 1935); Hugh T. Swedenberg, *The Theory of the Epic in England, 1650–1800* (University of California Press, 1944).

61. Lionel Trilling, *Matthew Arnold* (W. W. Norton, 1939; new edition, 1949).

62. Elisabeth S. Schneider, *The Aesthetics of William Hazlitt* (University of Pennsylvania Press, 1933); Ruth Child, *The Aesthetic of Walter Pater* (Macmillan, 1940).

63. William Irvine, *Walter Bagehot* (Longmans, Green, 1939).

64. Walter J. Bate, *From Classic to Romantic: Premises of Taste in Eighteenth-Century England* (Harvard University Press, 1946).

65. Sidney Lanier, *The Science of English Verse* (Charles Scribner's Sons, 1880; new edition, Johns Hopkins Press, 1945).

66. John C. Pope, *Rhythm of Beowulf* (Yale University Press, 1942).

67. William L. Schramm, *Approaches to a Science of English Verse* (University of Iowa Press, 1935).

68. William K. Wimsatt, *The Prose Style of Samuel Johnson* (Yale University Press, 1941).

69. Uncollected. The most important pieces: an introduction to Morris W. Croll and Harry Clemons, eds., John Lyly's *Euphues: The Anatomy of Wit* (E. P. Dutton, 1916) and papers in *Studies in Philology* 16 and 18 (University of North Carolina Press, 1919, 1921); in *Schelling Anniversary Papers* (The Century Company, 1923); the Baroque piece in Kemp Malone and Martin B. Ruud, eds., *Studies in English Philology.* (University of Minnesota Press, 1929).

70. Josephine Miles, *Wordsworth and the Vocabulary of Emotion* (University of California Press, 1942).

71. Walter J. Bate, *The Stylistic Development of Keats* (Modern Language Association of America, 1945).

72. Mark van Doren, *Poetry of John Dryden* (Harcourt, Brace, 1920); the third edition appeared as *John Dryden: A Study of His Poetry* (Henry Holt, 1946.)

73. Henry W. Wells, *Poetic Imagery* (Columbia University Press, 1924).

74. Rosemond Tuve, *Elizabethan and Metaphysical Imagery* (University of Chicago Press, 1947).

75. Cleanth Brook, *Modern Poetry and the Tradition* (University of North Carolina Press, 1939) and *The Well Wrought Urn: Studies in the Structure of Poetry* (New York: Reynal & Hitchcock, 1947); Robert Heilman, *This Great Stage* (Louisiana State University Press, 1948).

76. Austin Warren, *Richard Crashaw: A Study in Baroque Sensibility* (Louisiana State University Press, 1939).

77. Robert P. Warren, "A Poem of Pure Imagination: An Experiment in Reading" in edition of Samuel T. Coleridge, *The Rime of the Ancient Mariner* (Reynal & Hitchcock, 1946).

78. Mark Schorer, *William Blake: The Politics of Vision* (Henry Holt, 1946). Another excellent book on Blake is S. Foster Damon's *William Blake* (London: Constable, 1924).

79. Francis O. Matthiessen, *The Achievement of T. S. Eliot: An Essay on the Nature of Poetry* (Oxford University Press, 1935; new edition, 1947).

80. Harry Levin, *James Joyce* (Norfolk, Conn.: New Directions Books, 1941).

81. Henry James, *The Art of the Novel: Critical Prefaces* (Charles Scribner's Sons, 1934).

82. Joseph W. Beach, *The Method of Henry James* (Yale University Press, 1918), *The Technique of Thomas Hardy* (University of Chicago Press, 1922), and *The Twentieth Century Novel: Studies in Technique* (The Century Co., 1932).

83. George P. Baker, *The Development of Shakespeare as a Dramatist* (Macmillan, 1907); Brander Matthews, *Shakespeare as a Playwright* (Charles Scribner's Sons, 1913).

84. A small selection from Elmer E. Stoll's publications, for example: *Shakespeare Studies* (Macmillan, 1927), *Poets and Playwrights* (University of Minnesota Press, 1930), *Art and Artifice in Shakespeare* (Cambridge, Eng.: The University Press, 1933), *Shakespeare and Other Masters* (Harvard University Press, 1940), *From Shakespeare to Joyce* (Doubleday, Doran, 1944).

85. Karl Young, *Drama of the Medieval Church* (2 vols., The Clarendon Press, 1933).

86. Henry C. Lancaster, *A History of French Dramatic Literature of the Seventeenth Century* (8 vols., Johns Hopkins Press, 1929 ff.)

87. For example: William P. Jones, *The Pastourelle: A Study of the Origins and Tradition of a Lyric Type* (Harvard University Press, 1931); Fredson T. Bowers, *Elizabethan Revenge Tragedy* (Princeton University Press, 1940); Frank W. Chandler, *The Literature of Roguery* (2 vols., Houghton Mifflin, 1907); Richmond P. Bond, *English Burlesque Poetry, 1700–1750* (Harvard University Press, 1932).

88. Howard Baker, *Induction to Tragedy* (Louisiana State University Press, 1939).

89. For example: Ashley H. Thorndike, *Tragedy* (Houghton Mifflin, 1908) and *English Comedy* (Macmillan, 1929); Felix E. Schelling, *Elizabethan Drama* (E. P. Dutton, 1908); C. F. Tucker Brooke, *The Tudor Drama* (Houghton Mifflin, 1911); John M. Berdan, *Early Tudor Poetry* (Macmillan, 1920).

90. Albert C. Baugh, ed., *A Literary History of England* (Appleton-Century-Crofts, 1948). A detailed review by René Wellek in *Modern Philology*, 47:39–45 (1949).

91. Norman Foerster, *The Reinterpretation of American Literature* (Harcourt, Brace, 1928).

92. Charles R. Anderson, ed., *The Centennial Edition of the Works of Sidney Lanier* (10 vols., Johns Hopkins Press, 1945).

93. Some examples of scholarly editions: Randall Stewart, *The American Notebooks of Nathaniel Hawthorne* (Yale University Press, 1932) and *The*

English Notebooks of Nathaniel Hawthorne (Modern Language Association of America, 1941); Ralph Rusk, ed., *The Letters of Ralph Waldo Emerson* (Columbia University Press, 1939); Francis O. Matthiessen and Kenneth Murdock, eds., *The Notebooks of Henry James* (Oxford University Press, 1947).

94. Stanley Williams, *Life of Washington Irving* (2 vols., Oxford University Press, 1935).

95. Arthur H. Quinn, *Edgar Allan Poe* (D. Appleton-Century, 1941).

96. Ralph L. Rusk, *The Life of Ralph Waldo Emerson* (Charles Scribner's Sons, 1949).

97. Odell Shepard, *Pedlar's Progress: The Life of Bronson Alcott* (Little, Brown, 1937).

98. Carl Van Doren, *Benjamin Franklin* (New York: The Viking Press, 1938); George F. Whicher, *This Was a Poet: A Critical Biography of Emily Dickinson* (Charles Scribner's Sons, 1938).

99. Vernon L. Parrington, *Main Currents of American Thought* (3 vols., Harcourt, Brace, 1927–1930).

100. Herbert Schneider, *The Puritan Mind* (Henry Holt, 1930).

101. Perry Miller, *New England Mind* (Macmillan, 1939). Cf. also Perry Miller, *Orthodoxy in Massachusetts, 1630–1650* (Harvard University Press, 1933).

102. Kenneth Murdock, *Literature and Theology in Colonial New England* (Harvard University Press, 1949).

103. Howard M. Jones, *America and French Culture* (University of North Carolina Press, 1927).

104. Harold C. Goddard, *New England Transcendentalism* (Columbia University Press, 1908).

105. Ralph H. Gabriel, *The Course of American Democratic Thought* (The Ronald Press, 1940).

106. Merle Curti, *The Growth of American Thought* (Harper & Brothers, 1943).

107. Ralph B. Perry, *The Thought and Character of William James* (2 vols., Little, Brown, 1935).

108. Oscar Cargill, *Intellectual America* (Macmillan, 1941).

109. Norman Foerster, *American Criticism: A Study in Literary Theory from Poe to the Present* (Houghton Mifflin, 1928).

110. George F. DeMille, *Literary Criticism in America: A Preliminary Survey* (Longmans Green, 1931); John P. Pritchard, *Return to the Fountains* (Duke University Press, 1942); William Charvat, *The Origins of American Critical Thought, 1810–1835* (University of Pennsylvania Press, 1936); Bernard Smith, *Forces in American Criticism: A Study in the History of American Literary Thought* (Harcourt, Brace, 1939).

111. Especially in Richard P. Blackmur, *The Double Agent* (New York: Arrow Editions, 1935) and *The Expense of Greatness* (Arrow Editions, 1940); Yvor Winters, *Maule's Curse* (Norfolk, Conn.: New Directions Books, 1938)

and *Primitivism and Decadence* (Arrow Editions, 1937); Cleanth Brooks, *Modern Poetry and the Tradition* (University of North Carolina Press, 1939).

112. Francis O. Matthiessen, *American Renaissance: Art and Expression in the Age of Emerson and Whitman* (Oxford University Press, 1941).

113. Francis O. Matthiessen, *Henry James: The Major Phase* (Oxford University Press, 1946).

114. Arthur H. Quinn, *American Fiction: A Historical and Critical Survey* (D. Appleton-Century, 1936) and *A History of the American Drama from the Civil War to the Present Day* (F. S. Crofts, 1936).

115. Horace Gregory and Marya Zaturenska, *History of Modern American Poetry, 1900–1940* (Harcourt, Brace, 1942; new edition, 1946).

116. Herbert B. Brown, *The Sentimental Novel in America, 1798–1860* (Duke University Press, 1940); Alexander Cowie, *The Rise of the American Novel* (American Book Co., 1948).

117. Carl Van Doren, *The American Novel, 1789–1939* (Macmillan, 1940).

118. Joseph W. Beach, *American Fiction, 1920–1940* (Macmillan, 1941).

119. Alfred Kazin, *On Native Grounds* (Reynal & Hitchcock, 1942); Maxwell Geismar, *Writers in Crisis: The American Novel between the Two Wars* (Houghton Mifflin, 1942) and *The Last of the Provincials: The American Novel, 1915–1925* (Houghton Mifflin, 1943).

120. Granville Hicks, *The Great Tradition* (Macmillan, 1933).

121. Ludwig Lewisohn, *Expression in America* (Harper & Brothers, 1932).

122. Van Wyck Brooks, *The Flowering of New England, 1815–1865* (E. P. Dutton, 1936), *New England: Indian Summer, 1865–1915* (E. P. Dutton, 1940), *The World of Washington Irving* (E. P. Dutton, 1944), and *The Times of Melville and Whitman* (E. P. Dutton, 1947).

123. William P. Trent, John Erskine, Stuart P. Sherman, and Carl Van Doren, eds., *The Cambridge History of American Literature* (4 vols., G. P. Putnam's Sons, 1917–1921).

124. Robert E. Spiller, Willard Thorp, Thomas H. Johnson, Henry S. Canby, eds., *Literary History of the United States* (3 vols., Macmillan, 1948). A detailed review by René Wellek in the *Kenyon Review*, 11:500–506 (1949).

125. The last sentences are the concluding sentences of René Wellek and Austin Warren, *Theory of Literature* (Harcourt, Brace, 1949).

V. Classical Scholarship

WALTER R. AGARD

1. *Classical Philology*, 3:384 (1908).

2. H. C. Lipscomb in "Humanistic Culture in Early Virginia," *Classical Journal* 63:203–208 (1948), gives an engaging account of the classical influence in early Virginia. According to the diaries of William Byrd II, that

Colonial planter began the day by reading a passage from Homer, Petronius, or some other classical author, and also wrote lengthy translations of several of them, from Greek into Latin as well as into English. The effect of such study on a later Virginian is made clear in Karl Lehmann's *Thomas Jefferson, American Humanist* (New York, 1947) and Louis B. Wright's "Thomas Jefferson and the Classics," *Proceedings of the American Philosophical Society* 87:223 ff.

3. George Sandys translated Ovid's *Metamorphoses* (1626), Ezekiel Cheever wrote his popular *Accidence, A Short Introduction to the Latin Tongue* (1709), James Logan published editions of Cato's *Moral Distiches* (1735) and Cicero's *De Senectute* (1744), and James Otis' *Rudiments of Latin Prosody* appeared in 1760.

4. See Talbot Hamlin, *Greek Revival Architecture in America* (Oxford University Press, 1944).

5. An excellent summary of this early period is given in R. F. Butts' *The College Charts its Course* (McGraw-Hill Book Co., 1939), in which the comments by Ticknor and Everett are cited. There are many other examples of American dependence on German scholarship. Theodore D. Woolsey went to Leipzig, Bonn, and Berlin for graduate study before he became professor of Greek at Yale in 1831: he later published texts of Greek plays based on German criticism. James Hadley was similarly indebted in writing his *Greek Grammar*. George M. Lane, after getting his Ph.D. degree in 1851 at Göttingen and becoming professor at Harvard, published his *Latin Grammar for Schools and Colleges*, and worked on Harper's *Latin Dictionary* with a reverential bow to his German teachers. At Columbia, Charles Anthon's *Classical Dictionary* and handbooks on classical culture and Henry Drisler's work in lexicography derived from those same sources.

6. Established in the eighteenth century by such scholars as Gesner, Reiske, and Heyne, the critical method was continued and developed by experts in exegesis like Wolf, Rischl, Dindorf, and Boeckh; comparative philologists like Bopp and George Curtius; students of culture like Niebuhr, K. O. Müller, Pauly, and Zeller; epigraphists like Kirchhoff and Dittenberger; and archaeologists like Jahn, Dörpfeld, and Furtwängler.

7. Basil L. Gildersleeve, *Essays and Studies, Educational and Literary* (Baltimore, 1890), p. 61; C. W. E. Miller, ed., *Selections from the Brief Mention of B. L. Gildersleeve* (The Johns Hopkins Press, 1930), pp. 272–73.

8. It includes William D. Whitney of Yale and Francis A. March of Lafayette, our first Sanskrit and comparative philology scholars, Albert Harkness of Brown, editor of texts of Caesar, Cicero, and Sallust and author of a widely used Latin grammar; William W. Goodwin of Harvard, vigorous editor and promoter of the classics, whose *Syntax of Moods and Tenses of the Greek Verb* was a contribution of the first order in its accuracy of analysis and clarity of statement; James B. Greenough of Harvard, a comparative philologist who collaborated with J. H. Allen in writing *Latin Grammar Found-*

ed on Comparative Grammar; F. D. Allen of Harvard, an authority on Greek and Latin inscriptions, whose *Remnants of Early Latin* won international recognition; Thomas D. Seymour of Yale, who specialized in Homeric institutions; Milton W. Humphreys of Vanderbilt, Texas, and Virginia, an authority on classical meters; Martin L. D'Ooge of Michigan; and John Williams White of Harvard, specialist in the verse and content of Greek comedy and author of the most widely used of all elementary Greek textbooks.

9. See L. E. Lord, *History of the American School of Classical Studies at Athens* (Harvard University Press, 1947).

10. The earliest series of Greek texts was edited by Thomas D. Seymour and John W. White, that of Latin texts by Basil L. Gildersleeve and Gonzales Lodge.

11. *American Journal of Archaeology*, 4:9 (1900).

12. *Bulletin of the American School of Classical Studies*, 5:49 (1902).

13. For American scholarship in perspective, see W. H. Rouse, et al., eds., *The Year's Work in Classical Studies* (London, 1907–).

14. Outstanding among them were William G. Hale, whose *Latin Grammar* was a scholarly achievement and whose analysis of the subjunctive and optative moods in *A Century of Metaphysical Syntax* was brilliantly stated, and C. E. Bennett, author of a popular Latin grammar and of *Syntax of Early Latin*, a work of considerable importance. Bennett also edited, with J. C. Rolfe, a college series of Latin texts. In more recent years Charles B. Gulick revised Goodwin's *Greek Grammar*: Herbert W. Smyth prepared a new Greek grammar and a study of the Ionic dialect, edited a series of college Greek texts, and trained generations of graduate students in his own exacting standards; and C. D. Buck's *Introduction to the Study of the Greek Dialects, A Grammar of Oscan and Umbrian, Comparative Grammar of Greek and Latin*, and *Reverse Index* won international recognition as standard works.

15. Kent is best known for his *Textual Criticism of Inscriptions, The Sounds of Latin*, and his edition of Varro, *De Lingua Latina*; Whatmough for his *Prae-Italic Dialects of Italy*; and Sturtevant for his *Studies in Greek Noun Formation, The Pronunciation of Greek and Latin*, and *Comparative Grammar of the Hittite Language*.

16. Rand's masterpieces in technical scholarship were his Boethius' *Opuscula Sacra* and *Consolatio Philosophiae, Studies in the Script of Tours*, and the Harvard edition of *Servii in Aeneidem I–II Commentarii*; but his reputation rests equally on his expert and devoted guidance of scores of research assistants. Notable work on medieval manuscripts has also been done by A. S. Pease and B. L. Ullman.

17. At the Catholic University of America a similar comradeship of researchers has made systematic and thorough studies of the Church

Fathers, under the direction of Roy J. Deferrari. The same group is also publishing a series of concordances to Latin authors.

18. Introductory studies of promise have recently been made by several young scholars, notably by John Finley on Thucydides and C. H. Whitman on Sophocles.

19. For example, the studies of Latin poets by Tenney Frank and E. K. Rand, and of Roman comedy by Henry W. Prescott; G. L. Hendrickson's papers on satire and literary style; John A. Scott's *The Unity of Homer* (in the notable University of California series of Sather Classical lectures), which overturned once and for all the extreme separatist theories of German critics, and his *Poetic Structure in the Odyssey;* Milman Parry's *Studies in the Epic Technique of Oral Verse-Making*, which threw fresh light on the vividness of the Homeric epics; Samuel E. Bassett's sensitive interpretation in *The Poetry of Homer;* William Ellery Leonard's translation and analysis of Lucretius; and Cedric H. Whitman's *Sophocles, a Study of Heroic Humanism.*

20. This program has been supported largely by the contributions of members of the Archaeological Institute of America. The membership grew steadily, until in 1930 there were over fifty branches in as many cities, with over three thousand members. After a sharp decline during the depression the membership is now increasing again.

21. For example: Allan Marquand's *Greek Architecture;* W. B. Dinsmoor's revision of Anderson and Spiers' *The Architecture of Ancient Greece*; G. M. A. Richter's *The Sculpture and Sculptors of the Greeks;* and M. W. Swindler's *Ancient Painting.* Pioneers in developing texts in archaeology were J. R. Wheeler, trained at the American School in Athens and under Charles Waldstein in the excavation and publication of the Argive Heraeum, who later wrote, with Harold W. Fowler, editor of the *American Journal of Archaeology*, the first comprehensive textbook on Greek art and archaeology; Frank B. Tarbell, who interpreted Greek art from the point of view of a trained archaeologist; Samuel B. Platner, who prepared a scholarly handbook on the topography and monuments of Ancient Rome; and R. B. Richardson, whose *Greek Sculpture* presented new data furnished by the archaeologists.

22. Published in the *University of Michigan Humanistic Studies.*

23. Important publications have also been made by W. L. Westermann and C. J. Kraemer of papyri in the Cornell collection, and by Allan C. Johnson and Henry B. von Hoesen of others in the Princeton collection.

24. *Classical Philology* 31:237 (1927).

25. *Sardis* (7 vols., Leyden, London, 1916–); P. V. C. Baur and M. I. Rostovtzeff, ed., *Excavations at Dura-Europos* (10 vols., Yale University Press, 1929–1947).

26. Fourteen volumes have been published so far, in the Johns Hopkins University *Studies in Archaeology* (Baltimore, 1929–).

27. They have been published in the *American Journal of Archaeology*

and in independent volumes, the most sumptuous of which is *The Erechtheum*. More comprehensive studies have also been published, such as D'Ooge's *Acropolis of Athens*, C. H. Weller's *Athens and Its Monuments*, and Grant Showerman's *Eternal Rome*.

28. J. C. Hoppin's *Handbook of Attic Red-Figured Vases* and *Handbook of Greek Black-Figured Vases*, Arthur Fairbanks' *Athenian White Lecythi*, and Miss Richter's *The Craft of Athenian Pottery*.

29. Other important studies in this field have been made by Frank F. Abbott and A. C. Johnson at Princeton. Although historians have been ruled by the Editor as outside the scope of this paper, special mention should be made of the studies in Hellenistic culture by W. S. Ferguson.

30. Bonner's major publication (with Gertrude Smith) was *The Administration of Justice from Homer to Aristotle*.

31. It is only fair to note that both Rostovtzeff and Jaeger had won their scholarly reputation in Europe before they came to this country.

32. In this connection the Institute for Advanced Studies at Princeton is performing a very useful service. On its staff are several leading scholars in archaeology, epigraphy, paleography, and philosophy, who are free to devote themselves to making comprehensive surveys of broad areas as well as conducting their own research and guiding the work of carefully selected younger scholars.

33. As Gildersleeve said, "No one, teacher or scholar, should so lose himself in grammatical studies as to become insensible of the deep truth which is embodied in the old term the 'humanities'." *Essays and Studies, Educational and Literary* (Baltimore, 1890, p. 123). In this connection tribute should be paid to many teachers in American colleges and universities who did not themselves engage largely, if at all, in specialized research or publication, but thoroughly steeped themselves in the life and literature of Greece and Rome, kept abreast of critical studies and investigations, and, with a genius for teaching, inspired generations of students to cultivate humanistic interests and values. Representative of many such scholarly teachers were Moses S. Slaughter of Wisconsin, H. de F. Smith of Amherst, Francis G. Allinson of Brown, and G. A. Harrer of the University of North Carolina.

34. For such courses many textbooks have been written, such as C. B. Gulick's *Life of the Ancient Greeks*, La Rue Van Hook's *Greek Life and Thought*, Grant Showerman's *Rome and the Romans*, F. G. Moore's *The Roman World*, H. N. Couch's *Classical Civilization: Greece*, and R. M. Geer's *Classical Civilization: Rome*. Mention should also be made of new translations, which have made the classics available in attractive modern versions, notably Richard Lattimore's *Iliad* and *Agamemnon*, Rolfe Humphries' *Aeneid*, and *Classics in Translation*, edited by Paul L. MacKendrick and Herbert Howe.

35. Basil L. Gildersleeve, *Essays and Studies; Educational and Literary*, p. 507.

VI. Philosophical Scholarship

ARTHUR E. MURPHY

1. Henry Adams, *The Education of Henry Adams* (Houghton Mifflin, 1922), ch. 25.

2. Josiah Royce, *The Spirit of Modern Philosophy* (Houghton Mifflin, 1892), ch. 12.

3. George H. Howison, *The Limits of Evolution* (Macmillan, 1901).

4. Josiah Royce, *The Religious Aspect of Philosophy* (Houghton Mifflin, 1885), ch. 11. James's opinion of the argument is reported in Ralph B. Perry, *The Thought and Character of William James*. (2 vols., Little, Brown, 1935), I, 798.

5. Josiah Royce, *The World and the Individual* (2 vols., Macmillan, 1899–1901).

6. Josiah Royce, *The Philosophy of Loyalty* (Macmillan, 1908).

7. Josiah Royce, "Provincialism," *Race Questions* (Macmillan, 1908).

8. Josiah Royce, *The Hope of the Great Community* (Macmillan, 1916).

9. G. H. Howison and Borden P. Bowne were the chief American representatives of Personal Idealism in this period. Edgar S. Brightman is perhaps its ablest defender in more recent times.

10. James's version of the pragmatic rule is given in *Some Problems of Philosophy* (Longmans, Green, 1911), ch. 4, Peirce's in *Collected Papers of Charles Sanders Peirce*, V (Harvard University Press, 1934), paragraphs 2 and 402.

11. See especially William James, *A Pluralistic Universe* (Longmans, Green, 1909), Lecture VII.

12. William James, *The Principles of Psychology* (2 vols., Henry Holt, 1890).

13. Cf. especially the title essay in William James, *The Will to Believe* (Longmans, Green, 1896).

14. Cf. especially Dewey's contribution to *Studies in Logical Theory* (University of Chicago Press, 1903).

15. Cf. his essay on "The Need for a Recovery of Philosophy" in *Creative Intelligence* (Henry Holt, 1917).

16. Cf. especially John Dewey, *Liberalism and Social Action* (G. P. Putnam's Sons, 1935).

17. The theory is fully developed in his lectures on social psychology posthumously published as *Mind, Self and Society* (University of Chicago Press, 1934).

18. Charles Hartshorne and Paul Weiss, eds., *Collected Papers of Charles Sanders Peirce* (6 vols., Harvard University Press, 1931–1935).

19. *Collected Papers*, V, bk. 2, ch. 5.

20. *Collected Papers*, I, paragraph 615.

21. Henry S. Commager, *The American Mind* (Yale University Press, 1950), p. 97.

22. Charles and Mary Beard, *The American Spirit* (Macmillan, 1942), p. 661.

23. Philip Wiener, *Evolution and the Founders of Pragmatism* (Harvard University Press, 1949), p. 190.

24. For Dewey's view of the danger of approach to human problems in terms of moral blame and approbation, see his *Logic* (Henry Holt, 1938), pp. 494–95.

25. Morton G. White, *Social Thought in America* (Viking Press, 1949), p. 7.

26. John Dewey, *The Influence of Darwin on Philosophy* (Henry Holt, 1910), p. 19.

27. White, *Social Thought in America*, p. 243.

28. Vernon L. Parrington, *Main Currents in American Thought*, Vol. III, *The Beginnings of Critical Realism in America* (Harcourt, Brace, 1930). The final essay, "A Chapter in American Liberalism," is particularly illuminating.

29. Houston Peterson, *The Melody of Chaos* (Longmans, Green, 1931), pp. 58, 269.

30. Henry Adams, *Education*, ch. 25.

31. George Santayana, *Realms of Being* (Scribner's, 1940).

32. Alfred N. Whitehead and Bertrand Russell, *Principia Mathematica* (2nd edition, 3 vols., Cambridge University Press, 1925–27).

33. The best of Cohen's philosophy is in *Reason and Nature* (Harcourt, Brace, 1931) and *The Meaning of Human History* (La Salle, Illinois: Open Court, 1947).

34. Edwin B. Holt, Walter T. Marvin, William Pepperell Montague, Ralph Barton Perry, Walter B. Pitkin, and Edward Gleason Spaulding, *The New Realism* (Macmillan, 1912).

35. Durant Drake, Arthur O. Lovejoy, James B. Pratt, Arthur K. Rogers, George Santayana, Roy Wood Sellars, and C. A. Strong, *Essays in Critical Realism* (Macmillan, 1920).

36. Arthur O. Lovejoy, *The Revolt Against Dualism* (W. W. Norton, 1930).

37. Cf. Montague's excellent essay, "The Story of American Realism," *The Ways of Things* (Prentice-Hall, 1940).

38. Ludwig Wittgenstein, *Tractatus Logico-Philosophicus* (Harcourt, Brace, 1922).

39. Clarence I. Lewis, *Mind and the World Order* (Scribner's, 1929).

40. Some of the best work of the analysts is collected in Herbert Feigl and Wilfrid Sellars, eds., *Readings in Philosophical Analysis* (Appleton-Century-Crofts, 1949).

41. For characteristic examples of this way of "doing philosophy," cf. Paul Schilpp, ed., *The Philosophy of G. E. Moore* (Northwestern University Press, 1942).

42. Cf. Susanne Langer, *Philosophy in a New Key* (Harvard University Press, 1942).

43. Charles L. Stevenson, *Ethics and Language* (Yale University Press, 1944).

44. Alfred N. Whitehead, *Science and the Modern World* (Macmillan, 1925).

45. Alfred N. Whitehead, *Adventures of Ideas* (Macmillan, 1933).

46. The speculative hypothesis is most fully worked out in Whitehead's *Process and Reality* (Macmillan, 1929).

47. Alfred N. Whitehead, *Modes of Thought* (Mamillan, 1938), p. 151.

48. The case for this educational theory is well stated in Hutchins' *Education for Freedom* (Louisiana State University Press, 1943).

49. Marxism had few orthodox representatives among the academic philosophers. Sidney Hook's *Towards the Understanding of Karl Marx* (New York: John Day, 1933) and Harold Laski's *The State in Theory and Practice* (Viking Press, 1935) show the influence of Marx in political philosophy.

50. Beatrice and Sidney Webb, *Soviet Communism: A New Civilization?* (2 vols., Scribner's, 1936).

51. Etienne Gilson, *The Spirit of Medieval Philosophy* (Scribner's, 1936), and *The Unity of Philosophical Experience* (Scribner's, 1937), are perhaps the most influential of his writings in this field.

52. Cf. for example, John Wild, *Introduction to Realistic Philosophy* (Harper & Brothers, 1948).

53. Etienne Gilson, *Christianity and Philosophy* (New York: Sheed and Ward, 1939), chs. 3–4 and especially pp. 77–78.

54. Cf. Fulton J. Sheen, *Communism and the Conscience of the West* (Indianapolis-New York: Bobbs Merrill, 1948), ch. 1.

55. His philosophy is most adequately stated in *The Nature and Destiny of Man* (2 vols., Scribner's, 1941–43) and in *Faith and History* (Scribner's, 1949).

56. The excellent translations of Kierkegaard's writings published by the Princeton University Press have been widely read in theological and literary circles. Of chief philosophical importance are *Philosophical Fragments* and *Concluding Unscientic Postscript* (Princeton University Press, 1936 and 1941).

57. Brand Blanshard, *The Nature of Thought* (2 vols., Macmillan, 1940).

58. Clarence I. Lewis, *An Analysis of Knowledge and Valuation* (La Salle, Illinois: Open Court, 1946).

59. Filmer S. C. Northrop, *The Meeting of East and West* (Macmillan, 1946).

60. Max Black, ed., *Philsophical Analysis* (Cornell University Press, 1950).

Contributors

MERLE CURTI, Frederick Jackson Turner Professor of History at the University of Wisconsin, has represented the American Historical Association in the Social Science Research Council and has been a member of the Board of Advisors of the American Council of Learned Societies. He has lectured on American History at the several universities of India under the auspices of the Watumull Foundation and at the first Fulbright Conference on American Studies at Cambridge University. He was president of the Mississippi Valley Historical Association in 1951–1952 and Vice-President of the American Historical Association in 1952–1953. He is a member of the American Academy of Arts and Sciences, the American Philosophical Society, and other learned societies. His books include *The Social Ideas of American Educators*, *The American Peace Crusade*, *The Roots of American Loyalty*, and *The Growth of American Thought*, which received the Pulitzer Award for History in 1943.

LOUIS WIRTH, who died on May 3, 1952, was Professor of Sociology at the University of Chicago and a former president of the American Sociological Society. He was an outstanding leader both in the development of theory and in the application of social science to practical problems, especially in the fields of housing, urban issues, and race relations. His role in the Social Science Research Council was a significant one, and he was influential in developing closer relations between American and foreign sociologists. His work on UNESCO committees was notable. His book, *The Ghetto*, is a classic, but the greatest part of his scholarly output is to be found in a long series of writings in which he collaborated with others. Professor Wirth was eminently qualified to evaluate the development of the social sciences in twentieth-century America.

W. STULL HOLT, Professor of History in the University of Washington since 1940, had previously been on the faculty of the Johns Hopkins University for ten years. He was President of the Pacific Coast Branch of the American Historical Association in 1951–52. His books include *Treaties Defeated by the Senate, Historical Scholarship in the United States, 1876–1901: As Revealed in the Correspondence of Herbert B. Adams*, and several published by the Brookings Institution. He served in the military forces during both World Wars.

RENÉ WELLEK is Sterling Professor of Comparative Literature at Yale University. Born in Vienna, Austria, of Czech parentage, he was first in the United States in 1927–1930. He returned to Europe to teach English at the University of Prague and Czech at the University of London. In 1939 he went to the University of Iowa, where he was Professor of English, and in 1946 joined the Yale faculty. He is the author of *Kant in England* and *The Rise of English Literary History* and coauthor (with Austin Warren) of *Theory of Literature.* A two-volume *History of Modern Criticism* is in preparation for the Oxford University Press.

WALTER R. AGARD, Professor of Classics at the University of Wisconsin since 1927, is a past member of the Board of Directors of the American Philological Association and is a lecturer for the Archaeological Institute of America; he has served as president of the Classical Association of the Middle West and South, and is now president of the American Classical League and a member of the board of directors of the American Council of Learned Societies. He is the author of articles on Greek art and institutions and of many books, among them *The Greek Tradition in Sculpture, Classical Gods and Heroes, The New Architectural Sculpture, What Democracy Meant to the Greeks,* and *Classical Myths in Sculpture.*

ARTHUR E. MURPHY has recently accepted an invitation to become head of the Philosophy Department at the University of Washington. He has been Susan Rinn Sage Professor in the Sage School of Philosophy at Cornell University and chairman of that School. Before going to Cornell he was head of the Department of Philosophy at the University of Illinois (1939–1945) and previously taught at the University of Chicago and at Brown University. He is editor of the *Philosophical Review,* author of *The Uses of Reason,* and coauthor of *Philosophy in American Education.* The latter book was the report of the American Philosophical Association's Commission on the function of philosophy in American education, of which he was chairman. In 1950 he was president of the Eastern Division of the American Philosophical Association. His main field of philosophical interest, aside from American philosophy, is in ethics and value theory.

INDEX

Index